Critical Essays on

IRIS MURDOCH

CRITICAL ESSAYS
ON
BRITISH LITERATURE

Zack Bowen, General Editor
University of Miami

Critical Essays on

IRIS MURDOCH

edited by

LINDSEY TUCKER

G. K. Hall & Co. / New York
Maxwell Macmillan Canada / Toronto
Maxwell Macmillan International / New York Oxford Singapore Sydney

G. K. Hall & Company
Macmillan Publishing Company
866 Third Avenue
New York, New York 10022

Maxwell Macmillan Canada, Inc.
1200 Eglinton Avenue East
Suite 200
Don Mills, Ontario M3C 3N1

Library of Congress Cataloging-in-Publication Data

Critical essays on Iris Murdoch / [edited by] Lindsey Tucker.
     p.   cm.—(Critical essays on British literature)
    Includes bibliographical references and index.
    ISBN 0-8161-8871-8
    1. Murdoch, Iris—Criticism and interpretation. I. Tucker,
Lindsey, 1936– . II. Series.
PR6063.U7Z634   1992
823'.914—dc20   92–28711
                                                          CIP

10 9 8 7 6 5 4 3 2 1 (hc)

Printed in the United States of America

Contents

General Editor's Note

♦

The Critical Essays on British Literature series provides a variety of approaches to both classical and contemporary writers of Britain and Ireland. The formats of the volumes in the series vary with the thematic designs of individual editors, and with the amount and nature of existing reviews and criticism. They are augmented, where appropriate, by original essays by recognized authorities. It is hoped that each volume will be unique in developing a new overall perspective on its particular subject.

Lindsey Tucker's introduction is an excellent distillation of the critical approaches to Iris Murdoch's work and at the same time an analysis of the complex philosophy that informs her writing. Tucker discusses the wide variety in Murdoch's work, from the formal technical virtuosity of plot in the early novels, through the rich body of mythic material, to the oddities of her characters, their psychology and their resulting comic or grotesque situations. Along the way Tucker touches on Murdoch's affinity for Freud, Christianity, Buddhism, Platonism, and realism.

The first group of Tucker's selected essays discuss broader perspectives involving a number of works, while the latter essays are focused on individual works. Original essays by Thomas Jackson Rice and Cheryl Bove are published for the first time in this volume.

ZACK BOWEN
University of Miami

Publisher's Note

◆

Producing a volume that contains both newly commissioned and reprinted material presents the publisher with the challenge of balancing the desire to achieve stylistic consistency with the need to preserve the integrity of works first published elsewhere. In the Critical Essays series, essays commissioned especially for a particular volume are edited to be consistent with G. K. Hall's house style; reprinted essays appear in the style in which they were first published, with only typographical errors corrected. Consequently, shifts in style from one essay to another are the result of our efforts to be faithful to each text as it was originally published.

Introduction

♦

LINDSEY TUCKER

Iris Murdoch is something of a phenomenon. As the author of twenty-four novels, four philosophical works, a number of plays, poems, and articles over the last thirty-eight years, her productivity alone makes her noteworthy. But it is because of her dual roles as moral philosopher and novelist that she appears as unique. Indeed, while her fiction has made her one of England's most popular novelists, her discussions on philosophy and aesthetics have generated some unease among her critics who have felt the need to understand and evaluate her art in relation to her philosophical pronouncements. As a consequence, reviews and scholarly studies of her work have expressed both high praise and angry dismissal. As Peter J. Conradi has aptly noted, "few writers divide their audiences as radically. Between her advocates and her detractors there is a gulf fixed."[1] However, the fact that her detractors have felt that she warrants such an expenditure of scholarly effort offers grudging evidence of her importance, for the truth is that Iris Murdoch cannot be easily dismissed. She is a superb storyteller and a creator of work that is energetic, original, imaginative, and serious.

Besides her philosophical writings there are numerous published interviews that have offered enough additional commentary of both a philosophical and aesthetic nature to make even the most enthusiastic reader cautious about venturing too intrepidly into areas uncharted by her nonfictional discourse. And because she is a formidable reader and a complex thinker, such caution has often proved sensible. Furthermore, while her first novel, *Under the Net*, was published in 1954, her first full-length philosophical study, *Sartre, Romantic Rationalist*, had appeared a year earlier, and this kind of interweaving of the fictional and the nonfictional has been the dominant pattern of her work for thirty years.

By 1961, for example, Murdoch had produced four additional novels— *The Flight from the Enchanter* (1955), *The Sandcastle* (1957), *The Bell* (1958), and *A Severed Head* (1961)—and critics had of necessity begun to take note of her. But during these same years a number of philosophical papers appeared on the scene, some of which were to become major sources for her ideas on her art and which have had no small influence on the way her novels would be read. Even today familiarity with these early writings is a useful starting point.

The first of these, "The Sublime and the Good" (1959), begins Murdoch's articulation of what is to be a continuing concern: 1) the relationship of the political and moral concepts derived from Romanticism to contemporary concepts of the human personality and 2) the effects of these views on politics, goodness, and the human subject upon the fate of the novel in the twentieth century.[2] In this paper Murdoch first outlines Kant's views on beauty and the sublime and then critiques his theories of art. She derives her own theories of art from the practices of Shakespeare and Tolstoy and from certain nineteenth-century novels, against which the writing of the twentieth century is seen as diminished. "The Sublime and the Beautiful Revisited" (1960) is a more lengthy and more powerful amplification of these views.[3] Here Murdoch's own theories of art are brought forward in more detail. "Against Dryness," published a year later, and subtitled "A Polemical Sketch," is almost exclusively a statement about art and the past and present state of the novel.[4]

Murdoch argues for the necessity of understanding the human subject against both a contingent world and a world of essences. Unhappily, however, the Enlightenment, Romanticism, and the Liberal tradition have all combined to leave us with "far too shallow and flimsy an idea of human personality" (ad, 16). This Liberal-Democratic theory of personality, as she calls it, to which we in the twentieth century are heirs, is responsible for what Murdoch perceives to be wrong with ourselves and our literature.[5] To trace the causes of our problems, Murdoch begins with Kant who, as "the father of all modern forms of the problem of freedom" (sbr, 247), has bequeathed to us the idea of the individual as a solitary willed being. This being, whom Murdoch describes as "morally speaking monarch of all he surveys and responsible for his own actions" (ad, 17), is possessed of a limited inner life comprised only of acts and chores. Kant's moral philosophy also privileges reason and argues for its ability to transcend the more problematic aspects of the human psyche, namely, emotion and desire.

Hegel's theories also problematize later concepts of the human personality. Murdoch seems to mistrust Hegel's view that human conflict cannot involve good and evil, but only different forms of good, so that the conflict engendered between two subjects involves only "private whims and passions" (sg, 50). What Hegel gives to Romanticism, Murdoch argues, is the idea of a conflict centered within the individual who, at war with him/herself, is part of a totality, but whose relationship to that totality is problematic because the individual is seen as a privileged consciousness. What Murdoch distrusts especially in Hegel is the notion of a private destiny that operates without that "world of essences" (sbr, 251) and conceives of a basically solipsistic individual as its center.

Murdoch's view of empiricist thinking is not any more positive. She argues that Hobbes and Locke established the subject as a political being, existing in a world of other subjects whose coexistence is inevitable and necessary, but whose liberalism never freed itself from Romanticism. While this early view of society was "undynamic and naive" (sbr, 252), its real impetus was scientific, and it perceived the world as a material construct. Eventually, she argues, the liberal tradition divides into two schools—linguistic empiricism (evolved by Wittgenstein) and existentialism (evolved by Sartre). Because the former valorizes the choice and reason of a subject who exists alone, yet is surrounded by a society constituted by language, Murdoch describes this school as behavioristic.

Existentialism is regarded by Murdoch as having much in common with linguistic empiricism because it also is hostile to metaphysics and "construe[s] virtue in terms of will" (sbr, 253). It is true that she seems to have found Sartrean existentialism relevant to conditions in postwar England,[6] but she comes to regard it as linked to Hegalianism in that both mandate the continued privileging of the individual. Although existentialism is anti-system, the individual still acts out a solitary struggle for freedom by way of willed action. She concludes that "existentialism shares with empiricism a terror of anything which encloses the agent or threatens his supremacy as a center of significance" (sbr, 255). Worse, empiricism and existentialism have left us prey to two problematic conditions: convention and neurosis.

Convention is the dominant landscape of what Murdoch calls the Ordinary Language Man—so called because he is shaped by convention but is too arrogant to be overpowered by any structure larger than himself. He has a tendency toward abstraction and oversimplification, and although he exists in a network of difference, he still manages to operate self-sufficiently. The second condition—neurosis—is the most telling mark of the existential man, whom Murdoch calls the Totalitarian Man because of his supreme isolation. "Ordinary Language Man," she says, "is at least surrounded by something which is not of his own creation, viz. ordinary language. But Totalitarian Man is entirely alone" (sbr, 254). Totalitarian Man lives through a process of self-mythologizing, which casts the world and people in it as extensions of his own consciousness.

As one might suspect from the foregoing comments, Murdoch is skeptical about the human subject's ability to be either wise or good. In a later work, *The Sovereignty of Good* (1970), where she more fully outlines her questions about the human psyche, she argues that human beings are "naturally selfish," that they are egocentric, machine-like energy systems driven by forces incomprehensible to them.[7] Furthermore, this egocentric consciousness is inclined—even doomed—to falsify harsh realities through the generation of a variety of obsessional fantasies which she defines as a "proliferation of blinding self-centered aims and images" (*SG*, 67). In the end, she argues, we are "transient mortal creatures subject to necessity and chance" (*SG*, 79).

Murdoch has, of course, a lot to say about the world this human creature inhabits. It is rich, complicated, external, and—above all—contingent. Indeed, it is its contingent nature, its complexity, particularity, and messiness, that the fantasy-ridden egotists fear and attempt to control by imposing form and pattern upon it. In part Murdoch's view of the world is shaped by Kant's idea of the sublime, although in the end she qualifies certain aspects of his theory. As mentioned earlier, Kant privileges reason (one of Murdoch's false gods). Also, his philosophy assumes a conflict between reason and the imagination where reason fails, even as it is invigorated by its understanding of what it cannot master. This view of the human encounter with the awesome and appalling, contains for Murdoch hints of Romantic self-assertion and is therefore unacceptable. Having defined the sublime as a "vast and varied reality outside ourselves" (sbr, 268) that can both terrify and exhilarate, Murdoch sees beyond the conflictive aspects upon which Kant focuses too intently. Because the sublime (what she calls the true sublime) is a "real" experience, it can lead human consciousness to a nonviolent apprehension of difference, even an absence of self which is nonthreatening if properly understood (sbr, 269).

Most important perhaps, the understanding of the sublime is essential for the creation of great art. In "The Sublime and the Beautiful Revisited" Murdoch begins what will be an ongoing elaboration of what characterizes great literary works. Rejecting Kant's narrow concepts of art, which envision it as "hygenic," a "quasi-thing" that operates as a form of play only (sbr, 249), Murdoch counters that one's experience of the art of the novel is a "spiritual experience; and where spirit fails . . . art fails" (sbr, 268). Murdoch does not mean, however, that art should be didactic; good art requires that the artist have a realistic vision as well as compassion whereby s/he will be able to transcend the limits of personality and reveal the "minute and absolutely random detail of the world" (*SG*, 86). "Good art is good for people," Murdoch says in an interview with William Slaymaker, "because it takes them away from themselves."[8] It is a place where "all sorts of free reflection goes on."[9] Art is thus "the most educational of human activities and a place in which the nature of morality can be *seen*" beyond appearance (*SG*,87–88).

Nonetheless, for Murdoch much art is bad art—art that "fascinates and diverts," giving "magically induced satisfaction to the lower part of the soul,"[10] offering not knowledge but consolation, a particularly attractive but dangerous by-product that, by its very nature, distorts reality—always to Murdoch that which is "intolerably chancy and incomplete" (*SG*, 87)—by imposing pattern and form.

Where does Murdoch find good art? In some of the sprawling nineteenth-century novels, works that are not only un-Romantic, but that contain "a plurality of real persons more or less naturalistically presented in a large social scene, and representing mutually independent centers of significance which are those of real individuals" (sbr, 257). Novels that meet this major requirement are those of Dickens, Dostoevsky, James, Austen, and Proust.[11]

Murdoch's enthusiasm for Shakespeare and Tolstoy has become a commonplace, and her writings are filled with references to both.[12] Shakespeare, she has said, is great because his writing "abound[s] in free and eccentric personalities" that are not projections of his own mythology; for he is "the most invisible of writers" and thus the most "un-Romantic" (sbr, 261). Shakespeare defies the Kantian notion of art as play art for Shakespeare is serious and ultimately has to do with love. She concludes that the artist should be "the analogon of the good man . . . the lover who, nothing himself, lets other things be through him" (sbr, 270). For Murdoch, Shakespeare was this kind of artist.

The conditions of convention and neurosis that for Murdoch describe the general consciousness of modern and postmodern times also point to the kind of novels presently being written. Actually, it would be more accurate to say that the lesser literature of the nineteenth century subscribed to convention while that of the twentieth century is more dominated by neurosis. Conventional novels fall victim to stereotypical settings and stock characters; neurotic novels contain characters bound to the author's own psychological conflicts.

From this categorization of convention and neurosis, Murdoch amplifies her description of the serious modern novel by again seeing it in terms of two extremes: "either it is a tight metaphysical object, which wishes it were a poem, and which attempts to convey, often in mythical form, some central truth about the human condition—or else it is a loose journalistic epic, documentary or possibly even didactic in inspiration, offering a commentary on current institutions or on some matter out of history" (sbr, 264). In "Against Dryness,"[13] she evokes the term *crystalline* for the "tight metaphysical novel," and further describes it as a "small quasi-allegorical object" that is lacking in the kind of characters that were to be found in the better novels of the nineteenth century, but that are largely absent from the novel of the twentieth century (ad, 18). The persons Murdoch wishes to see can only occur in a novel in which contingency operates, where a character moves with freedom against a background of values, of realities which transcend him.

Having made use of a growing number of convenient dichotomies to describe the twentieth-century novel—crystalline and journalistic, formal and contingent, open and closed—Murdoch has often found herself occupying a problematic place in relation to them. What kind of novels was Murdoch herself writing? Many early reviewers and critics thought that she wrote both—or to be more precise, that she attempted to write open novels, but was, in fact, better at writing closed ones. In the judgment of many critics the early novels seem to conform to the description of the "crystalline" novel, where form overrides contingency. Indeed, it has been argued by some that most of the novels coming before *The Nice and the Good* (1968) fit this category. Dominated by gothic elements, these novels are described by Zohreh T. Sullivan as "allegories of power," in which Murdoch's solipsistic hero is demonized and placed at the center of a grouping of characters s/he has emotionally, spiritually, or physically enslaved.[14] Such novels as *Under the Net, The Flight from the Enchanter, A Severed Head, The Unicorn* (1963) and *The Time of the Angels* (1978) are particularly full of gothic landscapes, enchanter figures, and intricately plotted events. While such works have been the object of some negative criticism, they also have their defenders. Elizabeth Dipple, one of the most knowledgeable of the more recent scholars (and one who is far more positive about her later work), explains the failings of Murdoch's earlier plots as attributable to her enormous technical power which, in the early novels, takes over and ends in subordinating character and verisimilitude to plot.[15] Yet even these works, Dipple says, can tease the reader into thought. Furthermore, each novel is "entirely new and in a sense a continuation and elaboration of elements one thought one knew" (Dipple, 6). Robert Scholes develops a similar point in an early but still insightful reading of *The Unicorn*. Identifying Murdoch as one of his fabulators, a contemporary allegorist, he argues that in such novels as *The Unicorn* Murdoch forces us to "shift our interest from the fictional to the ideational," and he likens Murdoch's gothic structures to a cathedral "in which every spire and every gargoyle is packed with meaningful allusions to an invisible world."[16]

Accompanying the very obvious gothic elements in these works, even growing out of them, is a rich and complex body of mythic material. Murdoch has said that we are prone to live in myth and symbol, that "we're all constantly inventing symbolic images to express our situations" (Biles, 310). Certainly her richly allusive works support this statement. But care is needed here, for Murdoch, as a literary realist, resists symbolic readings of her novels.[17] It is important to note, for instance, that Murdoch's view of myth does not include the Jungian concept of archetypal configurations embedded in some kind of racial consciousness. Nor does she intend to use myth to impose form and thereby transcend contingency, as she sees the modernists doing.[18] Instead, myth is the product of the obsessive, fantasy-making operations of the deluded and deluding ego and should be situated within the consciousness of characters only. This mythmaking activity is especially obvious in the novels that contain first-person narrators—novels like *Under the Net, A Severed Head, The Black Prince* (1973), and *The Sea, the Sea* (1978). Nevertheless, myth harbors dangers for the artist too, and Murdoch understands her own inclinations to mythmaking. She has frequently commented on the fact that mythic structures can become capable of drawing characters "into a sort of spiral, or into a kind of form which ultimately is the form of one's own mind," and has cited *A Severed Head* as one instance where she has given herself to myth.[19]

Like the writers of the nineteenth century, Murdoch gives to the construction of characters the highest priority, and argues, "a novel must be a house fit for free characters to live in; and to combine form with a respect for reality with all its odd contingent ways is the highest art of prose" (sbr, 271). Although these words conclude her 1960 paper "The Sublime and the Beautiful Revisited" and were written over thirty years ago, they speak to Murdoch's ongoing struggle with her own form. A number of early critics have tested her work against the above statement and found much of it failing to offer characters who were genuinely free, but served instead as ideograms. One such critic, Linda Kuehl, has argued that Murdoch's characters are personifications of a theory possessed of "inexplicable motives and weird fantasies" which reduce them to "anomolous caricatures."[20] R. L. Widmann accuses Murdoch of using many flat characters and also of failing to give her more fully developed characters freedom from *her* control of contingency.[21] More generous critics have attributed her failing with character to an overuse of her comic gifts.

It is true that we can see her fiction as populated by grotesques and indict her either for exaggeration or for harshness. However, it has been Murdoch's contention that "real" people are "more eccentric than anybody portrayed in novels," that people are indeed "terribly odd" (Bellamy, 137). As she explains it: "It's an evident feature of human psychology that people have secret dream lives. The secrecy of people is very interesting, and the novelist is overcoming the secrecy and attempting to understand. Readers sometimes say to me that I portray odd characters; but the secret thoughts and obsessions and fantasies of others would amaze one, only people don't tell them" (Heffenden, 201–202). Because "real" people are driven by fantasies over which they have little control, motivation has, for Murdoch, little substance. Thus although her characters can spend pages constructing and examining motivation, their own explanations are always rendered suspect, not only in terms how their story is told (this is especially the case with Murdoch's first-person narrators), but also in terms of their responses to contingent events. The result is sometimes comic, sometimes horrific, but what we often regard as grotesque in her work is for Murdoch an ingredient of her realism. While it can also be argued that her gallery of characters comes from only the professional classes and is largely composed of civil servants, university professors, the literary and the artistic, this seemingly narrow social range belies an enormous assortment of individuals—a plethora of waifs, refugees, magicians, mystics, and demonic personalities—who experience the often bizarre events within the pages of her novels and who often write compulsively and at great length about those events.

Important to her characters' inability to understand their true motivations is Murdoch's use of the ideas of Freud. Indeed, it is her understanding of passion—both sexual and religious—that marks Murdoch's realism as dramatically different from that of the nineteenth-century writers whom she admires. Of course Murdoch's view of the human subject as a system of energy aligns her with Freud's determinist views regarding human consciousness. Murdoch's knowledge of Freud is, in fact, very much in evidence in her work and she has spoken of him as a "great and wonderful discoverer" (Slaymaker, 431). "I love reading Freud," she says, "because one gets all sorts of ideas from him" (Haffenden, 202). Some of these ideas surface in her satiric treatment of psychoanalysis in *A Severed Head*, *The Unicorn*, and *The Black Prince*, but also in her representation of dreamwork, oedipal struggles, and obsessional neuroses. What she seems to value most in Freud is his doctrine of *anamnesis*, his ideas concerning ego and id—"the unconscious mind, the deep, dark part of the soul which [in] Freud's view can be good and can be bad, from which ambiguous powers emerge" (Slaymaker, 431). Still, she denies being a Freudian and questions any " 'scientific' view about the structure of the soul" (Slaymaker, 427), nor does she accept Freud's foregrounding of the ego.

In a sense Murdoch can accept Freud to the extent that he derives some of his own philosophy from Plato. Where Plato and Freud converge in an important way in Murdoch's thinking is in their awareness of the importance of Eros as a "fundamental force" (*FS*, 34). In Plato's view this energy is to be perceived in terms of sexuality as well as in its transformation. In other words, sexual love is a cosmic power whose principle, Eros, "connects the commonest human desire to the highest morality" (*FS*, 33). Eros is thus a mediating spirit that takes human desire beyond the sexual to the good. For while passion can bind, it can also liberate and lead, and can ultimately be purified (*FS*, 34). It is this drive that is so important to Murdoch's work and that gives her novels their peculiar intensity. Eros explains why her characters fall in love in such bizarre ways, why passion can be obsessional and also platonic, and why sex can happen in totally meaningless ways. While falling in love is for Murdoch a way in which the dreaming ego is shocked into awareness of an Other, it can also be a dangerous desire that attempts to "de-realize the other, devour and absorb him, subject him to the mechanism of our own fantasy" (*FS*, 36). Eros is also a trickster; hence the representation of sexuality of every sort, including oedipal fixations and incest, in so many of her novels.

As Murdoch's maturer work has made its appearance, the oscillation between closed and open novels has become less pronounced.[22] Those novels appearing after *Nuns and Soldiers* (1981)—*The Philosopher's Pupil* (1983), *The Good Apprentice* (1985), *The Book and the Brotherhood* (1987), *The Message to the Planet* (1989)—offer evidence of her growing ability to combine the mythic and psychological, to evoke a "deeply darkly comic" world where Shakespeare's influence is powerfully but indirectly felt (Conradi, 159).[23] She has also become more of the realist writer she has so admired, but perhaps with a difference.

While it is true that she has consistently argued the need to recreate realism, it is also true that Murdoch's brand of realism departs in important ways from what we have come to know as literary realism—what Dipple calls historical realism—the kind of realism a writer can evoke when she pays "creative attention" to her/his civilization (Dipple, 31).[24] The word *attention* is one Murdoch has taken from the work of French mystic Simone Weil, and it represents to her the important need to see carefully and to read seriously. One ingredient in Murdoch's work that argues for such attention is her capacity for generous amounts of visual detail, especially that which is to be found in her later works (it has been often noted that her most recent fiction is the lengthiest). Attention is also involved because the duty of the creative realist is to be aware of the reader, of his/her need to be involved in this most important idea play. Yet such attention is difficult and involves the surrender of the reader's own fantasies—as they come to shape expectations and offer consolation—for the writer must move beyond her own conciliatory mythmaking if she is to succeed in drawing the reader into attending the world.

However, mimesis is not involved in Murdoch's definition of realism; she is too much of a Platonist to trust mere imitation. Murdochean realism involves seeing not only what is in the text but what lies beyond it, what is ultimately Platonic *reality*. Dipple marks Murdoch's important conflation of literary realism and reality as follows: "In Murdoch's work, the discovery of reality is both historical (generally, contemporary England) and transcendent—a curious and radical intermeshing which defines her idea of the operation of love" (Dipple, 34). In her more recent treatise, *The Fire and the Sun*, Murdoch declares that the "deep structures of reality" can only be reached by the good artist, and then only fleetingly (*FS*, 83).

It has doubtless become clear to readers only superficially familiar with Murdoch that the vocabulary in which both Murdoch and her critics become "enmeshed" suggests a disturbing tendency toward truism. Generalized concepts involving freedom, goodness, beauty, love, and reality seem out of place in this postmodern age, and yet it must be argued that whatever conceptual banalities reside in Murdoch's Platonic pronouncements, they become anything but banal when played out in the world of her fiction; and as she has moved away from her earlier, quasi-allegorical works, she has expanded not only her casts of characters, but also their potential for complicated ruminations and misadventures. There is, furthermore, an unusual (and for some, disquieting) preoccupation with religion which has become even more pronounced in her later work.[25]

Again, neither her theoretical pronouncements nor her representations of religion are simple. Her religious beliefs are a mixture of sacred and secular, with an emphasis on the latter. For instance, she has denied any belief in God many times; nor is she favorably disposed toward what she describes as the supernatural aspects of Christianity, even though she has also noted recently that she feels closer to Christianity than she once did. Yet she has always been interested in Christ, both as a human being and as a symbol, in the sense that he is associated in her novels with a grouping of often unimpressive, usually failed individuals, characters like Tallis Browne in *A Fairly Honorable Defeat* (1970) or Anne Cavidge in *Nuns and Soldiers*. However, what Murdoch seems to find artistically useful in the presence of Christ involves the need for her characters to understand the divine in terms of the everyday world, even if such an understanding is inevitably a limited one. Thus while critical of what she had described as the materialization of God (*FS*, 70), Murdoch seems comfortable with the domestication of Christ.

It would also seem that Buddhism has played an increasingly important role both in her ideas of religion and in her work. Frank Baldanza noted some time ago, in his discussion of *The Nice and the Good*, the presence of renunciating figures who had about them "a hint of Buddhist and Hindu values . . . in a secular context."[26] Practicing Buddhists have also appeared in a number of other novels of more recent vintage—Christopher Cather in *A World Child* (1975), Monty Small in *The Sacred and Profane Love Machine* (1974), and James Arrowby in *The Sea, the Sea*. However, it must also be noted that the enlightenment of these practitioners is as individualized as the characters themselves, and a believer in Buddhism is not automatically a better person.[27] Buddhism is a great religion, Murdoch says, because it concerns itself with a change of consciousness. What she endorses is the more "sophisticated" Buddhism, the Buddhism that, "very conscious of conceptual limitations," realizes how myths can be useful for addressing concerns that must be understood "in another way" (Haffenden, 207). What she seems to conceive of as even more acceptable of late is "some kind of Christian Buddhism," doubtless because of her reluctance to surrender the concept of Christ (Haffenden, 206).[28]

Accompanying Murdoch's acknowledgment of the role of religion in her art is a deeper fashioning of the ways in which art and religion come together: "there has always been a dangerous relationship between art and religion," she says (*FS*, 69), echoing her favorite nay-sayer in matters artistic. Yet that relationship fascinates her, and her recent remark to Slaymaker that her work was in the main concerned with the conflict between magic and the good (Slaymaker, 431) also echoes Plato's concern with magic as an aspect of consolation that appeals to the lower part of the soul (*FS*, 45). One important area of Plato's thought concerns images that can, Murdoch says, be "valuable aids to thought" as long as they are not used to focus desire on lower-order objects. Plato often uses "visual structures to understand non-visual" ones, she argues (*FS*, 68), yet he always reminds us that because art conspires with pleasure, an abandonment of the appropriate spiritual hierarchies is usually the result.

Perhaps the most stimulating source of ideas about images is to be found in Plato's own myth of the Cave, a myth Murdoch finds particularly suggestive for her own artistic strategies. Despite the ignorance of the prisoners who sit facing the back wall of the Cave, where only the shadows cast by the fire can be seen, it is their condition, and their gradual turning away from the shadows to the fire—their limited freedom from *eikasia*, the "vague, image-ridden illusion" that has shaped their consciousness—that the good artist can use for subject matter. Murdoch thus feels that Plato wants us to take the existence in the Cave seriously; there are lessons that the artist, as one of the prisoners, can learn and transmit as s/he traces the emergent understanding of the relationship of the fire to the shadows on the cave walls. However, where the obsessed, the envious, the neurotic consciousness resides, there also resides the artist who, as "naive fantasist" sees only shadows and thus "construes the world in accordance with the easy unresisted mechanical 'causality' of his personal dream-life" (*FS*, 76). There is also another kind of artist—the ironist—one who has moved out of the shadowy realm of *eikasia* but has not yet ventured past the fire,[29] which s/he still mistakes for the sun.

The myth of the Cave clearly supplies Murdoch with an invigorating view of the making of art, for it promises a journey that involves the release of spiritual energy along with a power that is always ambiguous. At the same time, the levels of illusion and the perceptions of the chained prisoners—who see images but remain unaware of their source—is the stuff of her novels. The myth of the Cave thus marks her own journey as an artist who has moved from the practice of an ironic to a more comic form.

In her development of that more comic form, Murdoch appears to have turned to Zen Buddhism as an alternative to Plato's seriousness, especially because of Zen's view of the comic as central to the journey. About the nature of Zen humor she has said "the *koan* often appears as some sort of wild joke. Of course there is a bad absurd (degrading, hurtful), but is there not also a good absurd? Loss of dignity need not be loss of moral stature, can be a surrender of vanity, a discovery of humility" (*FS*, 73). It would seem that Murdoch means these precepts to apply to both the artist and the artistic production, and they suggest that the surrender of control, which has produced the looser, longer work of her later phase, has also produced an artist who values the comic over the satiric.

As mentioned earlier, criticism of Murdoch's work has often found itself not just informed, but also constrained by her philosophical pronouncements. Earlier studies focused in the main on the problem of contingency and the form of her novels, as well as on her ability to construct free characters.[30] Besides the tendency of some to be highly evaluative (Widmann for example, indicts Murdoch's "light treatment of . . . serious problems" [12]), others seem angered by what they perceive to be, in one critic's words, "diverse meanings hard to perceive" (O'Connor, 38). Attesting further to her importance, however, was the arrival on the scene of some full-length studies and a couple of monographs. Of these the most influential and insightful was A. S. Byatt's *Degrees of Freedom*, a study of Murdoch's first seven novels in which Murdoch, as a friend, served in a kind of advisory capacity.[31] Byatt's own sensitivity, coupled with her familiarity with Murdoch's theories, makes her readings of the early works still useful, although her tendency to give too much attention to existentialism has grown increasingly problematic. While a few studies appeared in the 1970s, among them Richard Todd's *Iris Murdoch: The Shakespearian Interest* (1979), it was not until the 1980s that four more comprehensive full-length studies appeared: Elizabeth Dipple's *Iris Murdoch: Work for the Spirit* (1982), Angela Hague's *Iris Murdoch's Comic Vision* (1984), Peter J. Conradi's *Iris Murdoch: The Saint and the Artist* (1986), and Deborah Johnson's *Iris Murdoch* (1987).[32]

In compiling the criticism that follows, an attempt has been made to present discussions of as broad a range of Murdoch's novels as possible. Given the prolific nature of the Murdoch canon, as well as the number of critical studies done over the past thirty years, choice has been difficult. However, while a few articles reprinted here are of a more general nature and serve as an introduction to special areas of concern in Murdochean criticism, most of the essays included in this collection treat individual novels, especially those written in the 1970s and 1980s. Because most Murdoch studies include at least some reference to her philosophical and aesthetic concerns, it was felt that the need of the present time was for studies that are either narrower in focus or that treat more recent works.

Therefore, the introductory essays include Slaymaker's "Myths, Mystery and the Mechanisms of Determinism: The Aesthetics of Freedom in Iris Murdoch's Fiction," and Richard Todd's "The Shakespearian Ideal." The former, an elaboration of the ways in which Murdoch's concept of freedom differs from her philosophical predecessors, also discusses the influence of that concept on the metaphors of mechanism employed in her fiction; the latter explores Murdoch's interest in Shakespeare and the way in which obsessional ingredients, rare as they are in his work, enter *Hamlet*. Both critics use one of Murdoch's most successful novels, *The Black Prince*, as their fictional example. Slaymaker discusses the ways in which Murdoch's narrative strategies address freedom, especially through the construction of artist-narrator Bradley Pearson who, as a romantic and a mediocre artist caught up in his own obsessional fantasies, can nevertheless articulate aesthetic theories that often echo those of Murdoch herself. Todd examines the ways in which Pearson, as an embodiment of Murdoch's views on Shakespeare's achievement—particularly in *Hamlet*, his most obsessional play—is able to function as an acute observer of Hamlet's foibles, even as he recognizes his own.

Another selection of a more general nature is Deborah Johnson's chapter on Murdoch's questing heroes. In the light of Murdoch's own resistance to being considered a woman writer and her expressed identification with men,

Johnson's attempt to bring feminist questions to bear on Murdoch and her work is a difficult one.[33] Describing her as a female writer "who likes wearing male masks," Johnson focuses in particular on those several works where Murdoch uses a first-person male narrator, a rhetorical strategy suggesting Murdoch's preoccupation with power relationships that, because they involve men and women, are gender related.

The final more general study is Zohreh T. Sullivan's introduction to three of Murdoch's earlier novels, all of which are particularly noted for their darker themes and their use of gothic settings—a labyrinthian house in *The Flight from the Enchanter*, an isolated seacoast castle in *The Unicorn*, a ruined fog-bound rectory in *The Time of the Angels*—places that Sullivan argues are inversions of genuine community and that express the egoism and drive for power that dominate their protagonists.

The next grouping of essays are studies of specific works. In a recent reading of Murdoch's second novel, *The Flight from the Enchanter*, Thomas Jackson Rice offers a corrective reminder to critics who have themselves become trapped in the mythmaking patterns constructed by Murdoch's characters and who, as a consequence, tend to spin meaning out of appearances that are refracted through the prism of their own egoism and desire. Rice sets *Under the Net*—a text with one of Murdoch's first-person male narrators—against *The Flight from the Enchanter*—a text with a limited omniscience point of view, where the figure with power is viewed from the vantage point of those who are seemingly controlled by him. Rice then goes on to argue that even characters who perceive themselves as caught in systems of another's making are not thereby free from solipsism and egoism, but whereas in the first case Murdoch makes the artist the bearer of meaning, in the second case, meaning becomes the work of art itself.

Conradi's contention that *A Fairly Honorable Defeat* marks a new phase in Murdoch's career, makes his essay on this work an important one. His reading is informed by an emphasis on Murdoch's use of Eros and her debt to Freud's argument that the human psyche withdraws emotional investment in lost objects (via narcissism and aggression) and redirects them onto the world. Conradi examines the effects of these ideas on the formal aspects of the novel.

Angela Hague's "The Comedy of Contingency in *An Accidental Man*," draws on the comic theories of Cornford and Frye, among others, to examine an area of Murdoch's work that is too often subsumed in other concerns. She especially deals with the ways in which this "brittle comedy of manners" inverts comic convention and moves closer to irony.

Dorothy A. Winsor, working with psychological theories related to problems of mergence and separation, examines the ways in which infantile fantasies impinge on the later behavior of Murdoch characters who, to become enlightened and moral, must make a conscious attempt to recognize the positive uses of passivity. Examining *The Sacred and Profane Love Machine*,

Winsor sees a contradiction between the surrender of ego and aggressivity and the move toward mergence that Murdoch argues for in her essays, and the representation of such behavior in her novels. Passivity, she argues, seems a problematic form of goodness, and can itself become a means of keeping power.

Two selections offered here treat Murdoch's interest in religion. Dipple's comparison of *The Bell* and *Henry and Cato* (1974), demonstrates the evolution of Murdoch's style from a more repetitive skeletal plot to a more loose and complex one in which the ideal is less in evidence and characters are more spontaneous. But perhaps even more important is Dipple's argument that although Murdoch has grown increasingly interested in the difference between the artist and the saint in recent years, she has also been able to minimize the obstrusiveness of this oversimplified dichotomy. While *The Bell* is more successful in establishing the remoteness of religion from everyday life, *Henry and Cato* is able to show the remoteness of religious life from the spiritual life of her characters, all of whom represent different levels of the good. Tucker's study of *The Sea, the Sea* argues for the importance of a number of thematic concerns—Buddhist views of the phenomenal universe, the nature of art, and the surrender of magic—which, interwoven with ingredients from *The Tempest*, make this novel one of her richer blendings of the comedic and the gothic.

Nuns and Soldiers marks both the beginnings of another productive decade for Murdoch and a new creative phase as well, where her novels continue to get longer and looser, even as she brings formal patterning and ingredients of the gothic into more complicated conjunctions. Two final selections treat these more recent works. In "The Uses of the Past in *Nuns and Soldiers*," Margaret Scanlan examines Murdoch's thematic and formal uses of history. Cheryl Bove's "New Directions: Murdoch's Latest Women" argues that Murdoch's changes in narrative strategies have produced in her more recent work women characters who are more fully drawn and also less victimized.

Notes

1. Peter J. Conradi, *Iris Murdoch: The Saint and the Artist* (New York: St. Martin's Press, 1986), 3; hereafter cited as Conradi.
2. Iris Murdoch, "The Sublime and the Good," *Chicago Review* 13, no. 3 (1959): 42–55; hereafter cited in the text as sg.
3. Iris Murdoch, "The Sublime and the Beautiful Revisited," *Yale Review* 49 (Winter 1960): 247–71; hereafter cited in the text as sbr.
4. Iris Murdoch, "Against Dryness," *Encounter* 16, no. 1 (1961): 16–20; hereafter cited in the text as ad.
5. Frank Baldanza's "Iris Murdoch and the Theory of Personality," *Criticism* 7, no. 2 (Spring 1965): 176–89, is still useful on this subject.
6. Conradi suggests that it was her work with the United Nations Relief and Rehabili-

tation Administration and her work with displaced persons that influenced her interest in Sartrean existentialism because this philosophy "privileged the cultureless outsider hero" (11).

7. Iris Murdoch, *The Sovereignty of Good* (New York: Schocken, 1971), 78; hereafter cited in the text as *SG*.

8. William Slaymaker, "An Interview with Iris Murdoch," *Papers on Language & Literature* 21, no. 4 (Fall 1985):427; hereafter cited as Slaymaker.

9. John Haffenden, *Novelists in Interview* (New York: Methuen, 1985), 208; hereafter cited as Haffenden.

10. Iris Murdoch, *The Fire and the Sun: Why Plato Banished the Artists* (New York: Oxford University Press, 1977), 45. Hereafter cited in the text as *FS*. Murdoch's fullest development of her aesthetics appears in this text, where she at last confronts her perhaps most influential teacher, offering what is something of an apologia, even as she attempts to rescue the function of good art from its burial in Plato's negative commentary.

11. See Jack I. Biles, "An Interview with Iris Murdoch," *British Novelists Since 1900* (New York: AMS, 1987), 306; hereafter cited as Biles. Murdoch tells this interviewer that she feels much closer to Dickens and Dostoevksy than she does to Joyce or Woolf.

12. See especially Richard Todd, *Iris Murdoch: The Shakespearian Interest* (New York: Barnes & Noble, 1979). Speaking in reference to both her 1978 novel, *The Sea, the Sea*, and a more recent one, *The Philosopher's Pupil* (1983), about the influence of *The Tempest* on both, Murdoch argues that while this play influences her work, it is present only in shadowy ways. She goes on to say, "It has nothing to do with being dominated by Shakespeare or anyone else; it has to do with being dominated by myself and my own mythology, which is very strong" (Haffenden, 195, 198).

13. "Dryness" alludes to Hulme's preference for "beauty in small dry things" (sbr, 259).

14. Zohreh T. Sullivan, "The Contracting Universe of Iris Murdoch's Gothic Novels," *Modern Fiction Studies* 23, no. 4 (Winter 1977–78): 562.

15. Elizabeth Dipple, *Iris Murdoch: Work for the Spirit* (Chicago: University of Chicago Press, 1982), 84–85; hereafter cited as Dipple.

16. Robert Scholes, *Fabulation and Metafiction* (Urbana: University of Illinois Press, 1979), 59–60.

17. Perhaps this statement should be qualified. Murdoch has, for example, described *A Fairly Honorable Defeat* as a "theological myth," with Julius King as the Satan figure, an "old Testament 'instrument of justice,' " Tallis as the Christ figure, and Tallis's father as God the Father (Michael O. Bellamy, "An Interview with Iris Murdoch," *Contemporary Literature* 18 [1977]: 135–36; hereafter cited as Bellamy). But she warns readers against seeing patterns that aren't there. She also argues that she does not attempt to write allegorically, that "symbols must be very carefully controlled" (Biles, 310).

18. Murdoch also opposes twentieth-century critics of Romanticism—those whom she groups together as Symbolists. (See sbr, 261–64.) Although they appear as anti-Romantics, they are also antihumanist and, abhorring messiness, escape into "self-contained things"— into symbols that operate as a type of representation purged of its contingent ingredients. Also, their preference for poetry over prose is, for Murdoch, suspicious. Used as a "tool . . . for disclosures," Symbolist aesthetics privilege precision and clear definition—another sign of their need to control (sbr, 263).

19. Frank Kermode, "The House of Fiction: Interviews with Seven English Novelists," *Partisan Review* 30 (Spring 1963): 64.

20. Linda Kuehl, "Iris Murdoch: The Novelist as Magician/The Magician as Artist," *Modern Fiction Studies* 23 (1969): 356.

21. R. L. Widmann, "Murdoch's *Under the Net*: Theory and Practice of Fiction," *Critique* 10, no. 1 (1967): 14–15; hereafter cited as Widmann.

22. Murdoch has always been keenly aware of her own failings as an artist. At the same time she seems to have overcome much of her anxiety about her pattern-making tendency and more recently claims that "I have become more relaxed and, in a sense, more confident. There is more reflection in the later novels than in the earlier ones" (Biles, 307).

23. Conradi considers *A Severed Head*, *A Fairly Honorable Defeat*, *The Black Prince*, *The Sea, the Sea*, and *An Accidental Man* to be her best and argues for the 1970s as the time of Murdoch's "great flowering" (210).

24. I have borrowed generously from Dipple's chapter "Reality and Realism," 9–35.

25. In her interview with Slaymaker she has remarked that "I am more interested in religion than I used to be, and more concerned about religious belief, and this might suggest a move away from skepticism" (Slaymaker, 425).

26. Frank Baldanza, "The Nice and the Good," *Modern Fiction Studies* 15, no. 3 (Autumn 1969): 422.

27. Murdoch has noted, for example, that "Monty didn't get much out of Buddhism, but Theo did in a way."

28. Murdoch's exact words to Haffenden are, "It seems to me that some kind of Christian Buddhism would make a satisfactory religion because of course I can't get away from Christ, who travels with me."

29. Murdoch views the fire as representative of "the disturbed and semi-enlightened ego . . . consoled by its discoveries" (*FS*, 43).

30. See, for example, Ann Culley, "Theory and Practice: Characterization in the Novels of Iris Murdoch," *Modern Fiction Studies* 15, no. 3 (Autumn 1969): 335–45; William Hall, " 'The Third Way': The Novels of Iris Murdoch," *Dalhousie Review* 46 (Autumn 1960): 306–18. William Van O'Connor, "Iris Murdoch: The Formal and the Contingent," *Critique* (1960): 34–46; hereafter cited as O'Connor.

31. A. S. Byatt, *Degrees of Freedom* (New York: Barnes & Noble, 1969); other early studies include Peter Wolfe, *The Disciplined Heart: Iris Murdoch and Her Novels* (Columbia: University of Missouri Press, 1966), Frank Baldanza, *Iris Murdoch* (New York: Twayne, 1974), and Donna Gerstenberger, *Iris Murdoch* (Lewisburg: Bucknell University Press, 1975).

32. I am grateful to John J. Burke for notice of the following: Suguna Ramanathan, *Iris Murdoch: Figures of Good* (New York: St. Martin's Press, 1990), and Darlene Mettler, *Sound and Sense: Musical Allusion and Imagery in the Novels of Iris Murdoch* (New York: Peter Lang, 1991).

33. In a number of places Murdoch has expressed her discomfort over being labeled a woman writer, admitting, "I identify with men more than women" (Bellamy, 133). She adds, "I am a great supporter of women's liberation—particularly education for women—but in aid of getting women to join the human race." Many feminists would recognize such comments as, at best, an attempt to avoid the trap of essentialism, at worst added evidence of the humanists' resistance to the recognition of difference by which they practice exclusion of women.

GENERAL TREATMENTS OF
MURDOCH'S FICTION
◆

Myths, Mystery and the Mechanisms of Determinism: The Aesthetics of Freedom in Iris Murdoch's Fiction

WILLIAM SLAYMAKER

All of the twenty novels that Iris Murdoch has written and published since 1954 have to do in some way with the idea of freedom. The central focus of her philosophical essays is also the problem of human freedom. In the 1950s and 1960s Murdoch attacked both the romantic promethean freedom in Sartre's fiction, drama, and philosophy, and the careful rational analysis of freedom in Stuart Hampshire's *Freedom of the Individual*. She attempted to correct the false picture of freedom found in Kantian and Hegelian analyses.

By the 1970s, Murdoch's growing skepticism had developed into a belief in the severe limitation of human freedom. In her fiction, Christian, Celtic and classical myths play an important role in her fictional interpretations of freedom. The explanatory structures for human action and motivation found in Greek tragedy and epic—fate, destiny, doom, Ate, frenzy, nemesis, fury—are adumbrated in her novels. Murdoch has adapted the pagan world of irrational forces to modern life, not only as a literary device, but also as an explanatory system which emphasizes the mystery and opacity of human existence. Freedom appears as a suspect mode of that existence that, like human life itself, is so complex as to defy a total rational analysis; myths provide fictional frameworks to support her notion of the incomprehensibility and impenetrability of human action and motivations.

Important to the expression of Murdoch's views on freedom are the metaphors of mechanism, especially the machinery of the human ego with its uncontrollable psychical as well as physical/sexual energy. These mechanisms do not mean that there is no human freedom. Rather, they point out the difficulty of attaining to a state of freedom, and how deceptive that state is. Murdoch is quite skeptical about the possibility of human freedom, but she is not cynical. There are ways out of the labyrinthine human condition, and love and art are two of the most important. Love can be false, egotistical and sadistic; it can spoil as well as sponsor freedom. Similarly, bad and

From *Papers on Language and Literature* 18, no. 2 (Spring 1982): 166–80; © 1982 by the Board of Trustees, Southern Illinois University. Reprinted by permission.

shallow art spoils freedom. Nonetheless, love and art hold out the best possibilities for escape from the mechanisms that render human freedom impotent and useless.

In her philosophical essays of the 1950s, Murdoch made it quite clear that she could not accept totally Sartre's analysis of freedom. She argues that Sartre offers no analysis of the "world of ordinary moral virtues." Instead, he presents a promethean and romantic view of freedom. In Sartre's excess of emotion and ideological urgency, Murdoch senses an "impatience . . . with the *stuff* of human life" and a lack of understanding of the "absurd irreducible uniqueness of people and their relations with each other." Murdoch's rejection of the romantic freedom of Sartre does not necessarily make her more open to the rationalists' arguments for freedom. Her essay "Dreams and Self-Knowledge" provides evidence of her rejection of the view of man as a responsible and rational, free moral agent. As a skeptic about rule-oriented decision making, Murdoch sees the possibility of transcendent visions conditioning moral choices. Freedom becomes, then, a "mode of reflection" rather than just the power for decisive choices.[2]

In a pair of articles published in 1959, "The Sublime and the Good" and "The Sublime and the Beautiful Revisited," Murdoch turns her attention toward the place of freedom in an aesthetic theory based on love. Rejecting the systematic philosophical views of freedom of Kant and Hegel, Murdoch finds that freedom is possible for those persons who can love and accept an object (human or nonhuman) which is other and distinct from the loving subject. As she concisely puts it, "Freedom is exercised in the confrontation by each other, in the context of an infinitely extensible work of imaginative understanding, of two irreducibly dissimilar individuals. Love is the imaginative recognition of, that is respect for, this otherness."[3] Freedom becomes an imaginative confrontation with the mystery of otherness. The acceptance of this otherness in all its particularity and incomprehensibility is love which, as an aesthetic concern, is freedom to know, understand and respect things quite alien to familiar points of view.[4] The aesthetic principle of love must be applied in order to free the characters in the contemporary novel, and to respect their individuality and contingency.

In "Against Dryness" Murdoch summarizes her dissatisfaction with the theories of freedom of the 1950s. Modern novelists have lost the sense of man "against a background of values, of realities, which transcend him"; novelists write "crystalline" and "journalistic" novels that indulge in fantasy and do not show the complex reality of the world with its "degrees of freedom." She forcefully states her dissatisfactions with the ways freedom has been conceived by artists and intellectuals: "We are not isolated free choosers, monarchs of all we survey, but benighted creatures sunk in a reality whose nature we are constantly and overwhelmingly tempted to deform by fantasy. Our current picture of freedom encourages a dreamlike facility; whereas what we require is a renewed sense of the difficulty and complexity of the moral life and opacity of persons."[5]

In two essays in 1966, "Freedom and Knowledge" and "The Darkness of Practical Reason," Murdoch begins to limit the arena of human freedom. On the surface, the essays respond to Stuart Hampshire's philosophical assertions that freedom and free will are exercised in a factual external world which occasions rational decisions and choices. Murdoch argues that freedom is exercised more often in the interior world of imagination. Hence freedom is subjected to the world already made in the imagination and the values we impose on ourselves by attending to the imagination. We lack total control and freedom because "we have already partly willed our world when we come to look at it; and we must admit moral responsibility for this 'fabricated' world, however difficult it may be to control the process of fabrication." Her definition of freedom at this juncture of the development of her thought shows a constriction of the potency and scope of freedom: "To be free is something like this: to exist sanely without fear and to perceive what is real."[6] What is real and how it is to be perceived are difficult questions, but she suggests that for some—artists in particular—freedom is obtainable through an accurate perception and portrayal of the real.

A collection of essays, *The Sovereignty of Good*, and an appraisal of Plato's aesthetic, *The Fire and The Sun*, are longer works that extend arguments about freedom into the provinces of moral philosophy and aesthetic theory. In the first essay from the collection, "The Idea of Perfection," Murdoch defines in more detail the concepts of attention, vision, imagination and love, all of which figure in the concept of freedom. Her idea of perfection is moral progress, the movement toward a better vision of an object or person, and love coupled with knowledge, seeking out and attending to the reality of something or someone else.[7]

To some degree, the limits of the individual's attention are the limits on his freedom. Choices are restricted by what can be seen, and what can be seen depends upon the individual moral imagination and effort. Furthermore, the individual has only "slight control over the direction and focus of his vision" (*SG*, 40). While the idea of freedom is essential to Murdoch's analysis of moral progress or perfection, the concept of necessity enters with more emphasis and conviction than her earlier writings suggest. Freedom is a "kind of necessity": "if I attend properly I will have no choices and this is the ultimate condition to be aimed at." At least for the artist, art is an effort aimed at freedom by the recognition of necessity: "the idea of a patient, loving regard, directed upon a person, a thing, a situation, presents the will not as unimpeded movement, but as something very much more like 'obedience' " (*SG*, 40).

Murdoch recognizes and accepts the irrational and subconscious aspects of human personality. The freedom she allows, especially for the artist, is that of seeing these forces and recording them in all their reality. Love of reality rewards the artist who can record this vision of reality and thereby release psychic and other compulsive energies (*SG*, 43–4). This is the moral progress Murdoch seeks.

In "On 'God' and 'Good,' " the second essay in the collection, Murdoch describes human freedom as an energy system. This metaphor, introduced in the first essay, gives a new perspective on Murdoch's concept of freedom. "What we really are," she argues, "seems much more like an obscure system of energy out of which choices and visible acts of will emerge at intervals in ways which are often unclear and often dependent on the condition of the system in between moments of choice" (*SG*, 54). Love, a form of freedom open to the artist, is a reorientation of the selfish egocentric mechanism toward something other; and goodness, liberating because it frees us from our narrow personal fantasies, is attained by this redirection of attention. Good, not mediocre art reveals an ardent love for reality and liberates one from the mechanisms of fantasies. "Reality" in all its ambiguity is important for Murdoch because it is outside the self. She is skeptical about self-analysis and self-knowledge because "it is an attachment to what lies outside the fantasy mechanism, and not a scrutiny of the mechanism itself, that liberates. Close scrutiny of the mechanism often merely strengthens its power. 'Self-knowledge,' in the sense of a minute understanding of one's own machinery, seems to me, except at a fairly simple level, usually a delusion" (*SG*, 67). Murdoch stresses love and art because they are energy systems addressed to the outside, the other object. She cogently explains,

> It is in the capacity to love, that is to *see*, that the liberation of the soul from fantasy consists. The freedom which is a proper human goal is the freedom from fantasy, that is the realism of compassion. What I have called fantasy, the proliferation of blinding self-centered aims and images, is itself a powerful system of energy, and most of what is often called 'will' or 'willing' belongs to this system. What counteracts the system is attention to reality inspired by, consisting of, love. In the case of art and nature such attention is immediately rewarded by the enjoyment of beauty. In the case of morality, although there are sometimes rewards, the idea of a reward is out of place. Freedom is not strictly the exercise of the will, but rather the experience of accurate vision which, when this becomes appropriate, occasions action. It is what lies behind and in between actions and prompts them that is important, and it is this area which should be purified. By the time the moment of choice has arrived the quality of attention has probably determined the nature of the act. This fact produces the curious separation between consciously rehearsed motives and action which is sometimes wrongly taken as an experience of freedom.
>
> (*SG*, 66–67)

In Murdoch's analysis, Good becomes the object of attention which liberates. Will is merely a "natural energy of psyche" available occasionally for goodness, and soul is a "mechanism of attachments" which needs purification. Freedom neither guarantees good acts nor right and pure action. Except for goodness itself, will, soul and freedom are all subject to chance and necessity (*SG*, 69–74).

Murdoch is not a strict determinist in any sense. She claims there is no scientific or philosophical proof of total determinism. The small area of the human spirit "free from the mechanism of empirical psychology" is to be found in goodness. Goodness, as an abstraction, is art; as a concrete human relationship, it is love. Love expressed as art is best and most free because it is transcendent. It is separate from the messiness of ordinary love relationships, which become enmeshed in the mechanism of the possessive ego. Art is the vision of love. Murdoch concludes her second essay with a rather stirring assessment of aesthetic principles: "For both the collective and the individual salvation of the human race, art is doubtless more important than philosophy, and literature most important of all" (*SG*, 76). This is not a disclaimer for the effectiveness of philosophy; it is a bold statement of her belief in the liberating qualities of good art.

In the last essay, Murdoch attempts to get a firmer grip on the vague term 'reality', which is at the heart of her aesthetics and concept of freedom. It is not a photographic realism that Murdoch means to be the real subject of great art, but rather, "pity and justice" (*SG*, 87). Murdoch adopts the terminology and concepts familiar to platonic philosophy. In order to define reality, which is the aim and object of every great artist and a vision which is lovely and liberating, Murdoch resorts to such linguistic equations as: the authority of truth is reality, duty and virtue are reality, Good is transcendent reality, selflessness is realistic, and really looking or attending is reality (*SG*, 90–93). These equations add up to the formula, an old one for Murdoch, that what we seek is a vision of unity, a dream which is transcendent and liberating from the anchors of self. Quite obviously Murdoch's reality is a platonic, not a naturalistic one. Ultimately, the unified transcendent reality Murdoch seeks is love. It is the platonic love of a vision of goodness, truth and beauty which liberates and makes us open to the Good (*SG*, 102–3). Murdoch's reality is a vision which defines and redirects the energies and passions of the often misdirected psychic mechanisms. Seeking and finding reality are thus liberating experiences.

The Fire and the Sun: Why Plato Banished the Artists is not only an examination of Plato's aesthetics, but also an expression of Murdoch's ardent wish to replace Angst, alienation and isolation as central concepts in post-Kantian and existential philosophy with some gentler yet plausible concept of a human transcendent reality. Murdoch attacks Plato's contention that art is not reality but rather a fantasy of the falsely speculative imagination. She rejects his arguments that art is not true and that it is dangerous because it trivializes and undermines the truly spiritual. She cannot accept his portrait of artists and their art as irrationally seductive, base and morally weak.[8]

Using Plato's criticism of art and artists as a point of departure, she constructs a positive view that art serves to free the human being who is engaged in contemplating it. She agrees with Plato that the bad artist is a fantasiast who does not see external necessity, and who constructs the "mechanical 'causality' of his personal dream-life" (*FS*, 76), but good art can be like religion, and attending to it can be like praying. Art can lead to unselfishness. It is good and moral. The good artist recognizes necessity and helps purify the imagination so that it may contemplate the real world.

Necessity and reality are equated in *The Fire and the Sun* (45, 80, 83). In contrast to Plato's distrust of art, Murdoch believes that good art makes recognition of necessity (which is reality) a serious but playful exercise that does not turn one's attention away from the good, but focuses his vision on images of good. This exercise is a process of consolation in a world where religion and metaphysics are breaking down. Freedom has become the consolation of aesthetics—the free play involved in the creation of works of art with all their ambiguity and imaginativeness, their "voracious ubiquitousness," their "limitless connection with ordinary life," and their reflection of the mysteriousness and complexity of human existence (*FS*, 86).

At this point, Murdoch seems guilty of the accusations she has directed towards Sartre's art and philosophy. Her version of a transcendental aesthetic seems as far removed from the "stuff of human life" as his. But Murdoch is interested in the ordinary life and how freedom enters into it; she writes novels because literature describes in ordinary language the philosophical problem of freedom. Rarely, however, do Murdoch's novels include the quotidian existence of the average proletarian. The great majority of her characters are drawn from the middle classes with university educations and deep interests in art and its problems, interests coupled with the search for freedom. But rarely do the characters find it. The majority of her artists are mediocre practitioners of their crafts, caught in the same mechanical ways as everyone else, trapped in their own egoism and the excesses of psychical and sexual energies.

Murdoch shows the reader in her novels of the 1970s the inability of each character to attain to freedom through art or love or any other means. It is not that the characters are able only to attain to "degrees of freedom"; they are unable to be free because of the determining forces that rob them of any possibility of real and lasting freedom. Antonia Byatt's important study of Murdoch's novels of the 1950s and early 1960s accurately details the desperate attempts of Murdoch's characters to win some degree of freedom, and she is correct in her assessment that "all Miss Murdoch's novels can in an important sense be seen as studies of the 'degrees of freedom' available to individuals. . . ."[9] However, the novels of the 1970s show that freedom is severely limited by the frantic force of love, the impenetrability of human motivations, and the general opacity of human psychology. Expressed in mythical terms, love captures and binds humans in a net of error.

Actions are undertaken for very unclear reasons, almost as if supernatural agents were charged with biasing the decision making process. Whereas the philosophical essays show the theoretical possibility of freedom through a love of the good, true and beautiful, the recent novels show the failure of such a scheme. The determining forces of the overpowering, selfish ego and the mechanical psychical and physical drives combine to make freedom not a matter of degree but an unrealizable dream. Even Byatt seems to recognize this gradual change in the attitude toward freedom in Murdoch's earlier fiction. She argues that Jake of *Under the Net* (1954) is free, Nan in *The Sandcastle* (1957) achieves freedom, but Michael is only "tragically free" in *The Bell* (1958), and Randall finds "dubious freedom" in *An Unofficial Rose* (1962).[10]

In an analysis of the last novel Cyrena Pondrom is willing to grant the characters some measure of freedom. She maintains that even though "Murdoch's characters, in the course of their quests, find freedom an elusive goal . . . human will had a part in shaping events, and in this action of will lay a grain of freedom."[11]

The Black Prince (1973) illustrates Murdoch's more recent narrative development of the concept of freedom. One of her most complex novels, it not only contains long passages of aesthetic theory but constitutes one of Murdoch's few narrative experiments. The novel is a first-person narrative framed by an editor's and narrator's forewords and internal commentaries as well as five postscripts written by the editor, the narrator, and the main characters in the novel. The effect of the narrative experiment is to throw the narrator's story into question and thus to examine the possibility of truth and knowledge in a work of art.

The fictional editor of *The Black Prince* is P. Loxias, another name for the Greek god Apollo. Bradley Pearson is the author of the narrative section of the novel, entitled *The Black Prince: A Celebration of Love*. This novel, the title of which is slightly more complete than Murdoch's own, is written in prison. Hence the need of the intermediary Loxias as publisher and editor who gets the manuscript out of prison and publishes it with commentary. As the subtitle makes evident, the novel is about love: the Greek god Eros is epithetically the Black Prince. But the novel is also about the intricacies of art, and the fate, destiny or doom that plague the artist who must write what he considers to be the truth.

Loxias expresses the notion of the fatality of the artistic enterprise when he comments early in the novel that "art is a doom."[12] Bradley Pearson underscores this concept of fate when he recognizes that love and art are his "destiny" (*BP*, 210), and that "true art comes, with absolute necessity" (*BP*, 339). These statements are Murdoch's reminders that the creative human mind cannot help but create its own stories (myths) which are often the prevarications of reality she labels "fantasy." Fantasizing is an inescapable process of the human mind which colors human decision making and the perception of reality. As Murdoch revealed in an interview: "I think that people create myths about themselves and are then dominated by the myths. They feel trapped, and they elect other people to play roles in their lives, to be gods or destroyers or something, and I think that this mythology is often very deep and very influential and secretive, and a novelist is revealing secrets of this sort."[13]

Bradley Pearson's foreword to the novel is a revelation "of this sort." Even though the very nature of the confession is suspicious due to its overly refined sensibilities and purist attitudes toward art, nonetheless his ideas resonate sympathetically with many of those Murdoch has outlined in her essays. While Murdoch raises the suspicion that Pearson is a mediocre artist, ironically his aesthetic tenets about truth repeat some of her own: "good art speaks truth, indeed *is* truth, perhaps the only truth"; "art teaches one perhaps better than philosophy"; "only art explains, and that cannot itself be explained"; "without freedom there is no art and no truth" (BP, xi, xiii, xv, xviii).

Murdoch hopes to exaggerate, not fantasize, her characters' secrets to get at the truth. Even Pearson realizes that "art isn't chat plus fantasy. Art comes out of endless restraint and silence" (*BP*, 29). Nonetheless, the novel, *The Black Prince: A Celebration of Love*, is his release from the bonds of silence and an exercise in fantasy as the concluding postscripts show. Pearson confesses that he is fantasizing in his first lengthy aesthetic commentary after the foreword. He communicates his lack of restraint, his monomaniacal "delusions of grandeur." He realizes he is defending himself and his art through a "mound of words"; art becomes for him a fantasia of fears and mysteries: "We defend ourselves by descriptions and tame the world by generalizing. What does he fear? is usually the key to the artist's mind. Art is so often a barrier. (Is this true even of the greatest art, I wonder?) So art becomes not communication but mystification" (*BP*, 58).

Pearson holds neither his tongue, his pen, nor his imagination in check. One thing leads to another; irony is heaped upon irony. If Murdoch's straightforward definition of freedom is invoked here ("freedom is to exist sanely without fear and to perceive what is real") then Bradley Pearson does not measure up, and Murdoch reveals perhaps her own situation through the dilemma of Pearson. Freedom through art is a difficult achievement, given the mind-boggling complexity of sifting through motives and countermotives and finding the true and real ones. Art may reveal truth and freedom, but it is a mystery why this is so.

As in all of Murdoch's novels, love is one of the central themes. Marriage, as the institution of love, more often binds than frees. Murdoch simply calls it a "cage" from which lovers struggle to escape (*BP*, 72, 111, 127, 145). But marriage can be even more; it can be a "machine of mutual hatred" (*BP*, 67). Bradley Pearson's troubles begin with his search for love. His first marriage has been a hell. He retires and devotes himself to his art, but art does not come with this new freedom. Unable to write, he seeks some outlet for his energies. He cherishes the idea of selfless sacrifice as real freedom, but he can find no object of devotion. Since the love of God is out of the question, he seeks someone or something as an object of worship. The wife of his friend and artist-rival Arnold Baffin happens along, seduces him, and admonishes him to be free. But he feels he cannot act, worries about his feelings of destiny to be a great writer, and knows that art is a "doom" for him.

This knowledge throws Bradley into a frenzy: "What was this, love, sex, art? I felt that strong urge to do something, to act which often afflicts people in unanalysable dilemmas" (BP, 117). Unlike Stuart Hampshire's rational man who acts consistently with his willful perception of the world, Bradley is determined by uncontrollable urges and ideas that surge through him. The mystery and opacity of personality are unanalyzable and incompletely explainable. A feeling of fate and doom is Bradley's explanation for his confusion and inaction.

In another one of Pearson's lengthy narrative interruptions, he expatiates on the themes of freedom, goodness and art. Because the "natural tendency of the human soul is towards the protection of the ego," Pearson argues, the average person desires goodness in the comparative sense of being "better," "richer" or "cleverer" than others (BP, 152). Genuine goodness is intolerable to most men. But occasionally ordinary men, and often artists, desire true art, which is virtue. Pearson claims he desires it, and so writes little, in contrast to Baffin, who writes voluminously but with little interest in good art or moral goodness. Pearson claims he has the will to hold out against such seductive invitations to write, and resists the women who want him to write. Their reasons and admonitions are specious.

Pearson also argues that there is a discrepancy between subjective self-awareness and objective knowledge. This discrepancy makes truth almost impossible to discover. He suggests that "some kind of integrity of the imagination, a sort of moral genius" is necessary in order to find truth (BP, 157). This "moral genius" is a "Shakespearean" consciousness that preserves itself through will yet does not blind itself with its protective power. Pearson speculates that perhaps Eastern philosophy is right to advocate the "total destruction of the dreaming ego" (BP, 157), but only art and love hold out even the remotest possibilities of moral orientation of the consciousness: "almost all our natural preoccupations are low ones, and in most cases the ragbag of consciousness is only unified by the experience of great love or intense love" (BP, 158). Such a unification would be the truth and transcendental reality that Murdoch describes in her essays. It would be freedom.

Shakespeare is introduced into Pearson's "ragbag" aesthetics because he produced ingenuous yet highly conscious art. He functions as the medium through which Bradley is introduced to his great love for Julian Baffin, the daughter of Arnold Baffin and thirty-eight years his junior. But while Murdoch is herself serious about Shakespeare—she used his art as a touchstone in her essay "The Sublime and the Beautiful Revisited"—Bradley Pearson's interpretation of *Hamlet* is simply incredible. Murdoch maintained in an interview that while "some of Bradley's observations [about *Hamlet*], I think, are quite acute; others are dotty."[14]

From this confrontation with *Hamlet* and his meeting with Julian comes another of Pearson's analyses of love. Bradley sees love as a "demonic force engaged in continuous creation and participation," an act of creating the beloved, like a work of art (*BP*, 173). Unlike great art, the claims of love are overbearing, overpowering and blinding. Love can even "dim the dream of art and make it seem secondary, even a delusion" (*BP*, 174). In mythical terms, the "black arrow" of love is fearfully destructive in its power to delude, and Black Eros inspires Bradley to write his book which, as the postscripts show, may be based on a complete delusion. The freedom that comes through the unifying experience of great art or great love is unrealized, because both art and love turn out to be, if not completely delusory, at least unobtainable for Bradley Pearson.

In one of Pearson's shorter narrative disquisitions are echoes of Murdoch's favorite subject, platonic love. Pearson finds Plato right: love brings with it a "vision of selflessness." How wonderful and good to "will another rather than oneself" (*BP*, 176). While Pearson is experiencing the delusions of love, he is also experiencing love as freedom even though he knows it is also the cage that leads to marriage. Love is described as a marvelously powerful tool, a mechanism, a lever by which to move the world. It is also a spinning mechanical force, centrifugal and bent on crushing the "machine of flesh and bones" (*BP*, 265). Love is Bradley's destiny; no escape is possible; it becomes his cage.

When Bradley runs away with Julian, he discovers his love is not only his destiny but also his nemesis. Impotent to consummate his love for Julian, he believes he has ensured his love and liberation from doubt by willing a violent consummation; and he explains the violence of his attack on Julian in terms of anger or fury against fate which seizes him, maddens him, and makes him rapaciously take Julian. Bradley calls it Black Eros when Julian asks him why he acted so strangely and forcefully, and from this mythical explanation of the final consummation comes the further confession that art is now possible for him. He has been freed through sexual love, a release of sexual energy.

The love affair between Julian and Bradley is doomed. Julian leaves him. He desperately tries to win her back but becomes more deeply entangled in the strange relationship between Arnold and Rachel Baffin. Bradley's narrative ends when he tries to help Rachel after she has murdered her husband; he is blamed for the murder and is imprisoned. He is never able to sort out his different loves—the platonic, the sexual, and the artistic—and the love story of his life ends absurdly.

The first of five postscripts to the narrative is written by Pearson. In his account, fate is responsible for his willing complicity in the coverup of Arnold Baffin's death. He does not try to escape the blame, but to understand how his love for Julian has made art possible. He writes the book *The Black Prince: A Celebration of Love*:

> When I thought earlier that my ability to love her *was* my ability to write, my ability to exist at last as the artist I had disciplined my life to be. I was in the truth, but knew it only darkly. All great truths are mysteries, all mortality is ultimately mysticism, all real religions are mystery religions, all great gods have many names. This little book is important to me and I have written it as simply and as truthfully as I can. How good it is I do not know and in a sublime sense I do not care. It has come into being as true art comes, with absolute necessity and with absolute ease. That it is not great art I dare say I am aware. What kind of thing it is is dark to me as I am dark to myself. The mechanical aspects of our humanity remain obscure to us until divine power has refined them absolutely, and then there is no anxious knower any more and nothing to be known.
>
> (p. 339)

Even though Bradley Pearson is a suspect narrator and an ironic commentator on Murdoch's ideas, much of this conclusion to the postscript can be found in her essays. That truth is a mystery best revealed through art derives from Murdoch's aesthetic of freedom. The only substantial difference is that the novel employs Greek myth in order to show the confusion and lack of freedom Bradley Pearson experiences. The myth represents the determining forces of love, fate, psychic confusion and the forces of physical attraction that tie humans together in love affairs seemingly beyond their rational control.

While some of Bradley Pearson's aesthetic is a reliable expression of the author's, Iris Murdoch makes it clear that Bradley is an emotional romantic. The postscript ends with such ardour and passion for art and the memory of Julian, both as escapes from Bradley's prison of doubt and illusion, that it is hard not to feel that Murdoch purposefully made her narrator less than sympathetic. While he is not quite the passionate Sartrean hero of freedom, he shares an excess of romantic cerebral isolation and alienation that Murdoch had found unrealistic and unacceptable in Sartre.

The remaining four postscripts are rejections of Bradley Pearson's account of his love affair. Christian, the first wife of Pearson, claims that the business about art in the narrative and in his postscript is just that: good business intended to sell his memoirs. She sees the narrative as an exaggeration of the truth for the purpose of sensationalism. Francis, a psychologist and homosexual brother of Christian, sees Pearson's story as a classical example of the latent homosexual paranoia involved in psychological disguises in his narrative. Rachel Baffin finds the book "dreamy-fantasy-nonsense" and pities his need for an art of fantasizing. Even Julian rejects his account of her love for him. Since she has become a writer, she finds his analysis of art totally false and erroneous. True art is not related to Eros: "love is concerned with possession and vindication of self. Art with neither" (*BP*, 360). Art is a cool, dispassionate master of itself. Murdoch probably intends for us to see Julian's aesthetic assessment of Pearson's narrative to be partially correct, but she also reveals Julian's shallow aestheticism as an indictment of her youth and fickleness.

Each character thus sees the truth of Bradley's story according to his interests at the time. We suspect that Pearson's art, as he himself confessed, was not good or great art. His love for Julian was no doubt exaggerated and romanticised. If indeed Pearson's story is mainly fantasy, then the keys to freedom—true love and good art—require close scrutiny in the novel. The comic chorus of voices at the end of novel shows that Murdoch is skeptical of Bradley's love and theories of art. We have only the final postscript by the editor Loxias to convince us that Bradley was right after all and the others totally false in their remarks on the narrative. Loxias claims that it is Julian's aesthetic which is overly romantic, not Bradley's. Loxias' final words are significant for the whole novel: "Art is not cozy and it is not mocked. Art tells the only truth that ultimately matters. It is the light by which human things can be mended. And after art there is, let me assure you all, nothing" (*BP*, 336).

We may conjecture that this statement, taken in the light of Bradley Pearson's love affair and his imprisonment and death, is partially Murdoch's own. In his dissertation on the aesthetics and ethics of Murdoch's fiction, Michael Bellamy argues that Murdoch shows the escape from solipsism, from imprisonment in self, and the possibility of communication through art and the resultant freeing of the self by communion through art with others.[15] In spite of Bellamy's optimistic reading of Murdoch's fiction, the freedom realized by Pearson through love or art remains open to question, given that he is fantasizing in his own mediocre way. Pearson's dilemmas are as much examples of inauthentic freedom and self-delusion as they are of true freedom and true perception of reality. The concepts of fate, destiny, doom, necessity, frenzy, nemesis, blindness and confusion—all painted on a backdrop of myth, mystery and psychological and physical mechanisms involving sex and organic energy—underscore Murdoch's growing skepticism about the possibility of freedom. In the more recent novels her characters do not match the power and sublimity of freedom through art or love that radiates from *The Fire and the Sun*.

The novels after *The Black Prince* contain similar pessimistic accounts that offer little hope for a complete realization of freedom. *The Sacred and Profane Love Machine* (1974) is concerned with the mythical determining forces of gods and fate, as well as the mechanisms of the ego involved in messy love affairs. The old problem of artistic freedom resurfaces and is again left unresolved. Like *The Black Prince*, none of the characters finds freedom in any significant way. All turn away from a moral freedom based on good art and love. *The Word Child* (1975) is a bleak and disheartening description of a young man who never finds love or security. While the novel has little to do with the problem of freedom or the concerns of the artist, it does nothing to relieve the pessimism of the dark comedies which Murdoch continues to write. *Henry and Cato* (1976) recounts a search for freedom and God in the lives of tortured and twisted characters who rehearse the sordid existences made familiar by the previous novels. Several of the main characters attain to a gratuitous happiness at the end of the novel, but not because of any disciplined resolve or willful action. *The Sea, The Sea* (1978) describes the artistic ego. The novel reveals little about the problem of freedom. An account of the life and fantasies of a retired actor and director, it describes the deformation of reality through the wiles of the protective ego. *Nuns and Soldiers* (1980) is more felicitous and less tragic. Murdoch repeats her theme that love and good art liberate. But since the major characters are very rarely comfortable with their love affairs and the artists types are appallingly confused and disoriented, freedom is left unrealized.

As an artist concerned with reality, Murdoch does not think it true or aesthetically honest to show life as merely a confrontation of ideas. As she has argued in "Against Dryness," she does not intend to write "crystalline" novels where ideas and ideals correct and order the chaos of human existence. She is not likely to write a novel where any character obtains freedom, love or artistic inspiration in the pure form exposed in *The Fire and the Sun.* Nonetheless, it is also true that Murdoch has become increasingly critical and skeptical—in her novels at least—about the possibility of obtaining freedom. Freedom remains an ideal which is incompletely realizable in both life and art. The degrees of freedom have become smaller, fewer, and harder to attain.

Notes

1. *Sartre: Romantic Rationalist* (New Haven, 1967), pp. 23, 25, 41, 112.
2. *Proceedings of the Aristotelian Society* (London, 1956), supp. 30: 35, 50, 53, 55.
3. "The Sublime and the Good," *Chicago Review* 12/13 (Autumn 1959): 52.
4. "The Sublime and the Beautiful Revisited," *Yale Review* 49 (1959): 270.
5. *Encounter* 16 (1961): 18, 20.
6. "The Darkness of Practical Reason," *Encounter* 27 (1966): 50.
7. (New York, 1970), pp. 28, 34. Subsequent references are cited by page in the text.
8. (Oxford, 1977), pp. 5–6, 30, 41–2, 65–6. Subsequent references are cited by page in the text.
9. *Degrees of Freedom: The Novels of Iris Murdoch* (London, 1965), p. 11.
10. Ibid., pp. 38, 71, 103–4, 121.
11. "Iris Murdoch: An Existentialist?" *Comparative Literature Studies* 5 (1968): 410, 416.

12. (New York, 1973). All page references in the text are to this edition. The novel is loaded with references to doom, destiny, necessity and fate. Coupled with these are nemesis, fury, frenzy, delusion, blindness and other forces often encountered in Greek tragedy and epic. Cf. pp. ix, xii, 3, 66, 117, 149, 210, 272, 283, 289, 339, 340. This is only a partial list: the uses of these concepts require a separate study.

13. Michael Bellamy, "An Interview with Iris Murdoch," *Contemporary Literature*, 18 (1977): 138.

14. Jack Biles, "An Interview with Iris Murdoch," *Studies in the Literary Imagination*, 11 (1978): 124.

15. "The Artist and the Saint: An Approach to the Aesthetics and the Ethics of Iris Murdoch," *Dissertation Abstracts* 36 (1976): 6110-A.

The Shakespearian Ideal

- Richard Todd

A recent interview of Iris Murdoch's suggests that Shakespeare's 'marvellousness', which she feels should interest any novelist writing today, lies in his combination of 'real character' and 'magical pattern'.[1] The implication is that these two features of art do not normally co-exist, and we are reminded of her earlier and famous distinction between 'large shapeless quasi-documentary' novels and 'small quasi-allegorical' ones: the 'journalistic' and the 'crystalline'. This distinction was formulated in 'Against Dryness' (1961),[2] but on the evidence of more recent discussions Murdoch is now somewhat reticent about it. Indeed, in the 'House of Fiction' interview with Frank Kermode, less than two years after the publication of 'Against Dryness,' she was already regarding it as:

> one of those epigrammatic distinctions which are probably themselves rather inexact. The distinction was suggested to me in a way by worrying about my own work and about what was wrong with it.[3]

On the evidence of the interview referred to at the beginning of this paragraph, with Malcolm Bradbury in 1976, Iris Murdoch now feels the distinction to be 'too simple'. However, it has often been felt, and she does not herself appear to deny this, that it is her own novelistic aim to steer a middle course between the two terms of the distinction, or something like them, but that this aim has proved almost impossible to realise in practice and what has occurred instead is that she has too frequently submitted to the temptation of form, to the extent that character has tended to be sacrificed to pattern. She herself remarks, in the interview with Bradbury, that if she could create the people she would sacrifice the pattern.

To try to find out why Iris Murdoch feels that this Shakespearian ideal combination of character and pattern eludes her novelistic grasp, we may respect in this chapter her attitude towards 'Against Dryness' and turn instead to some of her later theoretical writing. It seems that her failure in this creative respect is one which she feels that she shares with her contemporaries, and it is a matter of continuing interest to her whether this failure is simply

From *Iris Murdoch: The Shakespearian Interest* (New York: Barnes & Noble, 1979), 24–42; © Richard Todd. Reprinted by permission.

a question of collective contemporary novelistic incompetence, or whether it is really possible to detect underlying reasons in the history of language and thought since Shakespeare's time for an inability to combine character and pattern. A full and precise statement of the characteristics of good art is to be found in an essay entitled 'The Sovereignty of Good over Other Concepts'.[4] Here we find extremely high claims being made for form in art: it 'is properly the simulation of the self-contained aimlessness of the universe' (*The Sovereignty of Good*, p. 86). It must be emphasised that the claim is made with reference to purely imitative criteria; what is to be represented is a conception of human life in the universe which Murdoch describes unflatteringly as follows:

> I can see no evidence to suggest that human life is not something self-contained. There are properly many patterns and purposes within life, but there is no general and as it were externally guaranteed pattern or purpose of the kind for which philosophers and theologians used to search. We are what we seem to be, transient mortal creatures subject to necessity and change. . . . Our destiny can be examined, but it cannot be justified or totally explained. We are simply here.
>
> —*The Sovereignty of Good*, p. 79

This is not all however. Murdoch offers what she admits to be a 'rather depressing description' of the human psyche in relation not only to its conception of the universe but also to its dealings with other human psyches:

> The psyche is a historically determined individual relentlessly looking after itself. In some ways it resembles a machine; in order to operate it needs sources of energy, and it is predisposed to certain patterns of activity. The area of its vaunted freedom of choice is not usually very great. One of its main pastimes is day-dreaming. It is reluctant to face unpleasant realities. Its consciousness is not normally a transparent glass through which it views the world, but a cloud of more or less fantastic reverie designed to protect the psyche from pain. It constantly seeks consolation, either through imagined inflation of self or through fictions of a theological nature. Even its loving is more often than not an assertion of self.
>
> —*The Sovereignty of Good*, pp. 78–9

Murdoch feels that this natural selfishness and universal pointlessness are a logical bequest of philosophical and scientific thought since Kant (indeed, she had already developed this idea to some extent in 'Against Dryness'), and as characteristics of human life considers that they may be more profitably assumed or asserted than actually argued. What is particularly at issue is that natural selfishness and universal pointlessness are non-consoling matters, and it is ideally the task of art to represent them in a way that does not falsely console by its form. Bad art only too obviously possesses form;

'the forms of bad art . . . are recognizable and familiar rat-runs of selfish day-dream' (*The Sovereignty of Good*, p. 86). The form which characterises good art, on the other hand, is not in this sense wish-fulfilling but 'resists the easy patterns of the fantasy' and so therefore 'often seems to us mysterious' (*The Sovereignty of Good*, p. 86). All consolation which we offer ourselves for the 'intolerably chancy and incomplete' characteristic of human life involves us in the creation of forms; these may be theological, mythical or anecdotal; even classification is difficult and these and various other kinds probably overlap in certain ways. However, though all consolation involves us in the creation of forms, it is possible to conceive of form which, according to Murdoch, is mysteriously not primarily the result of consolation. Shakespeare is one of the few artists who habitually manages, in her opinion, to offer artistic form which is non-consolatory. This conception, of form which does not console, must be examined since it does, I think, represent a further development in Iris Murdoch's thought from that voiced in 'Against Dryness', where she remarked:

> Real people are destructive of myth, contingency is destructive of fantasy and opens the way for imagination. . . . Too much contingency of course may turn art into journalism. But since reality is incomplete, art must not be too much afraid of incompleteness.
>
> —Ed. Bradbury, p. 31

The polemic of the phrase 'art must not be too much afraid of incompleteness' does seem to have developed further, in 'The Sovereignty of Good over Other Concepts', into speculation about what might be involved in conceiving of form as being non-consolatory. There is admittedly a brief but tantalisingly obscure remark at the end of 'Against Dryness':

> Perhaps only Shakespeare manages to create at the highest level both images and people; and even *Hamlet* looks second-rate compared with *Lear*.
>
> —Ed. Bradbury, p. 31

The later essay suggests that, rather than simply regretting that so much art does console, we should try more positively to attend to the kind of completeness which only the greatest art possesses, mysterious and demanding contemplation, not conforming to the consoling patterns of the fantasy.

Discussion of such a notion is not, it must be admitted straight away, made easy by Iris Murdoch's somewhat ciphered use of the term 'form' in contexts in which her reader may be excused for feeling that greater explicitness is wanted. The reader who comes to *The Sovereignty of Good* fresh from a reading of *An Unofficial Rose* (1962), for instance, where he will have had to consider Randall Peronett's repeated remarks to the effect that his wife Ann lacks 'form', may already be agreeing with A. S. Byatt that knowledge seems necessary of Iris Murdoch's esoteric use of the word in order to see 'what relevance it has at all' in this novel,[5] and this will make the argument of the later essays that much harder to grasp. It may be felt, however, that in *The Black Prince* (1973) Iris Murdoch has been triumphantly successful in finding a mode of discourse in which to *show* what she means by 'form', or lack or superabundance of it, and to show what might be implied in its consoling or non-consoling nature. *Telling* the reader rather than showing him—as she seems to do in *An Unofficial Rose*—means that the reader must assume, for example, prior knowledge of Murdoch's work on Sartre; it does seem that the success of *The Black Prince* connects this achievement of 'showing' with her success in engaging in 'first-person' narration. Whether or not this is actually true, it remains the case that the 'requirements' for nonconsolatory form, insofar as these are exemplified in Shakespeare, do seem to be set out even more accessibly in this novel than in the more theoretical writing; however it seems appropriate to work towards Bradley Pearson's remarks on Hamlet in *The Black Prince* by way of some more of the theoretical writing, if only in order to remove any doubt that what Pearson says, and what Murdoch herself appears to believe, stand in a close and interesting relationship. A. S. Byatt stresses rightly that '[Pearson] says much that [Murdoch] has said herself' on these matters.[6]

In her essay 'On "God" and "Good" ' Murdoch again discusses the consoling tendency of art, this time in order to illustrate the truth that the human psyche finds the apprehension of reality extraordinarily difficult; even though such apprehension is problematic it is 'better . . . than to be in a state of fantasy or illusion' (*The Sovereignty of Good,* p. 64). She puts the matter in this way:

> Art presents the most comprehensible examples of the almost irresistible human tendency to seek consolation in fantasy and also of the effort to resist this and the vision of reality which comes with success. Success in fact is rare. Almost all art is a form of fantasy-consolation and few artists achieve the vision of the real. The talent of the artist can be readily, and is naturally, employed to produce a picture whose purpose is the consolation and aggrandizement of its author and the projection of his personal obsessions and wishes. To silence and expel self, to contemplate and delineate nature with a clear eye, is not easy and demands a moral discipline.
>
> —*The Sovereignty of Good,* p. 64

What is implied here is that one of the criteria for 'good art' is that it should be *impersonal* in the way in which it avoids projecting its creator's 'personal obsessions and wishes'. In this achievement lies the ability to present reality, and the consumer of art must show, as the human psyche in contact with other psyches should ideally show, sufficient 'moral discipline' in order to apprehend reality. Murdoch then qualifies this statement slightly, and while the qualification is quickly offered at this point in her essay, it assumes far greater dimensions in Bradley Pearson's remarks. The passage in 'On "God" and "Good" ' runs as follows:

> Of course great artists are 'personalities' and have special styles; even Shakespeare occasionally, though very occasionally, reveals a personal obsession. But the greatest art is 'impersonal' because it shows us the world, our world and not another one, with a clarity which startles and delights us simply because we are not used to looking at the real world at all. Of course, too, artists are pattern-makers. The claims of form and the question of 'how much form' to elicit constitutes one of the chief problems of art. But it is when form is used to isolate, to explore, to display something which is true that we are most highly moved and enlightened.
>
> *—The Sovereignty of Good,* p. 65

The phrase 'the world, our world and not another one' may appear to suggest that Iris Murdoch does not subscribe to any heterocosmic theory of the art object. . . . I believe that this suggestion would be incorrect, and that what this extract shows is, in fact, her realisation that Shakespearian 'plausibility' brings the analogous nature of the artefact, and our apprehension of the world about us, so close as actually to identify them with each other.

We may return to what is meant in Shakespeare by a 'special style' after considering the point that these remarks invite us to see that Shakespeare's lapses into 'personal obsession', rare though they may be, are examples of that 'masochism' which is the 'greatest and most subtle enemy' of the artist (*The Sovereignty of Good,* p. 87). But Murdoch does not say this outright at any stage in these essays—though the comparison between *Hamlet* and *King Lear* at the end of 'Against Dryness' is in the light of these later essays rendered rather less obscure. It is left to Bradley Pearson, the curiously perceptive though deluded narrator of *The Black Prince,* to account for the 'second-rate'-ness of *Hamlet,* by suggesting that in this play, and to a lesser extent in the *Sonnets,* Shakespeare reveals himself in what is tantamount to a 'personal obsession'. Bradley Pearson's own name alludes to the influential line of criticism of a concentration on Shakespearian characters to which adherence in our own time must be accompanied by considerable sophistication if it is not to seem reactionary. In speaking of Shakespeare's obsession, Pearson reveals plenty of his own, and Murdoch's handling of the narrative is, it must be said at the outset, astonishingly skilful. Although we learn practically nothing of the *Sonnets* from Pearson, what we learn about *Hamlet* is of high interest since it carries the suggestion that this revelation of Shakespeare's self, though masochistic, is somehow not at variance with a conception of *Hamlet* as a supreme artistic achievement. How is this position reached?

There is no doubt that the allusion to *Hamlet* in *The Black Prince* is extraordinarily complex, partly because we are never entirely sure to what extent to associate the character of Hamlet with Pearson himself, or with Julian Baffin, the twenty-year-old daughter of Pearson's friend and (in Pearson's mind) literary protégé Arnold Baffin. During the course of his narrative, Pearson falls in love with Julian; this event is itself complicated by Pearson's often-described apprehension of Julian in what must be admitted to be markedly fetishistic terms.[7] One of the characters, Pearson's degenerate ex-brother-in-law Francis Marloe, his name too a Shakespearian allusion (in its reference to two of the chief 'contestants' in the foolish debate over Shakespeare's identity), points out that Pearson first meets Julian in the narrative when she is dressed in such a way as to be mistaken by Pearson for a boy, that he reveals himself to have fallen in love with her after a tutorial on the play during the course of which it transpires that she had once played the part of Hamlet (the part which, according to Pearson, every actor wants to play, and indeed the Shakespearian character with whom everyone identifies himself), and that he achieves sexual intercourse for the only time in the novel when she has, for a joke, dressed up in the costume of Hamlet. Perhaps, it is true, Julian's androgyny (present even in her name) shows her to be, as has been pointed out, the 'master-mistress' of Pearson's passion.[8]

Certainly Pearson's own vision of the events in his narrative is highly masochistic, though whether this masochism is comparable with Shakespeare's is an interesting question. Pearson's masochism culminates for the reader in the episode towards the end of the novel in which Arnold Baffin finally detects Pearson and Julian on their remote 'honeymoon', primarily in order to take Julian away; it turns out that Arnold is the first to tell Julian of the suicide of Pearson's sister Priscilla, about which Pearson himself had known since the previous afternoon. Francis had managed to contact Pearson by telegram, asking Pearson to telephone him, and on Pearson's return from the phone-box with the news, he had found Julian dressed as Hamlet. At this point the reader might well have sympathised with Pearson, and might have been caught up in Pearson's confrontation with the 'dark god', Eros, the other 'black prince' of the narrative (a composite figure, still other of whose dimensions are suggested by the Clown in *All's Well That Ends Well*, IV, v). The reader may have seen Pearson as in a way sexually liberated, after the previous failures which his narrative implies, by this confrontation with Eros-Hamlet. Later, the reader may come to realise that Pearson may also have been actually invigorated by Priscilla's death, and to share Arnold's view of a man who is 'totally callous. His sister dies and he won't leave his love-making'[9] the whole affair, indeed, begins to look suspiciously like 'the sexual gratification of an elderly man' (*The Black Prince*, p. 287), particularly as Arnold inadvertently reveals to Julian that Pearson had also deceived her over his age. Pearson's protestations will now be seen as inevitable in their powerlessness; his brief and glorious moment of potency is over, the spell is finished, and he has been completely unmanned by Arnold:

'Julian, I was going to tell you tomorrow. I was going to tell you everything tomorrow. I had to stay today. You saw how it was. We were both possessed, we were held here, we couldn't have gone, it had to happen as it did.'
—*The Black Prince*, p. 287

This account of matters, then, indicates that we are being invited to see Julian as Hamlet, and Pearson's contact with her in this role as temporarily invigorating, providing him with the impetus to resolve his 'writer's block'. Yet Bradley's very delay over embarking on his writing, and in particular the doubts it offers over the extent to which such delay could be considered indulgent, might itself recall Hamlet's conduct, and if most other resemblances in character are not very obvious (this would be in keeping with Pearson's deluded narratorial stance), there are some strikingly comparable effects in pattern.

It is often observed that the plot and subplot of *Hamlet*, as of so many of Shakespeare's plays, are organically linked, so that in one the death of Hamlet's father brings about Hamlet's own mental agony, and in the other, the death of Ophelia's father Polonius (at Hamlet's hands) brings about Ophelia's madness. Hamlet is therefore at least provided with a means by which his own suffering may be got into a tolerable perspective, since he is given the opportunity of attending to that of Ophelia; at one level the play is 'about' Hamlet's efforts to realise this, and certainly one of the crucial effects of the graveyard confrontation with Ophelia's brother Laertes, himself of course doubly bereaved, is finally to provoke Hamlet out of his irresoluteness. In *The Black Prince* two pairs of characters are linked in a comparable way through the central character; Pearson and his sister Priscilla are matched by Pearson's ex-wife Christian and her brother Francis. The difference is that there is arguably less economy in the novel than in *Hamlet*, and the reasons for this technical departure are interesting to speculate on since they may provide some grounds for speaking of Iris Murdoch's 'contemplation' of her Shakespearian interest. Neither of this matching pair, Christian and Francis, provide Pearson with the possibility of getting his own conduct into perspective by attending to it in others, as Ophelia and later Laertes do in the case of Hamlet. This function is performed by Priscilla's ex-husband Roger and his much younger girl-friend Marigold. Pearson certainly notes what he sees as the ludicrousness of the general stereotype, but the effect of his observation is firstly to anger him (*The Black Prince*, pp. 75 ff.), and later to increase (admittedly despite himself) the general repulsiveness and forgettability of Priscilla (pp. 184–87, 209). But his judgement is not equal to the circumstances, and he never 'attends' to the relationship between Roger and Marigold in that he takes nothing from his observation of it to his own relationship with Julian. Whereas Hamlet is finally moved into action by the consequences of attending to Ophelia and Laertes (*Hamlet*, V, i), Pearson, though faced with comparable material for attention, fails to respond to its challenges, and relapses into self-pity (represented, one might say, by Julian-Hamlet).

A comparable point might rapidly be made about the relationship to be discerned between another Murdoch novel, *A Fairly Honourable Defeat* (1970), and Shakespeare's *Othello*. Patrick Swinden has suggested that Julius King in that novel might be compared with Iago in having for much of the time no observable motive for the actions he undertakes in respect of the other characters in the novel, except possibly his detestation of Rupert Foster's book and the emotional pomposity of Rupert and his sister-in-law (and Julian's ex-lover) Morgan. If this comparison is accepted, we must ask with Swinden whom it is that Julius King plays Iago to, and the answer must be that the Othello figure in *A Fairly Honourable Defeat* is a composite one (as are the Ophelia and Laertes characters in *The Black Prince*); in this case both Rupert himself and Axel, the lover of Rupert's brother Simon, are involved; furthermore, Julius/Iago operates not on the 'husband' of each relationship but on its 'wife': both Rupert's wife Hilda and Axel's lover Simon. Four people, therefore, assume the role, in relation to Julius, which Othello alone is made to assume in relation to Iago.[10] Swinden is not himself concerned to underline the lack of economy here, but I feel that the effect is comparable with that of the *Hamlet* references in *The Black Prince*. Lack of economy at the level of pattern in *The Black Prince* (and the same could presumably be said, by extension, of *A Fairly Honourable Defeat*) is not primarily or even interestingly a matter of authorial incompetence or of an indulgent insistence on pattern for its own sake; in the case of this novel it is nothing less than functional to the creation of the character of Pearson.

In this respect the question of the precise nature of the allusion to *Hamlet* in *The Black Prince* is at its most compelling. The question is not simplified by a further question of the relative levels of seriousness of some of the points of allusion. For instance, Hamlet's 'sickness', in that he realises that he cannot arouse any passion in response to the Player's speech (II, ii), compares perhaps a little too neatly with Pearson's inability to arouse a different kind of passion until faced with Julian dressed as Hamlet. And there is probably no other play of Shakespeare's except *Coriolanus* in which the hero is so persistently at its centre, whether on-or off-stage, and in which the attention of all on stage is so constantly drawn to the hero; Pearson, too, is utterly at the centre of his own narrative and, what is more, at the centre of the Editor's remarks and of the Postscripts from four of the characters. What can be said is that these Postscripts, which distance the extremely sophisticated plot of *The Black Prince,* each undermine any claim to veracity of Pearson's own narrative, and in addition all undermine each other. Hamlet's concern is that Horatio should 'report me and my cause aright / To the unsatisfied' (V, ii, 331–2). If, as is fair to suppose, Pearson by means of his narrative makes a similar plea, the text of *The Black Prince* as we have it does not respect this. Instead, as a result of the narrator's delusions and of these conflicting Postscripts, the text is self-inflictedly pitiless to Pearson. This bare assertion can be supported further by sharpening some of the points of contrast between the characters of Hamlet and Pearson.

At a quite early stage in the novel, Francis refers to Pearson's 'thing about smells', of which there has indeed been evidence since the first page of the narrative (in relation, in this first instance, to Francis himself). It is possible to feel that this alludes to such features of Hamlet's character as his disgust at 'the rank sweat of an enseaméd bed' (III, iv, 92); here Murdoch's question of 'how much form to elicit' comes interestingly to the fore. If Shakespeare's reader feels Hamlet's disgust to be a neurosis, it is one which can be explained in terms of a sickness brought about by successive shocks, dramatically presented: his father's death, his mother's remarriage, its over-hasty nature contrasting with Hamlet's own tendency to procrastinate, and later horribly underlined by confirmations of her sexual submission to the murderer of Hamlet's father. If Pearson's disgust at the older women in his narrative is to be apprehended as operative, it comes to be seen as more of an obsessive neurosis; his 'thing about smells' is hard to rationalise and is indeed everywhere in his narrative, recurring in the highly resonant scene of the *Hamlet* tutorial with Julian. Pearson's obsession is formally insisted upon, and this contributes to the effect of a masochistic showdown since the reader is by its means constantly invited to confuse the values of 'love' and 'mere sex'. The room in which the *Hamlet* tutorial takes place is extremely hot, as is the weather; Pearson discovers that Julian had once played Hamlet at school:

> I had closed the book and had laid my two hands flat on the table. I stared at the girl. She smiled, and then when I did not, giggled and blushed, thrusting back her hair with a crooked finger. 'I wasn't very good. I say, Bradley, do my feet smell?'
> 'Yes, but it's charming.'
>
> —*The Black Prince*, pp. 164–65

In this way 'charm' becomes a morally suspicious concept, since Pearson later says that love (in the context of his love for Julian) 'generates or rather reveals something which may be called *absolute charm*. In the beloved nothing is gauche' (p. 170). Since Pearson has earlier, on his own admission to Julian, found the smell of her feet 'charming,' the reader can never ascertain whether Pearson's love for Julian is a result of his obsessive neurosis coming to exhibit a sexual attraction for him (whether, in other words, his love is really an expression of selfhood), or whether Julian really does genuinely liberate him. 'Never', that is, until the masochistic showdown with Arnold, when the mere presentation of a given and humiliating stereotype, one which arguably Bill Mor in *The Sandcastle* shows (and one which finds supreme literary expression in William Hazlitt's *Liber Amoris* [1823])—the sexual infatuation of a middle-aged or elderly man—does not even need the explicit detail of a 'thing about smells' to succeed in its effect of turning Julian against Pearson.

Iris Murdoch's achievement in *The Black Prince* is demonstrably more sophisticated than in the much earlier *The Sandcastle* (1957), but it can be briefly pointed out here that the two novels share not only the theme of this kind of sexual infatuation but, more importantly, a view of the moral demands which such infatuation imposes. What Pearson shows his reader impulsively and obsessively in *The Black Prince* is very similar to what Murdoch's philosophical mouthpiece in the earlier novel, the eccentric art-master Bledyard, tells Mor about his attachment to the young artist Rain Carter. In the words which are the most usually quoted from this (curiously unsatisfactory) novel, Bledyard speaks of Mor's inability to 'apprehend the distinct being' of either his wife or his beloved.[11] This seems an accurate assessment of Pearson's inability as well, and it is hard to resist the temptation to put the relative unsatisfactoriness of Mor's crisis in *The Sandcastle* down to a snobbish unease at the dullness of the general milieu in that novel, and to the contrasting excitement for Mor at Rain's entrance into that milieu, which imparts an air of fantasy-release to the whole affair as Mor apprehends both it and her. But Pearson's editor P. Loxias would dismiss this as unworthy ('Art is adventure stories'), recognising that an adventure story only appears as such in a life which is ordinarily dull. Pearson's own life, it is remarked in more than one Postscript (though never, of course, by Pearson in his narrative), is also dull. It is more to the point perhaps to recognise that what is imposed on the narrative of *The Sandcastle* by Bledyard is incorporated in an incomparably more functional way into *The Black Prince* by means of the narrative technique in that novel. In fact the achievement in *The Black Prince* allows the conclusion to be reached that whereas Hamlet's disgust genuinely reveals his character, Pearson's obsessive 'thing about smells' is formally insisted upon in a way which reveals his character but in a masochistic light. In this sense *The Black Prince* 'contemplates' *Hamlet*.

Pearson's comments on *Hamlet*, therefore, occur in the very context of a narrative insistence on features of Pearson's own character which may come to suggest that too much form has been elicited. If this is so, it may not be, it must be repeated, a matter of authorial incompetence that we find in *The Black Prince* so much as a novelistic consideration of what 'too much form' might entail. Pearson's failure must not be mistaken for Iris Murdoch's failure.

It seemed necessary to establish that Pearson's comments on *Hamlet* occur in a context of some immediacy, in that novelistic consideration is being given to matters of theoretical interest to Iris Murdoch herself and that Pearson to some extent embodies these matters, before moving on to consider these comments. The kind of distinction between Hamlet and Pearson which seems to emerge from the texts as such is that whereas Hamlet's suffering is *presented*, Pearson's is insisted upon. Pearson himself perhaps goes further, and thereby lays himself open to further charges of masochism: he shows himself to be impotent in his role as artist too. Shakespeare tells us, according to Pearson, more about himself in *Hamlet* than anywhere else:

> '*Hamlet* is nearer to the wind than Shakespeare ever sailed, even in the sonnets. . . . How does he dare to do it?'
> —*The Black Prince*, p. 163

Pearson demonstrates that for him the answer lies in an achievement which 'purifies' the language of the drama to an extent that conceptualisation and reality become one and the same thing. *Hamlet* and Hamlet are both linguistic triumphs: '*Hamlet* is words, and so is Hamlet' (p. 164). Pearson's identification of artefact and character seems virtually unverifiable, though he defends it by calling the play a monument of words, and by calling on its unequalled quotableness, which has the effect of making the play both accessible (everyone can quote it) and private (the obsession is particular to Shakespeare). However, what can perhaps be demonstrated is something of the dramaturgical aspect of Pearson's remarks, and the reason for this is that the 'dramaturgical' can be seen as figurative of what Pearson is saying about Shakespeare's rhetoric in *Hamlet*. There is a sense in which we can speak of Shakespeare's particular attitude in *Hamlet* to the 'language' of dramatic convention. Firstly, however, we should perhaps see that for Pearson *Hamlet* represents a vision of the Good in art (this vision need not be the same for everyone), and that the allusions in Pearson's own narrative show, quite functionally, the simultaneous accessibility and privateness of this vision. They do this by revealing the way in which attending to the Good may or may not (as Iris Murdoch herself sees it) induce virtue:

> The difficulty is to keep the attention fixed upon the real situation and to prevent it from returning surreptitiously to the self with consolations of self-pity, resentment, fantasy and despair. The refusal to attend may well bring about a fictitious sense of freedom . . .
> —'The Sovereignty of Good over Other Concepts', p. 91

It is extraordinarily illuminating to attempt to see Pearson's relationship with Julian in the light of these theoretical remarks.

Pearson's vision of *Hamlet* enables him to arrive at a conception of Shakespeare's 'special style' and to say that though Shakespeare is 'the king of masochists' (p. 164) what saves him is that 'his god is a real god and not an *eidolon* of private fantasy'. Shakespeare's art in *Hamlet* is, according to Pearson, supreme because it has arisen from a genuine apprehension of reality, an apprehension so rare that it allows Shakespeare to invent, through the power of love (which is this apprehension), 'language as if for the first time'.

Shakespeare not only avoids the second-hand in his depiction of experience; he actually gets under the net to the extent that language no longer 'signifies' but 'is'. It will not be the primary business of the 'form' in *Hamlet* to console, because it is presented as reality.

Where Bradley Pearson and Iris Murdoch differ, then, if one can put it like this, seems to be in the extent of their daring. Murdoch elsewhere offers a vision of the Good in art which Pearson says applies to Shakespeare's achievement in *Hamlet*. Where they do not differ is that both of them conceive of it as being a Shakespearian ideal of the relationship between the form of art and the contingency of character, between 'images' and 'real people'. Murdoch says that this ideal fails her in practice, partly because developments in the history of thought since Shakespeare's time have made it so difficult to conceive of the latter, and because we therefore lack a satisfactory theory of human personality. Pearson reveals that the ideal fails him as an artist, and he also reveals by means of his illusions *how* it fails him as an artist. What is more is that in doing so he suggests why this ideal did not fail Shakespeare as an artist in *Hamlet*. One effect of his narrative is to show that it is possible to integrate pattern, the 'form' of art, and character, true respectfully contingent apprehension. Pattern can be conceived of as not primarily consoling but as a function of character. Seen against Pearson's own failures, the patterns in *Hamlet* appear as things which do not console Hamlet but to which he attends in order to be able to enter on a decisive course of action, one which (though tragically destructive) brings about a real and not fictitious sense of freedom.

It therefore seems best to ask to what extent the 'purification of language' which Pearson detects in *Hamlet* can be seen as figurative of a sense of dramaturgical self-examination, which it is now rightly fashionable to see in this and in other Shakespearian plays. There is no doubt that *Hamlet* seems to possess a persistent applicability: Philip Edwards has written of 'its astonishing power to haunt every generation'.[12] This power seems to have to do with the way in which one could say that Shakespeare is looking, in *Hamlet*, not only at what it is to revenge, but at what it is to commit the concept of revenge to drama. . . . To return to *Hamlet* a few examples from the 'language' of dramaturgical convention, insofar as this language is at times exploited in the play, may finally be offered in order to give some figurative idea of what might be involved in Shakespeare's 'purification of language'.

Sufficient examples to give some idea of this exploitation may be found conveniently assembled, for present purposes, in Dover Wilson's account of the play,[13] though Wilson's conclusions from these examples were naturally different in emphasis from what now follows here. Wilson was the first to look deeply into the implications of Shakespeare's creation of the Ghost in *Hamlet*, and in addition arrived at a highly ingenious explanation for Hamlet's attitude to Ophelia in III, i and subsequent scenes by suggesting that Hamlet overheard in II, ii, Polonius's plan to 'loose' Ophelia to him. On the surface this may sound like one of A. C. Bradley's more elaborate 'Notes', and it should certainly be said that those who are sceptical of Wilson's explanation point out that the audience is thereby required to remember II, ii, for a considerable period of time. But Wilson's explanations do in fact raise matters of dramaturgical interest.

Though the Ghost is a persistent feature of the genre of 'revenge tragedy', a genre whose popularity was to reach a peak in the years following the appearance of *Hamlet*, Hamlet himself seems to have been the first character in the period to doubt the authenticity of the Ghost. Dover Wilson, making this fact widely available, resorted to a theory of audience Protestantism, and of the Protestantism of the Denmark which is really a vision of seventeenth-century England, to account for this. Though it may to a large extent account for the doubt, this line of reasoning is not much assistance in explaining the extraordinary address of Hamlet to the Ghost in the 'cellarage' scene:

> GHOST. Swear.
> HAMLET. Ha, ha, boy! say'st thou so? Art thou there, true-penny?
> Come on. You hear this fellow in the cellarage:
> Consent to swear.
>
> (I, v, 149–52)

It has been more than once observed that the 'cellarage' is in fact the term for the area under the Elizabethan and Jacobean stage, where the player playing the Ghost would be standing. It is therefore possible to offer a dramaturgical explanation for the curious tone of this exchange and to say that for some reason Shakespeare is examining convention at this point, and making Hamlet address not the Ghost in the play, or at least not primarily, but the player who plays him. The motives for this attitude to convention seem hard to arrive at, though the *effect* is very likely to be humorous. Such a distinction between motive and effect will not itself directly account for Hamlet's reference to the 'old mole' (I, v, 162), but scrutiny of motive will suggest another dimension, the 'extradramatic' in which convention's language is deliberately upturned. Hamlet can be seen thus in his 'antic disposition' (I, v, 172) which is exemplified from these exchanges onwards. It is in this disposition that Hamlet enters in II, ii just after Polonius and Claudius have been discussing both Hamlet and his behaviour, and Polonius has revealed his plan to 'loose' Ophelia to Hamlet. If Wilson was right in his suggestion that Hamlet overhears this, the scene may offer further evidence of Shakespeare's dramaturgical self-examination, since the scene exploits the convention by which an aside may be spoken on stage by one character in another character's physical presence but which the silent character must for the purposes of the drama, effect not to hear, though he must of course hear it since it provides him with his cue. The words of the Queen, 'But look where sadly the poor wretch comes reading' (II, ii, 167) are the words which

on might expect to form the cue, but in fact Hamlet is already onstage at
these words. His cue must be seen as having been provided by these earlier
words:

> POLONIUS: At such a time I'll loose my daughter to him.
> Be you and I behind an arras then;
> Mark the encounter: if he love her not,
> And be not from his reason fall'n thereon,
> Let me be no assistant for a state,
> But keep a farm and carters.
> KING: We will try it.
> (II, ii, 161–66)

(Polonius's last reference is a reminder of what Dover Wilson discovered,
that the term 'loose' in this sense was and still is current on stud-farms.)
Hamlet therefore, against all convention, treats his cue not only as simply a
cue, but incorporates its sense and uses it in the drama. Hamlet 'in fact'
hears the words (that is, the player playing Hamlet hears them, since they
are his cue to enter) but the character Hamlet then assumes knowledge proper
only to the player and uses the words of the cue to provide him with a further
impetus for the sustaining of his antic disposition. In this way the roles
of 'player' and 'character' are deliberately confused. The point was not,
presumably, of interest to Dover Wilson, whose own emphasis was in terms
of a Bradleyan psychology of character-realism which would account, by
means of the 'eavesdropping' explanation, for the cruelty of Hamlet to Ophelia, which he felt could not be accounted for in any other way.

Why Shakespeare moved, in the character of Hamlet, into realms outside the terms of the play itself but still inside the theatre, thereby creating
an effect in which a 'concept' or 'image' (the player Hamlet) is made to be
seen as functional of a 'real person' (the character Hamlet), it would be fairly
pointless to speculate on, short of saying, as Pearson himself says, that the
play is 'about someone Shakespeare was in love with' (*The Black Prince*,
p. 166); we may feel that it is most productive to consider Pearson's remarks,
spoken in the context in which they are spoken, as *figurative* for the impulse
of Shakespeare to achieve what he achieved in *Hamlet*. Such a view of Shakespeare's achievement is of some assistance in trying to arrive at an idea of
what is meant by Iris Murdoch's conception of Shakespeare's rare 'personal
obsession', and my own belief is that this conception is expanded more fully
by Bradley Pearson in *The Black Prince*, and applied by him, as Iris Murdoch
in her own person seems reluctant to do, to *Hamlet*. She has herself elsewhere
suggested that the achievement is more difficult for a twentieth-century
novelist partly because of a loss in the richness, availability and generally
referential quality of language since Shakespeare's time; nevertheless, Shakespeare's ability to master a kind of language which can be regarded as a

matrix which does not 'cramp the style' of individual characters is, for her, miraculous, and to be aspired towards by the twentieth-century novelist, herself included.[14]

This paper has been concerned with trying to find terms to speak of the way in which I believe we should see Iris Murdoch's overtly Shakespearian fiction in relation to her theoretical Shakespearian interest. What seems to emerge from her conception of a form which need not console is that it must involve a functional combination between character and pattern, and I have tried to suggest that she is at her most brilliant as a novelist when she manages to show this functional combination at work, as I believe she manages to do with the character of Bradley Pearson.

Notes

1.   'Iris Murdoch in conversation with Malcolm Bradbury', recorded 27 February 1976, British Council Tape No. RS 2001.

2.   This essay first appeared in *Encounter*, XVI (1961), and is now available in *The Novel Today*, ed. Malcolm Bradbury (London, 1977), pp. 23–31.

3.   Frank Kermode, 'The House of Fiction: Interviews with Seven Novelists'; first published in *Partisan Review*, XXX (1963), and reprinted in *The Novel Today*, pp. 111–35.

4.   Iris Murdoch, *The Sovereignty of Good* (New York, 1971), pp. 77–104.

5.   A. S. Byatt, *Degrees of Freedom* (London, 1965), p. 127.

6.   A. S. Byatt, *Iris Murdoch* London, 1967), p. 37.

7.   I have attempted to investigate this particular matter elsewhere: see 'The Plausibility of *The Black Prince*', *Dutch Quarterly Review*, VIII (1978), 82–93.

8.   For this suggestion I am indebted to A. S. Byatt.

9.   Iris Murdoch, *The Black Prince* (London, 1973), p. 287.

10.   Patrick Swinden, *Unofficial Selves* (London, 1973), p. 253.

11.   Iris Murdoch, *The Sandcastle* (London, 1957), p. 216.

12.   Philip Edwards, *Shakespeare and the Confines of Art* (London, 1968), p. 84.

13.   J. Dover Wilson, *What Happens in Hamlet* (Cambridge, 1935).

14.   Iris Murdoch uses this phrase herself in an interview with Ronald Bryden and A. S. Byatt, recorded by the BBC as part of 'The Lively Arts' programme and transmitted on 13 February 1968.

[Iris Murdoch's] Questing Heroes

DEBORAH JOHNSON

Iris Murdoch's novels pose in new and tantalising ways the question of what it means to write as a woman, to read as a woman. They disconcert and fascinate both female and male readers by continually questioning gender identity and transgressing gender boundaries. At the same time they have notably not attracted the attention of feminist critics. I am concerned to ask in this study why this is so and to suggest how and to what extent a reading of these texts may be modified and enriched by a feminist critical perspective. . . .

In the most obvious sense of the phrase Iris Murdoch does not 'write as a woman'. Unlike so many of her sister-novelists, Doris Lessing and Margaret Drabble for example, she has not apparently been concerned to explore what Elaine Showalter has called the 'wild zone' of female experience, that area where women's experience does not overlap with men's.[1] On the contrary the fictionalised masculine perspective is everywhere apparent in her novels. She is a female writer who likes wearing male masks. In the seven novels where she employs a dramatised narrator from her earliest novel, *Under the Net* (1954) to her latest but one, *The Philosopher's Pupil* (1983), that narrator is invariably male. These seven novels, which also include *A Severed Head* (1961), *The Italian Girl* (1964), *The Black Prince* (1973), *A Word Child* (1975) and *The Sea, The Sea* (1978), cover the thirty-odd years' span of Iris Murdoch's career to date; they constitute, it will readily be agreed, some of her most distinctive and thoughtful work.[2]

The phenomenon of Iris Murdoch's male narrators is one which I wish to explore at the outset. Elizabeth Dipple in her important and illuminating study of the novels, *Iris Murdoch: Work for the Spirit* (1982), bears, I think, unwitting testimony to the powerful interest of this phenomenon in the few sentences where she touches upon it:

> One more technical issue is worth brief mention: the frequent presence of a male first-person narrator, and the absence of a corresponding female voice. . . . It is unprofitable to conjecture *why* Murdoch does it (because all the first-person narration takes place through corrupted male psyches, is this

From *Iris Murdoch* (Bloomington: Indiana University Press, 1987), 1–19; c. Deborah Johnson. Reprinted by permission of Indiana University Press.

a veiled indication that men are more likely to be debased than women?), especially since she has said she is more comfortable there, and that seems to be that, since this study does not aspire to a psychoanalysis of the author.[3]

The writing here betrays the critic's deep interest in the topic which she proclaims is so peripheral. The topic is clearly not a 'safe' one; the text silently questions the sense of the term 'comfortable' (whose comfort is involved here?). In fact, a study of Iris Murdoch's narrators should not involve a psychological study of the author. What is in question here is a rhetorical strategy; her novels pose their own questions and do not need to be explained with reference to some supposedly more authoritative text.

Elizabeth Dipple does, however, go on to make an explicitly helpful comment about the phenomenon of male narration; it is 'something that should not work and does' and thereby she admits that the question of sexual difference does matter. I hope to show in the course of this discussion why Iris Murdoch's use of the male narrator works as well as it does.

Her curious preference for the male narrator is, I think, interestingly illumined by a passage from her philosophical work *The Sovereignty of Good*, in one of those apparently random connections between the non-fiction and the fiction which help to draw attention to the more puzzling elements in the fiction. In *The Sovereignty of Good* Iris Murdoch implicitly links the subjection to illusion, fantasy, the state of entrapment in the dreaming ego (which Plato calls *eikasia* and symbolises in the flickering, shadowy firelight of the Cave), with the gift of articulateness, the ability to manipulate language in order to have power over other people, and with the aesthetic fascination that language holds, the glamour of words. Inevitably her attitude to language partakes of her attitude to art in general; if art can all too easily degenerate into false patterns, lying consolations, then this must be true of language. *Goodness* (the generously disinterested awareness of the world outside the self) then becomes linked with silence and, even more revealing, with femaleness: 'Goodness appears to be both rare and hard to picture. It is perhaps most convincingly met with in simple people—inarticulate, unselfish mothers of large families—but these cases are also the least illuminating'.[4] Of course this statement, from a feminist political perspective, makes a number of problematical assumptions. Why should these cases be the least illuminating? Does this statement simply reflect the middle-class intellectual assumption that there is only one culture and that 'inarticulate mothers of large families' don't have access to it and are therefore not 'interesting' from a philosophical point of view? Are the self-sacrifices and apparent silence of such women rather too readily approved of as 'goodness', a necessary underpinning of an all-too-corruptible social fabric? But it is misleading to isolate this single statement from its context in Iris Murdoch's work in general. Her writings elsewhere explore (implicitly and explicitly) what this statement seems to take for granted.

In her fictional versions of 'the pilgrimage from appearance to reality (the subject of every good play and novel)',[5] Iris Murdoch chooses as protagonist the figure most directly opposed to the simple inarticulate mother of a large family—that is, the childless male professional who is indeed articulate to the point of volubility—who has power and, in the full sense of the word, glamour (a glamour which Iris Murdoch illustrates, not always convincingly, by the sexual spell he wields over the various women who surround him). He is always in love with words and is often concerned with language as an instrument of power. He is usually artistically or intellectually highly gifted; he may be a theatre director (Charles Arrowby in *The Sea, The Sea*), a novelist (Jake Donaghue in *Under the Net* and Bradley Pearson in *The Black Prince*), or a well-known philosopher (Rozanov, the central power-wielder though notably not the narrator in *The Philosopher's Pupil*). However his gifts are always in some measure frustrated: Charles Arrowby finds that power over others involves guilt and so attempts to escape from his theatrical past, Jake Donaghue and Bradley Pearson are for different reasons 'blocked' and John Robert Rozanov has come, it seems, to the limits of philosophy; he is now 'tired of his mind'. Martin Lynch-Gibbon (*A Severed Head*) and Hilary Burde (*A Word Child*) are highly cultivated men who are, again for different reasons, scholars *manqués*. They have failed to pursue their true enthusiasms (history, languages), taking up instead jobs which palely reflect and even parody their creative and/or intellectual needs. All these characters are impelled by their sense of failure to some degree of deeper self-examination and an attempt to break some of the false patterns which have so far dominated their lives.

The status of the quester is from the start very much open to question and, more challengingly, so is the nature of his quest. All Iris Murdoch's word-children are unreliable narrators, flawed reflectors of the fictional worlds they inhabit. Patrick Parrinder, writing of the novels of B.S. Johnson, has this very apposite comment to make about the quest *topos* in modern English fiction:

> The more strictly religious the writer's temperament the more wary he is likely to be of the inauthentic, external fictions that surround him. At the heart of English Puritan culture is *The Pilgrim's Progress* with its image of the quest for righteousness as a constant and perilous confrontation with the phantoms and illusions met by the wayside. Only by exploding innumerable fictions does the steadfast pilgrim arrive at the truth.[6]

But there is always the possibility in Iris Murdoch's novels that the pilgrim's sense of his quest may turn out to be yet another illusion, another gratifying fiction. This is what happens to Hilary Burde in *A Word Child*. His original quest, in which he saw himself (as so many Murdochian heroes do) as a knight-errant, was the freeing of himself and his sister, Crystal, from the poverty and deprivation of their childhood through his ambitious and single-minded studies at Oxford: 'I was *busy*. Like a knight upon a quest I was dedicated, under orders. I had to rescue myself and Crystal, to get us out of the dark hole in which we had grown up and out into sunlight, into freedom' (p. 116). But he abandons his career after his affair with Anne Jopling and the driving accident through which he kills her together with her unborn child. In trying to redeem his past for the second time he ironically seizes upon another 'quest', this time a disastrous one, the entanglement with Gunnar's second wife, Kitty, who is seeking to arrange a reconciliation between Hilary and Gunnar, now twenty years after Anne's death. Hilary describes the second quest in ironically almost identical terms: 'I now had a task, I was like a knight with a quest. I needed my chastity now, I needed my aloneness; and it seemed to me with a quickening amazement that I had *kept* myself for just this time' (p. 200). This is a characteristic illusion of the Murdochian hero. For Hilary there never was a quest, apart from a T. S. Eliot-like return to the point of departure to 'know the place for the first time'.

Such fiction-making is portrayed by Iris Murdoch as a predominantly male activity. The women in her fictions are often given the role of undermining (comically or tragically) these sustaining fictions. Hilary, caught up in his Kitty/Gunnar quest and the obsession with his past, decides to 'cashier' (to use his own term) his fiancée, Tommy, so as to preserve his 'chastity' for the quest. In the final ironic twist of the plot it is Tommy who, jealous and disappointed, betrays Hilary to Gunnar and so unwittingly brings about the events which lead to Kitty's death. Tommy is not to be so easily tidied away. In *The Black Prince* Bradley Pearson's quest, his 'ordeal', as he calls it, the confrontation with the Black Eros, is prematurely closed by the suicide of his sister, Priscilla. Her wrecked life has been revealed in brief and poignant glimpses while Bradley, Hamlet-like, has occupied the centre of the stage.

In her book on Sartre (*Sartre: Romantic Rationalist*) Iris Murdoch interestingly draws attention to the significant silences which occur in Sartre's novels due to his preoccupation with the existentialist quest and the isolated heroic questing consciousness:

> The lesson of *L'Etre et le Néant* would seem to be that personal relations are usually warfare, and at best represent a precarious equilibrium, buttressed as often as not by bad faith. We find nothing in the novels which openly contradicts this view. It is not only that the relationships portrayed in *Les Chemins* are all instances of hopelessly imperfect sympathies. . . . This in itself is nothing to complain of. Indeed it is in Sartre's ruthless portrayal of the failure of sympathy that we often most feel his penetration and his honesty. What does deserve comment is that Sartre acquiesces in the lack of sympathy in a way which suggests that his interest is elsewhere. He is looking *beyond* the relationship; what he values is not the possibility which this enfolds but something else. One feels this particularly perhaps in the treatment of Marcelle, who is dealt with hardly not only by Mathieu but by her author. Sartre

is not really very interested in the predicament of Marcelle, except from the technical point of view of its effect upon Mathieu. Similarly we feel a touch of hardness in the portrayal of Boris's relations with Lola. We are not moved by Lola's situation—whereas we are pierced to the heart by the somewhat similar situation of Ellénore in *Adolphe*. And a part of the reason is that Lola's author does not care very much either; he *accepts* the position. It is not *here* that he has entered absorbingly into his work.[7]

Iris Murdoch sees these gaps in Sartre's work in general terms as a failure to give us 'a concrete realisation of what George Eliot called "an equivalent centre of self from which the shadows fall with a difference." ' But it is no accident that the spaces where she sees that Sartre 'has not entered absorbingly into his work', where 'he *accepts* the position', concern the portrayals of female characters. The heroic male consciousness in modernist fiction is particularly inclined to see the women it loves as objects in its mental landscape; their importance lies in the shape and direction which they give to the all-absorbing quest.

The male narration obviously de-centres the female point of view. As a woman writing, Iris Murdoch is clearly aware of what she is doing and can both seriously and playfully exaggerate this de-centring effect. Some of the reflections which she gives to her male narrators (as, notably, Charles Arrowby in *The Sea, The Sea*) are almost Jacobean in their intense misogyny, their habit of generalising about 'women'. In their arguments with the women who love them the narrators are forever drawing upon misogynist generalisation in order to score points (as Hilary does with Tommy in *A Word Child*). This is not to imply that Iris Murdoch's women don't generalise about 'men'; they sometimes do, but such generalisations are somewhat rare and impotent, set as they are in an age-old tradition of misogynist *sententiae* and the overall dominance of the male viewpoint in the novels. The male lover continually expresses his sense of superiority through his sheer powers of articulation, his marked tendency to cap and better or simply to interrupt the utterances of his 'mistress' (who is in any case usually younger and/or of inferior social status). Iris Murdoch is clearly preoccupied by the unequal power relationships which exist between men and women as she is by other kinds of unequal power relationship. Often she shows two inequalities reinforcing each other as they do in *A Word Child* when Hilary's crude sexual bullying of the beautiful and mysterious half-Indian girl, 'Biscuit', turns into an obliquely racist bullying: ' "What's your name, Miss Mukerji?" I did not expect her to tell me' (p. 55).

Iris Murdoch shows all human beings, men and women alike, as subject to *eikasia* and particularly to that form of *eikasia* which renders other people invisible. But it is much more likely to be a woman than a man who exclaims in exasperation, as Georgie does to Martin in *A Severed Head*, 'you've got to *see me*' (p. 105). Part of the reason why Iris Murdoch's male narrators fail to 'see' is precisely because they talk too much. Like Plato's bad art-object they cherish their volubility.[8]

This brief survey suggests that connections between the male hero, articulateness, power and the quest *topos* are presented with a considerable degree of deliberate irony on Iris Murdoch's part. Before exploring the novels any further I would like to raise some general questions about the device of male narration, questions to which we have been re-alerted by recent feminist criticism.

In terms of the current psychoanalytically-based theories of sexual differ-ence, notably the work of Luce Irigaray, this 'male mimicry' can be seen as a potential means of undoing the repressive (patriarchal) structures encoded in language itself (Lacan's 'symbolic order'),[9] as a way of 'exposing through imitation'. As such it can point the way forward to a possible recovery of the operation of the 'feminine' in language. I shall briefly expound these ideas.

The thorny question of what *does* constitute the 'feminine' in writing has been well addressed by Mary Jacobus in an essay which opens with an excellent brief introduction to some current theories of sexual difference.[10] She writes that

> Utopian attempts to define the specificity of woman's writing—desired or hypothetical, but rarely empirically observed—either founder on the rock of essentialism (the text as body), gesture towards an avant-garde practice which turns out not to be specific to women, or, like Hélène Cixous in 'The Laugh of the Medusa', do both. If anatomy is not destiny, still less can it be language.[11]

She then goes on to suggest a possible way forward:

> A politics of women's writing, then, if it is not to fall back on a biologically based theory of sexual difference, must address itself, as Luce Irigaray had done in 'Pouvoir du discours, subordination du féminin' to the position of mastery held not only by scientific discourse (Freudian theory, for instance), not only by philosophy, 'the discourse of discourses', but by the logic of discourse itself.

For Irigaray, notes Mary Jacobus, the systems of representation at work in discourse are 'masculine' in that they are self-reflexive and specular (woman is either ignored or seen as man's opposite) and so 'disappropriate women of their relation to themselves and to other women'. So the 'feminine' is that which is repressed or elided in discourse. A feminist politics in these terms 'would attempt to relocate sexual difference at the level of the text by undoing the repression of the "feminine" in all systems of representation for which the Other (woman) must be reduced to the economy of the Same (man)'.[12]

Luce Irigaray, notes Mary Jacobus, sees role-playing as central to the female subverting of male discourse:

> Given the coherence of the systems at work in discourse, . . . how is the work
> of language of which she speaks to be undertaken at all? Her answer is
> 'mimetism', the role historically assigned to women—that of reproduction,
> but deliberately assumed; an acting out or role playing within the text which
> allows the woman writer the better to know and hence to expose what it is
> she mimics.

and she goes on to quote from Irigaray's 'Pouvoir du discours':

> To play with mimesis, is, therefore, for a woman, to attempt to recover the
> place of her exploitation by discourse, without letting herself be simply reduced
> to it. It is to resubmit herself . . . to 'ideas', notably about her, elaborated
> in/by a masculine logic, but in order to make 'visible', by an effect of playful
> repetition, what should have remained hidden: the recovery of a possible
> operation of the feminine in language. It is also to 'unveil' the fact that, if
> women mime so well, they do not simply reabsorb themselves in this function.
> *They also remain elsewhere*.[13]

Such playfulness is, Mary Jacobus stresses, political in effect; the quest for
specificity, for an elusive *écriture féminine*, takes its impetus from the political
and social realities of women's experience: 'To postulate, as Irigaray does, a
"work of language" which undoes the repression of the feminine constitutes
in itself an attack on the dominant ideology, the very means by which we
know what we know and think what we think'. The very term 'women's
writing' serves 'to remind us of the social conditions under which women
wrote and still write—to remind us that the conditions of their (re)production
are . . . the sexual and material organisations of society, which rather than
biology, form the crucial determinants of women's writing'.[14]

These theoretical insights certainly suggest ways of exploring theatri-
cally and role-playing in Iris Murdoch's novels: they also help illumine the
significant gap which separates the fiction from the philosophy, given Iris
Murdoch's own insistence on the difference between philosophy and fiction
as modes of discourse, and the distinctive nature of her practice within each
mode. Although I shall not attempt to re-cast Iris Murdoch as an exponent
of *écriture féminine*, I want to examine how far role-playing and male narration
in her novels can be read as liberating devices, subversive of male-dominated
structures and modes of perception.

An entirely opposite view of 'male impersonation' has been put forward
by the more traditional literary-historical approaches implied in what has
largely been Anglo-American feminist criticism. (The convenient distinction
between French and Anglo-American feminist criticism is becoming increasingly out of date.) This criticism sees male impersonation as a form of
evasion, an ultimately false bid for the universality, the neutrality historically
carried by the male voice, a bid which literary and socio-economic history
has made to a large degree necessary (an obvious instance being the adoption

by early nineteenth-century female novelists of the male pseudonym). So Annis V. Pratt writes:

> Many woman novelists have even succeeded in hiding the covert or implicit feminism in their books from themselves. . . . As a result we get explicit cultural norms superimposed upon an authentic creative mind in the form of all kinds of feints, ploys, masks and disguises embedded in the plot structure and characterization.[15]

Male impersonation in this view becomes an outstanding example of such feints, ploys, masks and disguises. And Sandra Gilbert and Susan Gubar discuss at length 'the aesthetic tensions and moral contradictions that threaten the woman writer who tries to transcend her own female anxiety of authorship by pretending she is male'.[16] However, while Charlotte Brontë's *The Professor* does seem to exemplify Gilbert and Gubar's theory, it might be argued that Emily Brontë's *ironic* use of male narration, Lockwood in *Wuthering Heights*, as one of several 'voices' in the narrative, is a much more flamboyant subversion of 'explicit cultural norms', and may be closer to what Iris Murdoch is doing with her male narrators.

How far, then, is Iris Murdoch's use of male narration a form of evasion, and how far is it a way of subverting the patriarchal structures and assumptions reflected in the texts? The problem is complex because so much more is involved in Iris Murdoch's use of male perspectives than mere ironic distance and implied didactic attitudes. There are various reasons why these perspectives compel a sympathetic reading.

The reasons in general terms are bound up with the relationship between narrative and desire, with what Roland Barthes has described as the Oedipal trajectory of all narrative, the drive towards origins and ends, the quest for knowledge:

> The pleasure of the text is . . . an Oedipal pleasure (to denude, to know, to learn the origin and the end), if it is true that every narrative (every unveiling of the truth) is a staging of the (absent, hidden, or hypostatized) father—which would explain the solidity of narrative forms, of family structures, and of prohibitions of nudity.[17]

The feminist semiotician, Teresa de Lauretis, in her book *Alice doesn't* (1984) has analysed the ways in which the discourse of Barthes (and of some other male structuralists) is ideologically loaded, or historically determined, so that the hero of narrative has to be seen as *male*, in obedience to a fundamental structuralist distinction predicated on sexual difference—the distinction between male-hero-human on the side of the subject, and female-obstacle-boundary-space, on the other.[18] Nevertheless, she writes sympathetically of the male Oedipal quest as it has been enacted throughout Western literature:

It was not an accident of cultural history that Freud, an avid reader of literature, chose the hero of Sophocles' drama as the emblem of Everyman's passage into adult life, his advent to culture and history. All narrative in its movement forward towards resolution and backward to an initial moment, a paradise lost, is overlaid with what has been called an Oedipal logic—the inner necessity or drive of the drama—its "sense of an ending" inseparable from the memory of loss and the recapturing of time. Proust's title, *A la Recherche du temps, perdu*, epitomizes the very movement of narrative: the unfolding of the Oedipal drama as action at once backward and forward, its quest for (self) knowledge through the realization of loss, to the making good of Oedipus' sight and restoration of vision. Or rather, its sublation into the higher order attained by Oedipus at Colonus, the superior being capable of bridging the visible and invisible worlds.[19]

This description fits many of Iris Murdoch's novels well enough. In general terms, these trace the journey of a male hero into a comic version of Thebes, where he either remains caught for good in the toils of erotic (self) deception (Edmund in *The Italian Girl* and, arguably, Martin in *A Severed Head*) or he manages to survive the process and move towards a modest version of Colonus—'the world transfigured, found' as Bradley puts it at the end of *The Black Prince* (p. 391)—into a state not bound by his normal, narrow ego-consciousness. His vision is enlarged through the destruction of some of his most cherished illusions.

Iris Murdoch's love-plots accordingly often work as a series of unveilings, of the discovery of erotic substitutions. Charles's often repeated question in *The Sea, The Sea*, 'Who is one's first love?' finds its echo throughout Murdoch's fiction. Peter J. Conradi has drawn attention to the repetition of Oedipal family situations: sibling rivalry in *Under the Net, The Flight from the Enchanter, A Severed Head, Bruno's Dream, A Fairly Honourable Defeat, An Accidental Man, The Time of the Angels*; mother-daughter rivalry in *An Unofficial Rose, The Black Prince*; father-daughter incest in *The Time of the Angels*; brother-sister incest in *A Severed Head, The Bell* and *The Red and the Green*.[20] And it may be added that where incest does not appear literally in the plot it can figure metaphorically. In *The Good Apprentice* (1985), for instance, Edward's quest for deliverance from his despair leads him to find his natural father (the father 'absent, hidden, or hypostatized' in Barthes' terms) who appears as a most ambiguous love-object:

> Of course Jesse was his father. But he was, as if now filled up to the brim, so much more: a master, a precious king, a divine lover, a strange mysterious infinitely beloved object, the prize of a religious search, a jewel in a cave.
>
> (p. 296)

Conradi, at one point in his book, discusses the novels in psychotherapeutic terms as an expression of 'the movement towards the saving of Eros, the clarification of passion or education of desire'.[21] He writes, 'Both growing up and paying attention for Murdoch are matters of struggling to perceive the world with less preconception, and to understand the provisionality of life-myths which lead us to repeat roles in emotional systems whose patterns are laid down early'.[22] In this sense the male questing hero is Everyman and following his progress involves a certain degree of libidinal investment on the part of the reader as well as the author.

But what particular forms of identification are available here for *female* readers? We might experience, as de Lauretis argues in her analysis of quest narratives, a double or split identification, finding ourselves caught between 'the two mythical positions of hero (mythical subject) and boundary (spatially fixed object, personified obstacle)', a split analogous to that which 'cinema offers the female spectator: identification with the look of the camera, apprehended as temporal, active or in movement, and identification with the image on the screen, perceived as spatially static, fixed, in frame'.[23]

I want to argue that the playfulness of Iris Murdoch's quest-narratives works precisely to expose or foreground such a splitting of the female subject. There are various general ways in which this happens. The first is, as I have already argued, the tendency of the narrative to reveal the quest *topos* itself to be inadequate or illusory as a model or metaphor for living. The hero's search for psychological and spiritual healing runs into conflict with the other characters' readings of their own life-stories. The *female* Oedipus conflict (never a direct or sustained object of authorial focus) makes its presence felt as a complicating subtext; so, in *The Black Prince*, Julian's attachment to her father throws a questioning light on Bradley's exalted reading of his own love-story, and in *The Sandcastle* (1954), Rain's incomplete separation both as woman and as artist from her dead father is a shadowy and enigmatic area for Mor in his bittersweet romance with her. This relatively simple early novel, a seemingly straightforward love-story, is particularly interesting. Although Rain is seen primarily as *object*, her colourful clothes in particular emphasising her desirableness as female image, she is implicitly re-instated as female *subject* by the terms of her own Oedipal family romance. Her little scene with the ageing and despotic Demoyte (Chapter Seven, pp. 93–8) is characterised by a complicity with Demoyte, an innocent yet knowing acceptance of his wistful gallantry, and suggests that Rain adopts this *pattern* of behaviour towards older men in general. With a beautiful structural subtlety this scene directly follows the more famous scene (Chapter Six) where Rain and Mor drive together into the woods and accidently overturn Rain's beautiful and expensive Riley into the river. (The car is a source of nagging anxiety to Mor; Rain has put it out of her mind when we next see her.) The juxtaposition of the scenes comments upon the enigmatic areas in Rain's personality, areas which remain closed to Mor's limited knowledge and awareness.

A final point which needs to be made about Iris Murdoch's handling of Oedipal situations is that the Freudian tensions are characteristically diffused by comedy. This is the case throughout the playfully Freudian novel *A Severed Head*. A pointer to the Oedipal logic of Martin's progress is provided in the (comically explicit) dream which Martin has at the beginning of Chapter 21 (pp. 137–8). The dream is constructed with an almost mechanical lucidity so as to point to Martin's hidden castration complex. Martin dreams that he is skating with his sister, whose image the reader sees implicitly but unmistakably to resemble Honor Klein. The condensed figure of Martin's sister/Honor gives way to a second condensed figure who represents both Martin's father and Honor. This mildly terrifying image is another 'severed head' (the sword is recalled from Martin's witnessing of Honor's Samurai sword display):

> . . . he glided on towards me with increasing speed, his huge Jewish face growing like a great egg above the silken wings of his gown. I swung the sword in an arc before him but as it moved the blade came away and flew upwards into the winter darkness which had collected above us. Clinging in fear and guilt to what remained in my hand I recognized my father.
>
> (p. 138)

The Freudianism of the dream is rather tongue-in-cheek, illustrating the suave psychoanalyst Palmer's theories concerning the 'mechanical' nature of the psyche. At the same time, it points to the underlying family drama in which Martin is caught, and which he keeps re-enacting with erotic substitutions. From a feminist viewpoint it is interesting that the most important of these erotic substitutions, Honor, should embody the division which according to feminist semiotic theory splits the female subject. Honor is the object of Martin's quest. She is taboo-object, sister in the royal incestuous brother-sister pair, severed head, Medusa as site of the original castration trauma ('the female genitals feared, not desired' (p. 45)). To that extent she remains opaque, veiled, within the story. But Murdoch gives Medusa a voice. Honor is highly articulate and is well qualified to explain her status as taboo-object to Martin: she functions as subject too. The logic of the interconnected events in the plot suggests that Honor is rather better than Martin at getting what she wants and it hints at an alternative reading of the novel in which Honor herself might function as a more canny female version of the questing hero.

These various feminist theories suggest some ways of articulating the complex relationship of the female author to her fictions. The question of how and to what extent Iris Murdoch inscribes her female presence into her text is, I think, central; it is related to what many critics and reviewers have seen as her 'comfortable' distance or detachment from her characters, her careful 'expunging of the self from the work of art' in A. S. Byatt's phrase, and consequent reluctance or inability to 'inhabit her action' as fully as she might.[24]

A closer look at the individual roles and masks presented through the dramatised male narrators (who, after all, differ very much among themselves) should reveal something of their function within these strangely elusive novels and begin to provide some answers to these questions.

Notes

1. Elaine Showalter, 'Feminist Criticism in the Wilderness', in *Critical Inquiry*, 8 (1981), 179–206; repr. in Elizabeth Abel (ed.), *Writing and Sexual Difference*, pp. 9–36; p. 30.

2. See, for example, Richard Todd, *Iris Murdoch* (London and New York: Methuen, 1984), p. 74: 'it does seem to be the case that the first-person narration suits not just Murdoch's technical gifts but the presentation of her theme in novel form'.

3. Elizabeth Dipple, *Iris Murdoch: Work for the Spirit* (London: Methuen, 1982), p. 88.

4. Iris Murdoch 'On "God" and "Good," ' in *The Sovereignty of Good* (London and Henley: Routledge & Kegan Paul, 1970), p. 53.

5. Iris Murdoch, *The Fire and the Sun: Why Plato Banished the Artists* (Oxford: Oxford University Press, 1977, reprinted 1978), p. 80.

6. Patrick Parrinder, 'Pilgrim's Progress: The Novels of B. S. Johnson (1933–73)', *Critical Quarterly*, vol. 19, no. 2, 45–59; p. 47.

7. Iris Murdoch, *Sartre: Romantic Rationalist* (1953; London: Fontana/Collins, 1967), p. 59.

8. 'The true *logos* falls silent in the presence of the highest (ineffable) truth, but the art object cherishes its volubility, it cherishes itself not the truth and wishes to be indestructible and eternal.' Iris Murdoch, *The Fire and the Sun*, pp. 65–6.

9. In Lacanian terminology the symbolic order is the order instituted within the individual human being by language. The child enters this order when it comes to language. Lacan contrasts the symbolic order, whose carrier is the father figure, with the imaginary order—the sensory 'given' of experience, the order of perception and hallucination.

10. Mary Jacobus, 'The Question of Language: Men of Maxims and *The Mill on the Floss*' in *Critical Inquiry*, 8 (1981), 207–22; repr. in *Writing and Sexual Difference*, ed. Elizabeth Abel (Brighton: Harvester, 1982), pp. 37–52.

11. Mary Jacobus, 'The Question of Language', p. 37.

12. *ibid.*, p. 38.

13. *ibid.*, p. 40.

14. *ibid.*, pp. 38–9.

15. Annis V. Pratt, 'The New Feminist Criticisms: Exploring the History of the New Space', in *Beyond Intellectual Sexism: A New Woman, A New Reality*, ed. Joan I. Roberts (New York: David McKay, 1976), p. 183.

16. Sandra Gilbert and Susan Gubar, *The Madwoman in the Attic: The Woman Writer and the Nineteenth-Century Literary Imagination*, (New Haven and London: Yale University Press, 1979), p. 70. For the relevant context see the whole of the chapter 'Infection in the Sentence: The Woman Writer and the Anxiety of Authorship', pp. 45–92.

17. Roland Barthes, *The Pleasure of the Text*, trans. Richard Miller (New York: Hill

and Wang, 1975), p. 10. Quoted in Teresa de Lauretis, *Alice doesn't: Feminism, Semiotics, Cinema* (London and Basingstoke: Macmillan, 1984), pp. 107–8.

18.   Teresa de Lauretis, *Alice doesn't*, Chapter 5, 'Desire in Narrative', pp. 103–57.

19.   *ibid.*, pp. 124–5.

20.   Peter J. Conradi, *Iris Murdoch: The Saint and the Artist* (London and Basingstoke: Macmillan, 1986), pp. 83–4.

21.   *ibid.*, p. 84.

22.   *ibid.*, p. 83.

23.   Teresa de Lauretis, *Alice doesn't*, p. 12.

24.   A. S. Byatt, *Degrees of Freedom: The Novels of Iris Murdoch* (London: Chatto and Windus, 1965), p. 204.

The Contracting Universe of Iris Murdoch's Gothic Novels

Zohreh T. Sullivan

Iris Murdoch's waifs, orphans, refugees, demons and saints, all share a common isolation, a loss of community, and the absence of close relationship to "a rich and complicated" group from which as moral beings they should have much to learn.[1] As a philosopher, Murdoch connects this loss of community to the inadequacies of existentialist and empirical thought that rely on self-centered standards of individual consciousness and sincerity, rather than on other-centered values of virtue, love, and imagination. As a novelist, she dramatizes her ethical concerns by increasingly demonizing the existentialist, solipsistic hero who rejects the "messy reality" of involvement with others in order to pursue what he perversely sees as freedom, abstraction, and romance.

> We no longer use a spread-out substantial picture of the manifold virtues of man and society. We no longer see man against a background of values, of realities, which transcend him. We picture man as a brave naked will surrounded by an easily comprehended empirical world. For the hard idea of truth we have substituted a facile idea of sincerity.
>
> (*AD*, 18)

By failing to see reality as worthy of loving exploration, Murdoch's benighted protagonist is compelled to rely exclusively on personal values as his sole guide to morality. The resulting psychological distortions to which such solipsism is liable cuts a man off completely from others and from society. She contends that the modern psyche is debilitated by such "ailments of Romanticism" as neurosis, solipsism, and obsession with power, a fear of history, and "a fear of the real existing messy modern world full of real existing messy modern persons, with individual messy modern opinions of their own" (*SBR*, 254). Such a sickness can be cured only by a therapeutic perception, by an act of imagination which she identifies with love. Murdoch's characters cannot see because they are enclosed in "a fantasy world of

From *Modern Fiction Studies* 23, no. 4 (Winter 1977–78): 557–69. © 1978 by Purdue Research Foundation West Lafayette, Indiana, 47907. Reprinted by permission.

our own into which we try to draw things from the outside, not grasping their reality and independence, making them into dream objects of our own" (*SG*, 52). Her protagonists, therefore, can redeem themselves only by discovering new ways of seeing reality and by resisting the false consolations of form and of fantasy which Murdoch defines as "the enemy" of that true imagination which is "Love, an exercise of the imagination" (*SG*, 52).

The response of Murdoch's characters to community is complicated by the paradox of their personalities: although her isolated characters long to be part of a familial, social, or national group, they are at the same time solipsists who rely chiefly on will, ego, and power in order to manipulate the behavior of others according to their own systems and beliefs. Where there is power, there can be no community. Murdoch's concept of community, reminiscent of E. M. Forster's "Love, the beloved Republic," is realized, therefore, only within a nexus of morality, imagination, selflessness, and love. It demands a recognition that morality grows out of actual encounters with others, that such encounters are difficult and complex, that the crucial quality necessary to succeed in such an encounter is an imaginative love that delights in the otherness of the other, and that such love is a knowledge to be equated with the highest morality because it demands the surrender of one's self. Only saints, lovers, and artists can belong to a community because they have learned not only to see what is real, but also to act rightly: "The artist is indeed the analogon of the good man and in a special sense he *is* the good man: the lover who, nothing himself, lets other things be through him" (*SBR*, 270). In spite of man's temptation to retreat from the disorders of a threatening world into the order of art, form, and isolation, Murdoch instead demands contact with the chaos, contingency, and elasticity of an unpatterned life that finds its richness in multiplicity and its meaning in communication. She agrees finally with Karl Jaspers' theory of community, which insists that the individual can understand himself only in interaction with others:

> The thesis of my philosophizing is: The individual cannot become human by himself. Self being is only real in communication with another self-being. Alone, I sink into gloomy isolation—only in communication with others can I be revealed in the act of mutual discovery.[2]

Murdoch's repudiation of the retreat from disorder has led to her creation of various images of man-made order as alternatives for isolation and as versions of community. Among these, the more important are such social patterns as work, erotic involvements, family entanglements, and the restricted inner spaces of houses within which relationships are explored and confined. Before moving to her three gothic novels, let us briefly glance at Murdoch's handling of two of these forms—work and rooms. In the first instance, work substitutes for community in three ways that serve to illuminate both character and theme. First, the vocation to which an individual is drawn in some cases reflects his psychological inadequacy or reveals an abortive effort to give order and meaning to an otherwise vacuous life. Anna's work with the Miming Theatre in *Under the Net*, for instance, suggests her need to fit herself into the theoretical world of Hugo Belfounder in order to win his approval and love; the utopian lay-religious community at Imber provides characters in *The Bell* with a chance to lose their personalities in pursuit of tidy lives, tidy gardens, and tidy goodness; such vocations serve as placebos for those who fear the contingency of real life. Second, work might reflect a character's demonic need to control and exert power over others. Such an elusive and magical character as Mischa Fox, the newspaper magnate in *Flight*, is supposed to have "at his disposal dozens of enslaved beings of all kinds whom he controlled at his convenience." In her darkest novel, *The Time of the Angels*, Murdoch illustrates a parody of work in the atheist defrocked priest Carel Fisher who spends his days listening to *Swan Lake*, reading Heidegger, and indulging in Black Masses and erotic relationships with his black "Anti-Maria" and with his illegitimate daughter. Third, work can also serve as a means for a protagonist to redeem himself and to work his way towards self-discovery: the changes in Rosa's jobs in *Flight* from factory worker to journalist and in Jake's jobs in *Under the Net* from hackwriter to hospital orderly to creative artist measure their movement towards selflessness, towards exorcism of their minds from the spells of fantasy and delusion, and towards becoming creative artists in their own right.

Not only work, but rooms and houses in her novels function metaphorically to define and be defined by the relationships within them. The L-shaped room with its presiding blind and deaf mother, with its empty bed frame within which the Polish brothers make love to and enchant Rosa (*Flight*), Mischa's labyrinthian palazzo (*Flight*), Hannah's multi-mirrored rooms where she is imprisoned by the misperceptions and expectations of herself and others (*The Unicorn*), Carel's bombed-out rectory, his dark basement, and Elizabeth's sequestered room whose mirrored, L-shaped nook conceals the incestuous secret of the household (*Time*) are all enclosures that reflect ailments of interiority as manifested in the character of their occupants and in the nature of their spell-bound, erotic, and frequently incestuous relationships.

Although each of Murdoch's seventeen novels experiments with a variety of communities, I have chosen to focus on the three Gothic novels, *The Flight from the Enchanter, The Unicorn, and The Time of the Angels*, because of their curious demonic inversions of community, in spite of which they also contain the recurring Murdochian theme of the struggle of love against the many guises of evil in everyday life. The elements of community in these works are Gothic extensions of similar concerns in her other novels. Here, the nets of fantasy are tighter, more difficult to escape, more terrifying, and cause more tragedy (disappearances, suicides, murders) than in her other novels.

Such "open" novels as *Under the Net* and *The Bell*, for instance, use characters appropriate to comedy and set them within a recognizable community against a background of accepted moral values. Although her darker novels use some familiar conventions of comedy such as unexpected and unorthodox action, in them the element of surprise looms incongruously larger in their portrayal of a society that no longer contains any secure moral framework or an understandable social hierarchy. In *Flight*, for example, we never do find out Mischa's actual relations with SELIB (the immigration board) or with Parliament; we merely sense his influence with each group and witness the reverberations of his choices in the unexpected disappearance of the Poles and in the death of Nina. Consequently, the communities in Murdoch's comic novels begin to disintegrate when the unpredictability of actions fills her Gothic works with terror rather than comedy, with threat rather than security. If the world-view of some of her characters in the darker novels begins as comic (Annette, in *Flight*, charging out of finishing school to find education in the "School of Life"), it swiftly develops into the pathetic and ironic when they realize they are victims in a world engineered by a power which they can neither control nor understand.

The fictional technique by which Murdoch pursues her ideas in these novels reveals a movement from an open to a closed structure.[3] The already limited mental and physical spaces inhabited by narcissistic and Faustian characters in *Flight* and *The Unicorn* contract still further into the final confines of madness and death in *The Time of the Angels*. While *Flight* focuses on several different levels of society and a variety of erotic relationships. *The Unicorn* focuses more narrowly on a few philosophical attitudes and relationships confined within two houses, and *The Time of the Angels* concentrates even more narrowly on the mostly incestuous relationships within only one isolated ingrown household—that of an atheist priest who lives in a bombed-out rectory. These novels, therefore, are dramatizing the consequences of solipsism: the psychological and sexual enslavement of oneself and others through fantasy, delusion, self-abnegation, and power. They study the possibility of knowing and loving others in a society held together by the willing bondage of enslaved individuals to demonic centers of power—to Mischa Fox in *Flight*, to Hannah Crean-Smith in *The Unicorn*, and to Carel Fisher in *The Time of the Angels*.

Murdoch's society in these novels resembles Northrop Frye's description of a demonic human world, a society dichotomized between the ruthless, inscrutable tyrant on one hand and the sacrificed victim or *pharmakos* on the other, a community held together by "a kind of molecular tension of egos, a loyalty to the group or the leader which diminishes the individual."[4] The setting in each novel also conforms to the requirements of both the demonic and Gothic traditions: the straight path and rich topography of what Frye calls the apocalyptic is contrasted in Murdoch against the labyrinth or wasteland of the demonic. In *Flight*, for example, Mischa's house is described as a labyrinth in whose basement his "minotaur" Calvin plans his fiendish deeds. In *The Unicorn*, the landscape is remote, empty, and bleak. Its coastline is "repellent and frightening," its bog-filled, uncharted terrain and its sea kill people, its earth produces no trees, and its fish desert the rivers. And in *Time*, the incestuous household that lives within a dark, ruined rectory far removed from London, surrounded by fog and by wasteland, suggests metaphorically the perils of intellectual, spiritual, and emotional solipsism. In all three works, unhealthy love that is "immersed, sealed-up" is a form of self-love or incest and can result in unexpected disaster and pathetic deaths or can engender other demonic relationships.

The *Flight from the Enchanter* may be read as an allegory of power, power willingly conferred by psychologically enslaved individuals upon those who seek to control them by force of their personal magnetism and ego. The plot centers on Mischa Fox's attempts to gain control of a small independent magazine, the *Artemis*, its owner's sister Rosa, and various other independent people he can't bear to see free from his control. The will to power, produced in part by the need for form rather than contingency, turns Mischa into a demonic enchanter who structures both human organizations and human emotions according to his own mysterious theories of society and psyche. Man's capacity to impose restricting patterns, fantasies, and myths on external reality is seen not only in his gods and leaders but in the ineffectual organizations he creates that also serve as unwitting accomplices of power and as instruments of evil. The characters in this novel, for instance, are set against a vast sociological spectrum spanning the barbaric social life of an East European village, the sophisticated life of the international jet set, the artificial life within a girl's finishing school, the exacting life of the scholar, and organizations as different as an industrial factory and the Special European Labor Immigration Board.

Each of the major characters in *Flight* is an orphan, an alien, or a refugee who attempts to compensate for his isolation by creating and controlling his own world, free from the accidents and threats of real life. Mischa Fox, the supreme enchanter of the novel, is both ruthless controller and passive innocent. His own self-image as melancholy lover of the world emerges in confessional talks with Peter Saward when he weepingly recalls incidents from his childhood in an East European village. But this strange region of sensibility within him contrasts drastically with his life as a sophisticated power-magnate who rescues refugees such as Nina, only to trap them into his deathly web, and who manipulates his alter-ego, henchman, and "minotaur" Calvin to carry out his evil designs. His seduction of Rosa is perpetrated through blackmail, but under the guise of a god-psychiatrist who desires merely to aid her "Protean" self-revelation. In the same vein, the Polish refugees, the Lusiewicz brothers, are more primitive versions of Mischa Fox, because they exude the same demonic, spellbinding air of the master enchanter, but with more directness and less finesse. In order to escape Mischa, Rosa flees to discover a new identity within a new family, as protector of what she perceives to be two dejected, "half-starved, half-drowned animals"—the Poles. At first she is the controller, to whom their response is one of primitive adoration—"like poor savages confronted with a beautiful white girl" (p. 49). She showers the brothers with love in return for feeling like "the princess whose strong faith released the prince from enchanted sleep" (p. 54). The power play gradually reverses itself when she finds the brothers assuming barbaric control of her body and mind.

From playing the role of mother, she is seduced into becoming their mistress, which for the Poles is not the role of wife-surrogate, but rather that of sister-surrogate. In Frye's terminology this incestuous relationship would be a demonic parody of marriage: " 'You are our sister,' he said. 'You belong to both.' The brothers often said this . . . 'Wife is nothing,' said Jan" (p. 70). Enchanted by their barbaric sensuality, Rosa agrees to become part of their primitive community and reenact the rite by which they initiated their first "sister" in their Polish village—a schoolteacher whom they seduced and finally drove to suicide. Such barbarism is seen also in the brothers' relationship with their blind and deaf mother whom they revere as an idol, before whom they make love to Rosa, and to whom they offer alternately testaments of undying love and threats of death by fire. After Rosa leaves them, the mother mysteriously disappears. Both Mischa and the Poles share a common disinheritance and isolation which at first results in a yearning for family and nationality but eventually evolves into a compulsion to control and to possess that which is denied them. Although they desire a place in the community of peoples, their essential self-centeredness and solipsism lead them to arrogance, intolerance, and the will to power that automatically destroys the relationships they most seek.

In the Murdochian credo, love is incompatible with power; it never involves the need to change another individual, but consists instead of "the non-violent apprehension of difference" and the delightful perception of the inexhaustible otherness of the other. In this novel, Peter Saward, historian of pre-Babylonian empires, is the only person capable of Murdochian selfless love, "the lover who nothing himself, lets other things be through him." Unlike Mischa, who needs to "place" people in order to control them, and Rosa, who fears intimacy as a threat to her independence, Peter is seen to be totally vulnerable to others, "a personality without frontiers" who never needs to defend himself against the powers of others. He is, therefore, the only character who does not need to flee enchanters, with whom Mischa can feel easily at peace, and over whom Mischa has no influence.

Written seven years after *Flight*, *The Unicorn* (1963) represents a significant development in Murdoch's handling of the closed Gothic novel—the novel of form, myth, and socio-religious philosophy rather than that of character. Reminiscent of *Wuthering Heights,* "The Lady of Shallot," and Mme. de LaFayette's *La Princesse de Cleves,* this story is about the self-imposed exile and imprisonment of a group of people at Gaze Castle who weave themselves into a web of enchantment designed in part by Hannah Crean-Smith and by Gerald Scottow, her demonic master-caretaker. Hannah is the enchanting and spell-bound center who attracts the devotion of, among others, the Platonic philosopher Max Lejour and his household, of Effingham and Marian, the two outsiders who represent the moral and emotional inadequacies of the liberal and romantic modern world, and of Dennis, the thirty-three year old Christ-figure and keeper of fish who voluntarily becomes heir to Hannah's suffering in order to free others from their bounds of guilt. Part of the ambiguity of the novel lies in the nature of the bonds that imprison Hannah—ambiguous bonds that are variously interpreted by others as superstitious, pagan, Christian, spiritual, evil, or sexual. Hannah is believed to be either under a seven-year spell or undergoing a seven-year period of spiritual suffering as expiation for her adultery and her attempted murder of her husband Peter. Peter, in turn, has long been involved in a homosexual liaison with Gerald, whose sexual prowess enthralls all whom he chooses to favor.

But the community is controlled by more than sexual liaisons. Max Lejour, the classical philosopher at Riders, usually sees Hannah's quiet acceptance of unverified guilt in terms of the Greek concept of *Até,* "the almost automatic transfer of suffering from one being to another. . . . It is in the good that *Até* is finally quenched, when it encounters a pure being who only suffers and does not attempt to pass the suffering on" (*Unicorn,* p. 99). But, like others, he is also tempted occasionally to see her as "just a sort of enchantress, a Circe, a spiritual Penelope keeping her suitors spellbound and enslaved" (*Unicorn,* p. 99). This is a community, therefore, held together by central enchanters, by quasi-religious ideals, and by the fantasies of Hannah's audience who adore, imprison, and transform her into a symbol, and upon whom she in turn battens "like a secret vampire." While Hannah claims she has lived in their "gaze" like a false god, they in turn use her as a mirror in whose reflection they see a redeemed and ideal image of their earthly inadequacies. Hannah and her jailer-prisoners continue to feed upon one another for mutual sustenance until the "Vampire Play" literally plays itself out in the final act of suicide, murder, recriminations, and a continued cycle of guilt and expiation through suffering. At the end of the novel, Hannah admits that she has gradually evolved into a "false God . . . a tyrannical dream" who lived by her audience's belief in her suffering:

". . . Ah, how much I needed you all! I have battened upon you like a secret vampire. . . . I lived in your gaze like a false God. But it is the punishment of a false God to become unreal. I have become unreal. You have made me unreal by thinking about me so much. You made me into an object of

contemplation. Just like this landscape. I have made it unreal by endlessly
looking at it instead of entering it."

—*Unicorn*, p. 219

Gazing at life instead of entering it, needing the fairy-tale Hannah to
remain a symbol rather than become a reality, desiring the neatness of form
rather than the contingency of substance, the shape of art rather than the
shapelessness of life—all these are "ailments of Romanticism" that contribute
towards the failure of the community at Gaze. Symptomatic of the inability
of the others to save Hannah, Effingham admits that his own "really fat and
monumental egoism" has saved him from suffering, from involvement, and
from love; Marian admits, "I did not love her enough, I did not *see* her
enough" (*Unicorn*, p. 197). The most frequently recurring image of the
mirror represents both the limitations of vision and the distortions of perception. Marian, for instance, sees Hannah's mirrors as idealized extensions of
her, which "seemed to change her, to change even the blue dress" (*Unicorn*,
p. 51). The communities in the novel, therefore, are composed not of singu-
larly independent centers of significance, but of actors who find safety in a
looking-glass world, whose eyes project on to Hannah their image of her,
and who see in her the reflections of spiritual, platonic, or courtly ideals.
She dies when their faith in her wanes along with their existence as mirror
images of her reality. And Marian wonders, "When at last Hannah had
wanted to break the mirror, to go out through the gate, ought she then to
have been her gaoler?" (*Unicorn*, p. 247). Hannah's mirror is finally a metaphor for her dependence on the introspective, self-contemplative code of
conduct that gradually leads her to utterly disregard all others as independent
and complex beings to be known, understood, or loved.

If the ability of a community to create its demonic controllers is seen
in *Flight* and *The Unicorn*, Murdoch's *The Time of the Angels* is about the
power of the demon to contaminate himself and others. In all three novels
the enchanter manipulates the fantasies of victims who need a dominating
figure to provide metaphysical meaning and dynamic tension to their otherwise vague drifting lives. In *Time* the need for some reconstructed value
system directs this enchanter figure towards mad Nietzschean fantasies of the
self as a potential Deity in a nihilistic world. Particularly in her central
figure, Carel Fisher, we understand Murdoch's perception of the demonic as
the inevitable result of conceptual and imaginative inadequacy in an age that
venerates power and solipsism.

Father Carel Fisher, a defrocked priest whose atheism is inspired by his
reading of Nietzsche and Heidegger, controls his ruined rectory and a household that consists of Pattie his Jamaican mistress, his mysteriously ill niece
Elizabeth (who turns out to be both his daughter and his lover), and his
daughter Muriel, who is attracted, among others, to her father and to her

cousin Elizabeth. The novel's plot centers on Carel's attempts to maintain his control over his family, on Muriel's and Pattie's attempts to escape from his domain, and on the pitiable struggles of various kinds of good against the dynamic evil of Father Carel.

Carel is Murdoch's modern representation of a Faust, who like Thomas Mann's Leverkühn, signals the end of a humane intellectual and ethical tradition. The parallels between Leverkühn and Carel (their similar philosophical backgrounds, their pacts with the inhuman, their sexual enslavement of others) emphasize their author's concern with those nihilistic and irrational elements in modern existentialist thought that Mann had earlier seen as responsible for the inhumanity of the Germans during the Second World War. As one who equates Heidegger with Lucifer, Murdoch sees his philosophy as depraved, negative, and demonic, and appropriately makes *Sein und Zeit* Carel's Bible and the source of all his ideas and sermonizing. As Mann's Leverkühn had reflected the sickness of Germany before World War II, so Father Carel, enshrined in his tower of darkness, embodies the demonic nihilism and interiority of his time. The sense of the ending of an age and of a dying mythology is reinforced by the use of decaying characters whose loneliness is accentuated by their dark, ruined settings and by an oppressive atmosphere of terror, melancholy, and evil. Within the rectory live the ruins of a diseased age—grotesque parodies of family, of religion, of sexuality, and of love. Carel's isolation in the darkness of his being corresponds to the setting of the rectory shrouded in fog: "Ever since their arrival the fog had enclosed them, and she still had very little conception of the exterior of the rectory. It seemed rather to have no exterior . . . to have absorbed all other space into its substance" (*Time*, pp. 19–20). The darkness of this fog multiplies in implication as it penetrates the house, unnerving its inhabitants and merging with the darkness of Carel's cassock, Carel's black masses, black humor, and blackness of being.

If the central image of interiority in *The Unicorn* was the mirror, here it is the cocoon. Carel's effect on others takes the form of a kind of spell that imposes on them his special brand of immobility and dehumanization: Pattie is described as "inert like a chrysalis, moving a little but incapable of changing her place" (*Time*, p. 29), and his daughter Muriel fears the consequences of disobeying him because

> she was even more frightened of something else, of an isolation, a paralysis of will, the metamorphosis of the world into something small and sleepy and enclosed, the interior of an egg.
>
> —*Time*, p. 130

Infected by the disease of her father's lust, Elizabeth languishes like "the soft chill of a wax effigy," "a cocoon of darkness," and Carel fears she is about to leave them by retreating entirely into her own mind. Analogous to the image of the egg and the cocoon is Carel's metamorphosis into the cocoon of his increasing madness in his rejection of normal human relationships. Carel's inhumanity is compounded by an increasing abstractionism that replaces his former faith in a loving God and by a rigid totalitarianism that demands obedience from others to strict patterns of behavior. His request, for example, that Muriel relinquish her freedom in service to Elizabeth strikes Muriel as part of a diabolical plot to involve her in "some unspeakable alliance":

> "Elizabeth is a dreamer who weaves a web. That web is her life and her happiness. It is our duty, yours and mine, to assist and protect her, to weave ourselves into the web, to be with her and to bear her company as far as we can."
>
> —*Time*, p. 125

Elizabeth, "the delicate pure heart of the household, its kernel of innocence," is also its symbol of physical decay. She combines the Gothic characteristics of the ravished innocent and the *femme fatale*, attracting and menacing all who come in contact with her. As Murdoch's most effective portrayal of the orphaned demon-child, Elizabeth uses her amorality and lovelessness as weapons and armor against the outside world. Her diseased body encased in a surgical corset, her insistence on staying within "the dark, unvisited cavernlike environment," and her self-imprisonment behind locked doors that admit others only at the summons of a bell are all facets of her increasingly inhuman behavior. Carel's effect on Elizabeth has been to infect her with his inwardness and his solipsistic fantasies, a state of being into which she gradually withdraws: "She has come to live much more in her mind. Everyday reality means less to her" (*Time*, p. 123). As Carel, deprived of Pattie's devotion, is committing suicide, his daughter Muriel begins to recognize her love for him, a love that might have saved him had she used it well. But because his was a love "immured, sealed up," it could result only in a damnation to be reenacted by both his daughters who finally realize that "Carel had riveted them together, each to be the damnation of the other until the end of the world."

Carel's black mistress, Pattie, however, does save herself from the effects of his corruption, first by recognizing his evil and rejecting it, and then by transcending her suffering through love and service to others in a different and more open community—an African refugee camp. Murdoch's choral use of Blake's "Introduction" to "The Songs of Experience" as part of Pattie's musings is intended to suggest a healthy Romantic norm, a positive Romanticism that emphasizes the regenerative power of wonder that accompanies the discovery of the external sensory world through goodness, love, and imagination. Murdoch's pursuit of true imagination as man's key to the discovery and love of others also recalls what Alfred Kazin calls the great theme of Blake's work—the search for imagination "that has been lost and will be found again through human vision."[5] Seen within a framework of Romantic theories of perception, her sudden recognition scenes (such as Muriel's chilling keyhole vision of her father's naked body entwined with Elizabeth's) may be understood as devices intended to startle the self-deceptive mind into seeing the truth of others, and occasionally understanding, as Pattie does, the "face of evil as a human face." Carel's evil then is the result of man's intellectual errors that are created by his inadequate imagination—what Blake would call lost imagination, and Murdoch fantasy.

Demanding a "new vocabulary of attention" from novelists, Murdoch's polemical essay "Against Dryness" expresses concern that "modern literature . . . contains so few convincing pictures of evil" and that it requires "a much stronger and more complex conception" of indefinable and impenetrable real people. Because Iris Murdoch reveres the openness and contingency of "Tolstoyan" characterization, she would like not to be a philosophical novelist trapped within a fixed schematic and allegorical vision. Her gothic novels, however, seem to belie her preferences. Yet, her critics are simply incorrect in reducing the merits of such novels to "grotesque" jokes "contrived by an author with a flare for sensationalism."[6] Indeed, what this essay has sought to show is that by restricting themselves within a well-established mode, these novels succeed both formally and thematically in revealing the tyranny of pattern over contingency in structure, subject matter, and characterization. Because they are novels of such dramatic intensity and because they not only explore but embody the problems of power, freedom, and solipsism, they justify her occasional excursions away from her more open novels of free and accidental characters.

Her three Gothic novels are crucial to an understanding of her treatment of evil, the dangers of fantasy, and the problem of the discovery of others which is the only means to achieve human community. Within the Gothic form Murdoch has also found powerful images and a "new vocabulary of experience" that capture her sense of the moral and emotional failures of this age: the ruined church as an emblem of the failure of conventional religion to cure the sickness of the age, the incestuous family as a demonic extension of egoism and solipsism, and the enchanter or Faustian priest as a manifestation of modern existential man who defines his own values in a world bereft of the community of men and of God. The retreat of her characters into mental and spatial enclosures that admit neither contingency, humanity, nor love is most perfectly embodied in the progressively inward movements and the enclosed structure of Iris Murdoch's Gothic house of fiction.

Notes

1. Iris Murdoch, "Against Dryness," *Encounter*, 16 (1961), 18. Hereafter page references to Murdoch's essays will be included parenthetically and abbreviated as follows: AD for

"Against Dryness"; SBR for "The Sublime and the Beautiful Revisited," *Yale Review*, 49 (1959), 247–271; SG for "The Sublime and the Good," *Chicago Review*, 13 (1959), 42–55. After their first mention, the titles of Murdoch's novels will also be abbreviated: *Flight* for *The Flight from the Enchanter* (New York: Viking Press, 1956); *Unicorn* for *The Unicorn* (Middlesex: Penguin Books, 1966); and *Time* for *The Time of the Angels* (New York: Avon Books, 1967). Criticism of these three Gothic novels has been negligible in recent years, though a few fine studies came out in the late 60s. For general surveys that include some of these works, see A. S. Byatt, *Degrees of Freedom: The Novels of Iris Murdoch* (London: Chatto & Windus, 1965); Peter Wolfe, *The Disciplined Heart* (Columbia: University of Missouri Press, 1966); Rubin Rabinowitz, *Iris Murdoch* (New York: Columbia University Press, 1968); Frank Baldanza, *Iris Murdoch* (New York: Twayne, 1974); Donna Gerstenberger, *Iris Murdoch* (Lewisburg, PA: Bucknell University Press, 1975); Robert Scholes, "Iris Murdoch's Unicorn," *The Fabulators* (New York: Oxford University Press, 1967); Jacques Souvage, "The Novels of Iris Murdoch," *Studia Germanica Gandensia*, 4 (1962), 225–252; Olga Meidner, "Reviewer's Bane: A Study of Iris Murdoch's *The Flight from the Enchanter*," *Essays in Criticism*, 11 (October 1961), 43–47; and Daniel Majdiak, "Romanticism in the Aesthetics of Iris Murdoch," *Texas Studies in Language and Literature*, 14 (1972), 359–375.

    2. Karl Jaspers, "On My Philosophy," trans. Felix Kaufmann, in *Existentialism from Dostoevsky to Sartre*, ed. Walter A. Kaufmann (New York: Meridian, 1956), p. 145, quoted in Peter Wolfe's *The Disciplined Heart: Iris Murdoch's and Her Novels* (Columbia: University of Missouri Press, 1966), p. 37.

    3. In her interview with William K. Rose ("Iris Murdoch, Informally," *London Magazine*, 8 [June, 1968], 9–73) Murdoch admits a preference for the Dickensian or Tolstoyan "open" novel, one whose pattern is casual and uncontrolled and whose characters are contingent, independent, and free. Her Gothic novels, however, are more "closed" in structure, more patterned, "crystalline and quasi-allegorical," their characters frequently imprisoned within the author's metaphysical construct.

    4. Northrop Frye, *Anatomy of Criticism* (New York: Princeton University Press, 1957), p. 147.

    5. Alfred Kazin, "Introduction," *The Portable Blake* (New York: The Viking Press, 1959), p. 141.

    6. Linda Kuehl, "The Novelist as Magician/The Magician as Artist," *Modern Fiction Studies*, 15 (Autumn 1969), 357. Kuehl also accuses Murdoch's characters of not progressing "beyond their initial benighted outlooks." My contrary belief is that most of her major characters do, in fact, learn more about themselves, about the impenetrability of others, and about a world whose mystery transcends neat and conclusive knowledge.

ON THE INDIVIDUAL WORKS

◆

The Reader's *Flight from the Enchanter*

THOMAS JACKSON RICE

Throughout her career Iris Murdoch has proved to be subtler than her critics, as a review of her critical reception will quickly show. Her situation vis-à-vis her readers and reviewers seems analogous to that of the inscrutable central figure Mischa Fox of her second novel, *The Flight from the Enchanter* (1956), whose ambiguous complexity is reduced to a falsifying simplicity in the perceptions, or "interpretations," of the novel's characters who persistently mythologize Mischa as "Some god or demon" (287).[1] Given the intricacy of the idea-play in a typical Murdoch novel, it should not surprise us that similarly "reductive" interpretations also seem to dominate the critical discussion of her fiction. Of course, criticism is often a benign form of reduction, for the sake of clarification, which confesses its necessary loss of subtlety. Conversely, the critic who is more subtle than the text he reads may become absurd, a comic figure like Charles Kinbote in Nabokov's *Pale Fire* (1962), who finds himself in (i.e., inscribes his own identity into) the text he reads. Yet, the reductive imposition of a scheme of interpretation in criticism is no less a form of egoism. As Murdoch herself has remarked, great art "invites unpossessive contemplation and resists absorption into the selfish dream life of the consciousness," and the worthy reader, in turn, resists the tendencies to inscribe the self into the work or to impose a self-gratifying interpretation upon it: in "the enjoyment of art . . . we discover value in our ability to forget self, to be realistic, to perceive justly."[2] Thus, one of the *enchanters* that the reader must flee is his own "obsessive ego," with its "facile merging tendencies" that shrink "reality into a single pattern."[3] One of the problems here, and in *The Flight from the Enchanter*, is that it is extremely difficult to know when reading and interpretation cease to be "just" and become selfish impositions of satisfying meanings upon intractable materials; the critic's problem resembles that of Rosa Keepe, who can never know whether her attempted flight is actually part of the enchanter's plan and, thus, a flight *to* the enchanter (281). Perhaps the best that can be sought is a criticism that recognizes the dilemma, that admits its vulnerability to the egoistic gesture of appropriation. In fact, this is the ultimate strategy for reading that *The Flight from the Enchanter* suggests, within and for itself.

From a study-in-progress entitled *Iris Murdoch: Platonic Realist*. Printed by permission of the author.

An overview of the reception of Murdoch's novels shows how rare such admissions are and how difficult this kind of "unpossessive" reading can be; for example, her first novel, *Under the Net* (1954), published shortly after her own critical study *Sartre: Romantic Rationalist* (1953), was greeted by her reviewers as an "existentialist" novel, with Jake Donaghue as an English Roquentin, modeled on the central character of Sartre's *La Nausée* (1938). That *Sartre* is not a celebration but a critique of existentialism and that Jake's progress toward "authenticity" is satirically undermined, rather than endorsed by Murdoch, seem to be missed altogether.[4] It is true, however, that her explicit indictment of Jake's egoism in the opening of *Under the Net*, her serio-comic attack on the solipsistic worldview of existentialism, is only implicit as a negative subtext in the novel's ambiguous close.[5]

The Flight from the Enchanter, too, has suffered its share of reductive readings; it almost seems that Murdoch invited misreading by loading this book with symbolic and mythological motifs that beg for a patterned interpretation. Zohreh T. Sullivan in her essay "Enchantment and the Demonic in Iris Murdoch,"[6] although one of the best discussions of the novel, imposes a strict integrating pattern in her reading (tracing Murdoch's "allegorical representation" of demonic power [80]), despite recognizing that the subject of the book is precisely the danger of such assimilations of reality into the "dream life of the consciousness": "If an abstract proposition is being tested in *The Flight from the Enchanter*, it is probably Murdoch's theory of the demonic reverberations that result from imposing restricting patterns, fantasies and myths on objective reality" (74). Thus, Sullivan's reading is seriously flawed by her failure to apply her recognition of the novel's "abstract proposition" to her own interpretation of the book that proposes it. I would argue that the resistance to such appropriative acts of interpretation, by reader as well as by character, is precisely what the book is about. While *Under the Net* is a warning against the artist's imposition of form in the work of art (which has been misread as the achievement of the "form" of selfhood by its central character), *The Flight from the Enchanter* is Murdoch's caution against the reader's reciprocal act of imposing "meaning" upon the work. *The Flight from the Enchanter* is a self-reflexive novel— strongly anticipating the directions of Murdoch's later fiction—which can be read as a text about how to read a text, written perhaps in reaction to the misreadings of her first novel (that she is aware of and responsive to the ways critics view her fiction, in fact anticipating some possible responses to *The Flight from the Enchanter*, will be shown below). *The Flight from the Enchanter* is both a counter-text and a complement to *Under the Net*, as its nearly systematic thematic and technical contrasts to the preceding novel suggest.

Under the Net and *The Flight from the Enchanter* are both explorations of the nature of art, though they differ sharply in their emphases and narrative techniques. *Under the Net* is concerned with the unavoidable falsification of reality by art, as its central character; the professional writer Jake Donaghue, comes to realize: "all stories [are] lies" (81).[7] *The Flight from the Enchanter* examines the varieties of response to the work of art in the complex and often contradictory multiple perspectives of an audience: art, like reality, "is a cipher with many solutions" (305). Because these two novels concentrate in turn on the individual artist and the community of the audience, Murdoch chooses the most appropriate narrative technique for each: the solitary first-person narrator for *Under the Net* and multiple limited-omniscience, shifting irregularly among the perspectives of six characters who variously "read" their worlds, for *The Flight from the Enchanter*. As readers themselves, then, the characters of the novel exemplify the varieties of just and unjust interactions with the "text" of their world, providing models for the reader's responses to the text that contains them.[8] *Under the Net* is tightly organized, as well as narrowly focused, each chapter presenting the day-to-day exploits of the narrator, Jake, for approximately two weeks in July, in the early 1950s. Conversely, *The Flight from the Enchanter* is an "amorphous"[9] narrative of the experiences of a group of characters, covering an unspecified period of time (probably several weeks), and suggesting more chaos than organization in its conflicting perspectives.

Taught to be wary of abstraction by his mentor Hugo Belfounder—"cut all speech, except the very simplest, out of human life altogether" (81)—Jake records his story in *Under the Net* as concretely as possible. Jake curbs his artistic impulse to use imagery, allusion, and symbolism, attempting to render his story in simple and exact words, as he has with his translations of the French novelist Jean Pierre Breteuil. However, Jake also learns from Hugo that no language can ultimately express truth—"The whole language is a machine for making falsehoods" (60)—and, despite his attempts, he periodically allows his figurative imagination to work in his narrative, to "Touch it up" (59). The perspective characters in *The Flight from the Enchanter* know no such restraint and tend to fantasize about their personal situations and relations to others. They combine to create a novel remarkable for its variety of mythological allusions, symbolic patterns, and imagery. Although the stylistic surfaces of *Under the Net* and *The Flight from the Enchanter* differ, there is a deeper consistency in Murdoch's use of figurative language in these two works. Their relative scarcity or abundance of imagery directly reflects the characters' varying compulsions to order their perceptions. As Murdoch has remarked about the "matter of symbolism" in her fiction:

> I certainly don't aim at any kind of, as it were, allegorical method of telling the story. That is, I think the symbols must be very carefully controlled and, very often, the symbolism in a novel is invented by the characters themselves,

as happens in real life. We're all constantly inventing symbolic images to express our situations.[10]

Thus, symbolism in Murdoch's novels is usually a matter of the characters' projection of patterned meanings upon random experience, something quite different from the conscious fabrication of the author, elaborating a deliberate network of symbolic associations to encode a "meaning" within the text.[11] The imagery and order of a Murdoch novel, of course, are ultimately created by the novelist herself, but she stands one step removed from the process, on another "plane" so to speak, more interested in the individual's desire for form, in character or in critic, than in perpetuating and sustaining the illusion that absolute form exists in life or in art.

In Murdoch's view, the *immoral* artist manipulates material to impose the illusion of absolute design and meaning upon the reader.[12] This is what Jake Donaghue has already done in *The Silencer*, his one creative work prior to *Under the Net*, and it is an entirely open question whether Jake has escaped from, or merely repeated, his solipsistic act of "self-creation" in *Under the Net*. There are no artists, however, among the six perspective characters through whom Murdoch presents *The Flight from the Enchanter*: Annette Cockeyne, Hunter Keepe, Peter Saward, Rosa Keepe, John Rainborough, and Nina the dressmaker. Rather, all these characters picture themselves as artistic *creations*, existing within an "obscure system," like a Murdoch novel, where they are "kept in continual and irregular motion, jerking past each other like wooden horses racing at a fair, all involved in the movement . . . governed by mysterious forces" (84). While the "mysterious forces" in this quote are Rainborough's notion of the shadowy figures that control the political bureaucracy of SELIB (the Special European Labour Immigration Board), where he is head of the Finance Department, he is the only character who does not exclusively identify the "press lord and general mischief-maker" (118) Mischa Fox as the governing power, the "artist" and "enchanter" who controls his existence. More typical is Nina's sense of Mischa's power:

He bore with him the signs of a great authority and carried in his indefinable foreignness a kind of oriental magic. She was ready from the first to be his slave, though it never occurred to her to think that she might take more than a very minor part in his life. . . . She had not been prepared for the curious role which she found herself . . . forced to play.

(140)

Yet even Rainborough accepts Fox's uncanny omniscience, when his attempted seduction of Annette is thwarted by Mischa (chapter 10), and acknowledges his omnipotent control over the world of the novel, as if it were his ordered work of art:

Mischa's parties, as Rainborough knew from experience, were as often as not carefully constructed machines for the forcing of various plots and dramas; and this knowledge made him nervous, although he did not imagine that in this case he was likely to be cast in any central role himself.

(179)

The perspective characters of *The Flight from the Enchanter*, then, differ from the artist Jake Donaghue by seeing themselves as existing in a universe created and controlled by an artist, rather than as creators of their own worlds. Their attempts to flee from the enchanter's system and create their own worlds lead to the appalling discovery that even their search for freedom is part of a larger, determined design. The paradox that Murdoch explores in *The Flight from the Enchanter* is that both solipsism and submission to another's designs are acts of egoism (like the two types of appropriative reading I described in my opening). To see oneself as an actor in an ordered and meaningful drama is as much a gratification of the individual's sense of self-importance as is Jake's solipsistic art.[13] The disillusionment of the role-playing egoist who sees himself as an integral part of a patterned world may be prompted by the discovery, similar to the conventional solipsist's, that other very real beings exist independently, outside the perceived pattern, as happens when Rosa and Hunter are confronted by the inscrutable political "aliens," the Lusiewicz brothers. Otherwise, the characters' egocentricity is punctured by their recognition that their roles are far different and much less significant than they assumed them to be. Such discoveries drive Nina to suicide, Annette to a suicide attempt, and Rainborough to flight.

Rainborough, "who would have liked to play the role of being unhappily in love with Rosa" that has been taken instead by Peter, has recast himself: "I have the reputation of being Mischa's friend" (29). However, he loses this part to Peter as well, much as he loses control of his SELIB office and his love life to his secretary Miss Casement. Rainborough, in fact, is left without any central role to play in *The Flight from the Enchanter*, save that of a secondary character, a comic foil to Rosa, Hunter, Nina, and Annette who are variously resisting their designated parts in Mischa's schemes. It is Rosa who discovers that even to resist may be to play a role in Mischa's drama:

"It's odd," she said, "in the past I always felt that whether I went towards him or away from him I was only doing his will. But it was all an illusion."
"Who knows," said Calvin [Blick], "perhaps it is only now that it would be an illusion."

(281)

Murdoch deliberately leaves unresolved the question of whether Mischa is truly manipulative or only appears so to others, creating a central ambiguity in the novel that resists interpretation ("appropriation"). The evidence in *The Flight from the Enchanter* equally suggests that Mischa may be objectively detached from the characters' destinies, or that, through his agent Calvin Blick, "the dark half of Mischa Fox's mind," he may be egoistically involved in their fates while maintaining a posture of aloofness: "That's how Mischa can be so innocent" (33). Murdoch invests Mischa with an exterior duality that matches the dark and light halves of his mind: "He had one blue eye and one brown eye" (79). She heightens his ambiguity by showing the characters' tendencies to picture him as both a malign and a benign power, depending on their circumstances. Mischa's only decisive action in the novel, prompting a Parliamentary question about the status of illegal aliens, balances evil and good, simultaneously driving Nina to suicide and freeing Rosa from the captivity of Stefan Lusiewicz.

Whether Mischa is an arch-manipulator or only perceived as such, in other words whether he is or is not an "immoral" artist of creation in the story, he is firmly established by Murdoch as an *artist* figure much like herself. Mischa's chief work of art is his town house, which Murdoch places at the novel's center in chapter fifteen. The maze-like structure and ornate design of Mischa's house correspond to the complex features of *The Flight from the Enchanter*. The novel's abrupt transitions in place and point of view find their architectural equivalent in a house with "no corridors and no continuous stairways. . . . the floors were joined at irregular intervals" (185). The book's variety of literary and mythological allusions resemble a house assembled out of parts of other structures, "antiques which had been ripped out of other buildings," decorated with "art treasures which had been procured illicitly by Mischa" (185–186). Even the critical reviews of Mischa's creation, expressed by his "foes and acquaintances according to taste," anticipate the responses Murdoch expected her unique novel would provoke: " 'mad,' 'sinister,' 'vulgar,' or 'childish' " (186).[14] Again like *The Flight from the Enchanter*, Mischa's house is impenetrable at its core; its "central structure," which no outsider has entered, excites wild "speculation" (185–186). The mysterious center of the novel is the figure of Mischa himself, and the speculations about his alien origins and inscrutable intentions, provided by the six perspective characters, are their individual attempts to determine his meaning. Thus, the characters of *The Flight from the Enchanter* view Mischa as if he were not only an artist, but himself a work of art. Their acts of interpretation reflect and guide the responses of readers in the act of reading the novel that contains him.

The most important of Mischa's interpreters is his closest friend, Peter Saward, through whom Murdoch introduces the idea of decoding an alien language as an analogue to the reader's attempt to fix the meanings of Mischa and *The Flight from the Enchanter*. Peter's obsession with deciphering the unknown language of the ancient Kastanic script initially seems a peripheral part of the story. Yet Peter, too, has cast himself in a role, that of the reader and interpreter of a text, within a text that is being read and invites interpretation. This implicit tie between Peter and the reader of *The Flight from the Enchanter* becomes explicit late in the book. After the discovery of a bilingual stone solves the puzzle of Kastanic, as predicted by the "omniscient" Mischa, Peter turns his attention directly to the enigma of Mischa, "a problem which, he felt, he would never solve—and this although he had got perhaps more data for its solution than any other living being" (206). Peter's data are the photographs of Mischa's native village that Mischa has asked him to arrange into an album, another text that requires decoding. In the final chapter, Peter, joined by Rosa, pores over the "green book of photographs" (287), like the reader of *The Flight from the Enchanter*, reading the book of Mischa Fox.

Alone among the perspective characters, Peter recognizes the arbitrary nature of assigning a meaning to an ultimately indecipherable text or unknowable person:

> He knew, from many distinguished examples, how easily such a thing can become a mania, and how the most sober and balanced of men, once this passion is upon them, can lose completely their sense of proportion and spend years in trying to establish a particular theory the evidence for which could be written upon a postcard.
>
> (23)

Until Rosa reaches a similar understanding late in the novel, Peter is also the only character to apprehend Mischa's duality, seeing him not as "Some god or demon" (287), but as an ambiguous mixture: "how strangely close to each other in this man lay the springs of cruelty and of pity" (208). Peter and Rosa realize that labeling Mischa as mischief-maker or lord, demon or divinity, will only console the perceiver with the illusion of an ascertained meaning. To invest another person thus with an "identity" fixes the other in the individual's self-created world. The fatalistic "Calvin" Blick[15] tells Rosa that such solipsism is predestined and inescapable: "You will never know the truth and you will read the signs in accordance with your deepest wishes. That is what we humans always have to do" (278). But what Rosa learns from Peter is that such acts of *reading* can remain valuable, if the reader remains objectively detached, aware of the danger of falsification:

> "Well, what can one do?" said Peter. "One reads the signs as best one can, and one may be totally misled. But it's never certain that the evidence will turn up that makes everything plain. It [is] worth trying."
>
> (287)[16]

Peter and Rosa, then, are left with the book of photographs from another's world, a text that is not their own creation, that gives them no roles to play within it, and that may yield meanings only through their unself-centered acts of attention. Rosa *becomes* and Peter *is* the ideal reader for *The Flight from the Enchanter*.

Notes

1. All page references for Murdoch's novels, incorporated into the text of this essay, are to the internationally available Penguin paperback editions.

2. See *The Sovereignty of Good* (London: Routledge, 1970), 85–86, 90.

3. *The Fire and the Sun* (Oxford: Clarendon, 1977), 79. Murdoch continues: "The prescription for art is then the same as for dialectic: overcome personal fantasy and egoistic anxiety and self-indulgent day-dream. Order and separate and distinguish the world justly. Magic in its unregenerate form as the fantastic doctoring of the real for consumption by the private ego is the bane of art as it is of philosophy." Of course, what Murdoch says of art and of dialectic applies equally to critical analysis.

4. For characteristic reviews of *Under the Net* as an existential novel, see *Commonweal* 60 (4 June 1954): 228 [Jean Holzhauer], and *New York Times Book Review*, 20 June 1954, 15 [Edmund Fuller], and representative later essays by Roy Morrell, "Iris Murdoch—The Early Novels," *Critical Quarterly* 9 (1967): 272–282, and John B. Vickery, "The Dilemmas of Language: Sartre's *La Nausée* and Iris Murdoch's *Under the Net*," *Journal of Narrative Technique* 1 (May 1971): 69–76. Even A. S. Byatt, in her influential early study, *Degrees of Freedom: The Novels of Iris Murdoch* (London: Chatto and Windus, 1965), reads the fiction in existential terms, seeing *Under the Net* entirely in the Sartrean mode. Ben Obumselu, ("Iris Murdoch and Sartre," *ELH* 42 [1975]: 296–317) is the first critic to suggest that *Under the Net* "echoes *La Nausée* in order to contradict it," although he simultaneously argues that "Murdoch remains . . . recognizably in the [existentialist] camp." Susanna Roxman ("Contingency and the Image of the Net in Iris Murdoch, Novelist and Philosopher," *Edda* 2 [1983]:66) argues that Murdoch "transcends Sartre" in *Under the Net*, but also sees Jake as positively transcending existentialism in the book's conclusion. Murdoch, however, clearly discredits Jake's progress in the novel, classing him as an artist with those "who attempt to impose form upon essentially uncontrollable nature" (Ruth Heyd, "An Interview with Iris Murdoch," *University of Windsor Review* 1 [Spring 1965]: 142). Murdoch's skeptical view of existentialism, beginning with *Sartre: Romantic Rationalist* (Cambridge: Cambridge University Press, 1953), thoroughly informs her essays on moral philosophy in *The Sovereignity of the Good*. Recently, Murdoch has become even more explicitly critical of existentialism, "a philosophy with which I disagree . . . [based on] an illusion" (interview with David Gerard, in Olga Kenyon's *Women Writers Talk* [London: Lennard, 1989], 143–44).

5. As Louis L. Martz has observed, "Jake has his head and his suitcases full of undigested modern thought, especially French existential thought" ("Iris Murdoch: The London Novels," in *Twentieth-Century Literature in Retrospect*, ed. Reuben A. Brower [Cambridge, Mass.: Harvard University Press, 1971], 71).

6. Zohreh T. Sullivan, "Enchantment and the Demonic in Iris Murdoch: *The Flight from the Enchanter*," *Midwest Quarterly* 16, no.3 (April 1975): 276–97. The most substantial discussions of *The Flight from the Enchanter* in the early, full-length critical studies tend toward "monocular" views of a thematic pattern of the novel: "flight," "evil," or "power" (see Byatt's *Degrees of Freedom*, 40–60, Frank Baldanza's *Iris Murdoch* [New York: Twayne, 1974], 43–56, and Peter Wolfe's *The Disciplined Heart: Iris Murdoch and Her Novels* [Columbia: University of Missouri Press, 1966], 68–88). Of the two distinguished recent studies of Murdoch, Peter Conradi, in *Iris Murdoch: The Saint and the Artist* (New York: St. Martin's Press, 1986),

52–55, cursorily notes the saint-artist dualism of his thesis in the relationship of Peter and Mischa, while Elizabeth Dipple, in *Iris Murdoch: Work for the Spirit* (Chicago: University of Chicago Press, 1982), 136–42, sees the central conflict of the novel (also dualistically) in "the warring opposition of men and women" (140).

7. In her interview with Frank Kermode ("The House of Fiction," *Partisan Review* 30 [Spring 1963]:65), Murdoch stresses the philosophical implications of this theme of the falsification of art in *Under the Net*: "In a very simple sense" it is "a philosopher's novel." *Under the Net* "plays with a philosophical idea. The problem which is mentioned in the title is the problem of how far conceptualizing and theorizing, which from one point of view are absolutely essential, in fact divide you from the thing that is the object of theoretical attention."

8. The tendency of Murdoch's characters to see themselves "as if" they were characters in a novel, or drama, is already well established in her early fiction. This habit of mind persists in Murdoch's later fiction as well, finding its most explicit expression in Edward Baltram's reflection that his experiences in *The Good Apprentice* (1985) seem to have been "a whole complex thing, internally connected . . . as if we were all parts of a single drama, living inside a work of art"; however, Murdoch suggests Edward's achievement of maturity (and completed apprenticeship to the good) in terms of his objective assessment of one's self-fictionalizing tendencies as "a kind of magic" which is nonetheless necessary: "It's dangerous, but I don't see how we could get on without it" (523). John Bayley (*The Uses of Division* [New York: Viking, 1976]) has generalized that "the modern reflective consciousness cannot in some sense but see itself as taking part in a novel, the novel being the standard literary reflection of the individual in our age" (18); I am indebted to Conradi for pointing out Bayley's observation in his *Iris Murdoch*, 55. One implication of this fictionalization of the self, not pursued by either Bayley or Conradi, is that the character thus becomes a "reader" of the text that contains him; the whole point of my essay is that Murdoch exposes the failures of readers to read justly and accurately within her text, as cautionary models for the readers *of* her text.

9. I have chosen to use the term "amorphous" here in its scientific sense, as in chemistry, to mean the appearance of discursive form in a substance that nonetheless possesses a "deep" (i.e. molecular) structure. The opposite of amorphous is "crystalline," a term Murdoch uses to describe the highly organized work of fiction. (See "Against Dryness: A Polemical Sketch," *Encounter* 16 [January 1961]: 16–20.) This word has an added appropriateness because amorphous substances (like Tallis Browne's kitchen floor in *A Fairly Honorable Defeat*), are plastic, gluey, or sticky, all qualities that Murdoch and Sartre, in *La Nausée* (1938), associate with "reality." In *Sartre: Romantic Rationalist*, she observes that "the viscous" is Sartre's "fundamental symbol" for the nauseatingly "contingent over-abundance of the world" (17). Murdoch employs amorphous structures resembling *The Flight from the Enchanter* repeatedly in her later fiction to reinforce the reader's sense of the contingent nature of reality.

10. Jack I. Biles, "An Interview with Iris Murdoch," *Studies in the Literary Imagination* 11, no. 2 (Fall 1978): 125.

11. It is this distinction that places Murdoch as "poststructuralist," akin to the later Joyce, and quite different from a regressive, traditional realist, as she has sometimes been described. Furthermore, as I will suggest in this essay, Murdoch's critique of the impulse to form within her own highly formal works, allows her to restore traditional fictional conventions in her novels *with a difference*: Murdoch's use of form to undermine the desire for pattern is, as she might say, a use of "magic against magic" (see, for example, *The Fire and the Sun*, 65–67, 78–84 and passim). And the moral value Murdoch sees in this dis-illusionment of fiction gives her particular brand of post-modernism an affirmative dimension that is rarely found among her contemporaries.

12. See *The Sovereignty of Good*, 64–65 and passim.

13. Murdoch comments on this particular variation of solipsism that takes the form

of the individual picturing himself as an "actor" in a play, in one of her interviews: "I think there is a kind of self-centeredness that takes a dramatic form, but I don't think it is the only kind. What I mean is that it is consoling to feel that you are taking part in an inner drama. In a way, psychoanalysis depends upon this idea, doesn't it? The patient is cheered up by the analyst's picturing a drama in which the patient figures" (Biles, "An Interview," 117).

14.   Murdoch's prescience is borne out by several reviews of *The Flight from the Enchanter*. See, for example, *Catholic World* 183 (July 1956): 313 [Riley Hughes]; *Christian Science Monitor*, 19 April 1956, 7; *Manchester Guardian*, 27 March 1956, 4 [Anna Bostock]; *New Statesman and Nation* 51 (31 March 1956): 315 [Maurice Richardson]; and *Times Literary Supplement*, 6 April 1956, 205, for representative examples, ranging from the equivocal, to the bemused, to the negative.

15.   Murdoch's fondness for symbolically appropriate names has been noted by many of her critics. *The Flight from the Enchanter* is particularly rich with such name associations, some obvious, some obscure. Calvin's first name connects him with the theology of predestination, and his last name, by sound and meaning, with his snap-shot photographs ("click" and the German *blick*: "glance," "view," or "peep"). Mischa "Fox" beleaguers "Hunter" Keepe. Agnes prepares a "Casement report" on SELIB, and so on.

16.   Peter's defense of reading anticipates both Edward Baltram's view of pattern-making ("It's dangerous, but I don't see how we could get on without it" [*The Good Apprentice*, 523], and the arguments made by contemporary literary theorists, such as Geoffrey Hartman: "For what survives in this [post-deconstruction] graveyard of meanings is not simply a will, but specifically a *will to write*. The surprising power, even richness of language in Nietzsche, Stevens, or Derrida betrays the inner relation of what is now called 'deconstruction' to the very activity of writing. And that is Derrida's point, *his* understanding of Nietzsche's yea-saying within a suicidal nihilism. Language itself, nothing else, or the Nothing that is language, is the motivating residue. Despite obsolete and atrophied words, and falsified, disputable, or undecidable meanings, the will to write persists" (*Saving the Text: Literature/ Derrida/Philosophy* [Baltimore: Johns Hopkins University Press, 1981], xxiv). I would only add that the "will" to *read* persists as well.

A Fairly Honorable Defeat

Peter J. Conradi

The subject of *A Fairly Honourable Defeat* is pointed to when the Satanic Julius says 'Human beings are essentially finders of substitutes' (233). This has always been a great Murdochian theme. We might take *A Severed Head* as exemplifying the *reductio ad absurdum* of its claim: in that work almost every coupling you might have thought of occurs, as well as (as Bradbury pointed out[1]) some you didn't. The hurt produced by the removal of one relationship is compensated for by the substitution of a new one. Latterly, in *Nuns and Soldiers* the theme is still there, but treated at its most leisurely and patiently with, in place of the multiple substitutions and repetitions of the novels of the 1960s, a *single* substitution at the heart of the book. There Gertrude Openshaw loses her authoritative husband Guy and falls in love with the young, feckless, innocent, Tim Reede. 'She married her father, now she's married her son' is how one choric character describes this process (307). The success of that novel depends on our learning to understand what happens both from inside, as painful 'free' drama, as it might seem if it happened to us, and then later from the outside, as a much more conditioned Oedipal transaction.

Ann Wordsworth has pointed out that the Freudian description of mourning is very different from the 'flattering' humanist description. Freud, in *Mourning and Melancholia*, gives a harsh assessment of our psychic life, where 'the work of mourning is to force the ego into a testing of reality which will prove that the beloved no longer exists and that therefore all libido must be withdrawn from the dead and reinvested. . . . Narcissism and aggressivity mark both the work of mourning and the writing of poems.'[2] But no amount of reading of Freud makes us *experience* mourning quite like this, just as no amount of reading of 'flattering' humanists makes us able to experience the pain of someone else's bereavement as if it were ours. On such dissonances great fiction has always fed; and Gertrude appears in the end like Petronius' widow of Ephesus in *The Satyricon*, right to covet a happy substitution, rather than the unhappy void for which she is not built.

The harsh assessment has its own truth too, of course. Murdoch's closed

From *Iris Murdoch: The Saint and the Artist* (New York: St. Martin's Press, 1986), 159–83; © Peter J. Conradi. Reprinted by permission.

novels, where the characters are 'slaves', are its kingdom. Humanists who admire Murdoch's work do not, it seems to me, always appreciate how much steel there is in her vision, coexisting, not always comfortably, with warmer and more romantic elements. In *A Fairly Honourable Defeat* the elements come together and produce a brilliant and decisive master-piece. *A Fairly Honourable Defeat* is an elegant open novel which tests out the premises on which the closed novels are based. In *A Severed Head* two brothers compete for women; in *Bruno's Dream* two sisters love the same man but the unmarried sister renounces her claim. In *A Fairly Honourable Defeat*, Julius tries to manipulate two sisters into such competition, and (partly) fails. The sequence is one of a gradual opening out of the incestuous plot. Perhaps the mechanical plot of *A Severed Head* insisted too much on a 'harsh assessment'. In *A Fairly Honourable Defeat* Murdoch tests out this harsh assessment through Julius King, who is Satan in person:

> Human beings are roughly constructed entities full of indeterminacies and vaguenesses and empty spaces. Driven along by their private needs they latch blindly onto each other, then pull away, then clutch again. Their little sadisms and their little masochisms are surface phenomena. *Anyone will do to play the roles.* They never really see each other at all. There is no relationship . . . which cannot easily be broken and there is none the breaking of which is a matter of any genuine seriousness. *Human beings are essentially finders of substitutes.* [my emphases]
>
> (233)

This is Julius preaching to Morgan in the Tate gallery, and his view becomes the subject of a wager between them which makes the tragicomic plot of the book. It is also the heart of Murdoch's grimly comic aesthetic, the law which governs the rapid erotic substitutions of the early work. Criticism of Murdoch has not always taken account of it. In both *The Fire and the Sun* (13) and *Henry and Cato* (397), she writes that 'human affairs are not serious, though they have to be taken seriously', ascribing this view to Plato's *Laws*. Clearly Murdoch does not endorse Julius' frivolity, which depends on his ignoring the second part of the maxim. She shows that the breaking of a relationship can yield a very powerful anguish, and that the cultivation of customary relationships combines pleasure and virtue. But the disturbing brilliance of the novel comes, once again, from the way that the devil is given the best tunes.

Julius' diabolism is contested by the novel's own peculiar achievement. 'What novelist ever succeeded in making a good man interesting?' Julius asks provocatively (223). Tallis, the book's Christ-figure, is both good and interesting. Rupert, whom Julius addresses here, and who gets destroyed, is both less good and less interesting. The book to that degree disconfirms what Julius knows. The characters are wholly persuasive and sympathetic creations, with a being which extends generously beyond the immediate requirements of the plot and idea-play. The depiction of a happy homosexual relationship between Simon and Axel is itself a small triumph. To the degree that any are dull, to that degree they are evidence for Julius' prosecution, since Julius sees human beings as profoundly conventionalised and tending to stock type. If the book fails for Murdoch it succeeds for Julius. The title, which refers to the defeat of good by evil, here enters oddly into the book's substance. The novel is a research into the substantiality of the self.

And these are not 'stock' characters. They are interesting, believable, even memorable. The hugely sympathetic Simon, 'sensitive and child-like and pleasure-loving' (18); Hilda the wife who put husband before career, intelligent without pretension, strong, and comfortable; Rupert her pompous well-meaning husband, the stiff Axel, the disturbed Morgan and Peter, the good Tallis: the characters are alive, and alive through the relationships which define them, and by virtue of which they exist. Hilda and Morgan's closeness and dependency which excluded and hurt their mother while she lived; Morgan and Simon's affectionate and flirtatious friendship; Hilda and Peter's mother—son love, frustrated and gone 'underground' now that he is adolescent. Perhaps more than in any other novel these characters give us that illusion of independent existence which their author so values. The network feels fully imagined wherever we test it, fully 'there', and because it is real for us as a small society, the novel has the 'feel' of its time and place in a way that is the opposite of limiting. From *Under the Net* on, Murdoch has always had an extraordinary gift for evoking time and place. Here this gift approaches some high point.

The structure of the book comes from religious allegory, but it is an enabling, not a determining structure. Julius King is Satan, Tallis a Christ figure, and Tallis' father God the Father who finds that it's all gone wrong. A draft for the novel makes clear that Chapter 6's discussions of birth-signs was to have included the information that Tallis was born, Christ-like, on December 25th. This is omitted in the published version, presumably because the story is, once you grant its marvellously artificial premise, realistic too. It is the expansion outward from the *psychomachia* that she wished to emphasise. The allegorical elements are partly disguised, where Tallis is concerned, by being ascribed to the quixotic Morgan, who represents the human soul for which the two spiritual magnates are battling.[3] It is for her that Tallis represents 'holy poverty or some such stuff' (221). 'Living in Malory', Morgan envisages Tallis as 'an Arthurian knight' (249).

*

The novel's opening words are 'Julius King'. Its closing words 'Life was good' apply, with considerable dryness, to Julius' Paris excursion through a series of small, real pleasures. Julius, who thus frames the book, is the Lord of this world. But the novel has two books, and the division between them is important. The first 'open' book involves a patient and wonderfully assured depiction of the small Murdochian court, precisely locating the characters in a believable South Kensington world. Hilda and Rupert Foster are rich, successful, happily married Old Guard Socialists who judiciously combine pleasure and virtue. Rupert, a Senior Civil Servant, has denied himself a knighthood but not a swimming-pool, makes payment to many charities, including Oxfam, which read both as genuine benefactions and also as talismans against loss of their superabundant good luck. By any normal standards the Fosters are good people, socially concerned, conscientious paragons of the virtuous intellectual bourgeoisie. They are, as Hilda puts it, the 'decent self-centred habit-ridden hedonists who keep society going' (131) and occupy that world where, in normal circumstances, 'money and good breeding precluded screams and blows' (112). The high social and moral tone of the book are necessary, as in Dorothea Krook's view of Henry James, to its comic enquiry: the fall from grace from within a high-toned world can be especially dramatic.

Rupert who is emotionally unstable and untested, as Axel suggests, calls himself a Sunday metaphysician and like Marcus is writing a treatise on morality in a secular age. He is twice referred to as a Platonist. He represents a cosy and uninhabited version of Murdoch's own philosophy, and Julius' is the wisdom his morality needs to accommodate if it is not to be vulnerable through its silly optimism. From another, equally valid, point of view it is the *point* about Murdoch's philosophy that no one can adequately inhabit it. 'Any man, even the greatest, can be broken in a moment and has no refuge. Any theory which denies this is a lie' a later narrator puts this (BP 19), and from this point of view the woolly Rupert is simply very unlucky. Being tested by Satan in South Kensington must count as bad luck.

The breakage of a series of social rituals provides the momentum: wedding anniversary, dinner party, birthday party, and party to celebrate the completion of Rupert's book. Two expository chapters, which introduce the cast with a great relaxed *bravura* reminiscent of the high confidence of a Victorian novelist, are followed by the Fosters' celebrating their twenty-year marriage. Hilda's sister Morgan, acting like a woman possessed, disturbs the idyll by arriving unheralded from America fresh from a failed love affair with Julius. A dinner party of Rupert's younger brother Simon, and Axel his homosexual lover, to celebrate Julius' subsequent return is then disrupted by the arrival, unannounced, of Morgan's estranged husband Tallis, trying to discover his wife's whereabouts. It is disturbed therefore by the inadvertent meeting of the rivals in love, both earthly and transcendental. 'What a very strange little person', Julius comments. 'He ought to be sitting on a toadstool' (85). It is disturbed, too, by Julius' bizarre, clandestine invitation to Simon to visit him in his Brook Street flat. A festive afternoon by the Fosters' new swimming-pool in Chapter 11 is disrupted by the arrival, again unsummoned, of the Fosters' only and disturbed child Peter, who has dropped out of Cambridge. After a series of mock-coronations with a rose-crown Peter offers a denunciation of the 'civilised' values by which his parents live. This denunciation is a dress-rehearsal for Julius' and Rupert's confrontation. For this first book ends with two disputations, one on the nature of morality between the devil Julius and the bland Rupert, a discourse on the speciousness of all human goods and the frailty of all human nature. This is followed by a more particular wager between Julius and Morgan about the giddiness of the human heart. Morgan bets Julius ten guineas that he cannot break off the relationship between Simon and Axel. He decides to make things more interesting by breaking off Rupert and Hilda's marriage as well, through engineering a love affair between Morgan and Rupert. A practical demonstration of morals in a Chinese restaurant ensues, where Tallis defeats a group of louts terrorising a Jamaican, while Axel blusters, Simon intervenes to little effect, and Julius watches with thrilled fascinated interest, his eyes gleaming with pleasure. This first part thus ends with evil suffering a dishonourable defeat at the hands of good.

The wager which is the plot's central device has a long pedigree in literature. It borrows from Shakespeare, Mozart, and the book of *Job*. Patrick Swinden has pointed out that the plot's detail comes from Shakespeare's comedies, but that the shape of the whole is tragic.[4] The book is a distressingly funny tragi-comedy or problem comedy. The masque in the Prince Regent Museum recalls the pleached bower in *Much Ado About Nothing*, Julius refers to midsummer enchantments, and Hilda, like the lovers in *A Midsummer Night's Dream*, wanders all night over the Pembrokeshire moors. The piquant humour and insouciant, puzzling ironies complicate this effect. The vision that the novel tests may be that of Benedick's final speech 'Man is a giddy thing and this is my conclusion'; but the gamble is unlike the good-humoured wager in *Much Ado About Nothing*. Julius does try, like Don Pedro, to join one couple and, like Don John, to separate another. But the mood is closer to the wagers in *Cymbeline*, *Fob*, or even *Cosi Fan Tutte*: what is contested is a harshly cynical and sour view of the inconstancy of the human heart. Julius, as prime mover of strategems which depend on jealousy, gullibility, and on physical concealment, is as close to Iachimo as to Iago. Like Iachimo too, he goes scot-free, and truth is arrived at through a fantastic plot.

This is also to admit that the comic elements succeed better than the tragic. Leonard's speech in Chapter 9 derives in its detail from *Job*, another nearly tragic story of Satan making a wager about the destruction of a good man. Though distressed by Rupert's destruction we are not, I think however, deeply moved. Rupert has been too much an ironic butt.

Northrop Frye has pointed out that the true descendant of Shakespearian romantic comedy with its twins, disguises, and concealments is Romantic opera, and this brings me to the third wager. References to opera abound in this book and are carefully chosen.[5] There is an early reference to *Don*

Giovanni, another story about the rewards of promiscuity. *Fidelio*, which deals with slavery and emancipation of the enslaved into the sunlight, figures in Chapter 6. There is a discussion of Mozart and *Die Entfuehrung aus dem Serail*, which again concerns erotic slavery and emancipation, and Julius is last and pointedly shown, as I shall explain, looking forward to Monteverdi. At one level the book is close to *Cosi Fan Tutte*, with its disturbingly frivolous and stylised morality, its concealed ironic depths, and its own bet about human inconstancy; (the women in *Cosi Fan Tutte* discuss male inconstancy too).

Book Two sees the acting out of the wager, isolating the romance elements implicit in the more realistic first part, and employing a Mozartian plot—The Purloined Letters, as it might be—to try out the values contested in the first, enquiring into the problematics of 'civilised' lying and intelligent hypocrisy, power, repression, love, sex. It is both a stylishly 'light' and a grimly dark comedy of manners, moving again from an integrated to a scattered court, and ending with the 'fairly honourable defeat' of good by evil, with Rupert dead of hubris; but, before that, the breaking of two feasts occurs in scenes which are more comic as they are also more distressing. Julius deliberately arrives late at Axel's birthday party, spoiling Simon's carefully prepared meal, ingeniously arousing Axel's jealousy, and crowning the event by presenting the fastidious, humourless Axel with a vast pink teddy-bear. The last of these disastrous parties is staged to celebrate Rupert's completion of his book on ethics, completed at exactly the moment when he has been apparently exposed to his wife and himself as bankrupt of precisely those values he has celebrated so fulsomely in print. Hilda, distraught at what she believes to be her betrayal by both her husband and her beloved sister, has decided that she cannot cancel the occasion 'without letting them know that you know' (351). Like Maggie in *The Golden Bowl* she hopes to save face, if not redeem everyone concerned, by sustaining her social role at a pitch of extreme suffering. The result is ludicrous, distressing, and wildly, painfully funny. Here relations between Simon and Axel have also broken down and are kept up in public as pure, agonising charade. Simon, tormented beyond endurance by Julius, pitches him into the swimming-pool though he cannot swim. Hilda rejects Rupert, while Simon and Axel learn to trust one another again. Julius, assisted by Peter, has meanwhile torn up Rupert's magniloquent moralisings into confetti.

This is the culmination of a series of decreations. Hilda twice upsets or breaks bottles of lotion. Morgan tears up at different points a photograph of Tallis, Simon's trousers, a letter from Tallis unread, a letter from Hilda, and breaks Tallis' amber necklace. Morgan at her most destructive acts always as the lieutenant or agent of Julius; his mode of breaking off his relationship with her seems calculated to derive the maximum of frenzy and restlessness in her. ('Tie me down' she asks Rupert when she first sees Julius.) Julius has seduced her by cutting up a newspaper, and in one of the novel's great *scènes-*

à-faire enthrals her by cutting up her dress, brassiere, pants and stockings. Morgan then destroys a T'ang horse, the Brook Street curtains and some of the plaster, in the effort to stay warm.

Such deconstruction reads as both real and metaphoric. Morgan early asserts when reunited with Hilda and Rupert that they make her feel continuous. 'One ought to feel continuous, oughtn't one?' (91). A persistent and reticent rhetoric endorses the sentiment. 'Human beings cannot live without custom' (441) reflects the quietly authoritative Tallis, though the book attempts a discrimination between good custom and bad. Thus when Morgan first visits Tallis and seeks a source of energy with which to fight her own love for him, she draws upon her own capacity to live 'existentially' (i.e. amorally), as though butchering her own moral consciousness:

> So long as I can keep it all dismembered, she thought. Keep everything small and separate and manageable. . . . Detail, detail, detail, keep everything small and separate.
>
> (120)

The breakage and disembowelling of the Pembrokeshire telephone at a critical juncture and perhaps also the subsequent failure of Hilda's car, evoked with the usual panache and vividness, belong too to this chain of *dégringolades*. Dismemberment has long been a commonplace Neoplatonic symbol of the fall into multiplicity.[6]

There is, similarly, a chain of immersions and near-drownings. At the start of the book Hilda instructs Rupert to rescue a bumble-bee from the pool. 'I do wish insects had more sense of self-preservation. I do hope our hedgehog won't fall in' (16). Later the hedgehog does indeed fall in and drown (353) and later still, lacking both common-sense and the instinct for self-preservation, so does Rupert, dead, as Julius cruelly puts it, of vanity as much as drowning. Tallis' rescue of a fly early in the book (180) from drowning in a glass of sherry evidences his own contrasting care for all of creaturekind.

*

In *A Fairly Honourable Defeat* the scattering of the court is paralleled by the destruction of specious goods incarnated in Rupert. It is a comedy because the ego is again seen not merely as the source of depravity but also, for all but saints, as the locus of stability, *amour propre*, and that 'self-preservation' whose absence destroys the hedgehog and Rupert as much as does his vanity. In a real sense Rupert's hedgehog-like lack of 'self-preservation' *constitutes* his moral vanity. He dangerously thinks himself tougher than he is.

The role of Julius is thus equivocal, and it is worth considering his literary pedigree in more detail. Murdoch has suggested that 'If Iago were just an embodiment of evil I think we wouldn't be so interested' (Bigsby,

1982). The same is true of Julius. He is a brilliant success within the book—a disturbing, uncanny creation, with his colourless hair and violet-brown eyes—exactly because his 'myth', to employ the term persistently used of him, is combined with just enough 'psychology' to tease curiosity. We early learn of him that he possesses the kind of style that would enable him to get away with wearing a monocle. And he in fact appears equipped with a silver-handled cane, and umbrella with an ivory handle and lotus design, and in an evening dress with an opera cape. He is given to such old-world gallantry as hand-kissing. He dresses *clerically* (a word twice used of him) and accompanies his sartorial dandyism with a verbal dandyism, a mock-sententiousness designed to generate unease:

> Hilda, what perfectly delicious fresh lemonade. What are the more vaunted pleasures of the flesh compared with the wild joy of quenching one's thirst on a hot day?
>
> (283)

He is a persistently witty and indeed funny demon. The fact that his manipulations cause real hurt and damage to those for whom we have been taught to feel is a part of his sinister and very uncomfortable appeal. When he replies to Rupert's remark: 'At my age, Julius, I don't worry too much about my motives. It's enough for me if I can see the right thing to do and do it.' 'That's beautiful. I hope it comes into your book' (221); or when he ripostes to Morgan's 'I'm beginning to see myself clearly at last'. 'A remarkable feat, if true' (229), the humour of the situation in each case depends on the ways in which Julius' viewpoint is close to that of the author, though not his mordant and Nietzschean cynicism. Murdoch makes quite clear how fruitless she considers the examination of one's motives to be, and also how undesirable and how little possible it is to 'see oneself clearly': the effort siphons off energy properly used for seeing all that is 'unself', and the attempt usually degenerates into prevarication and untruth.

But his challenge is deeper than this. In appearance he recalls the shabby genteel devil of Book II of *Karamazov*, flashy, beringed, be-lorgnetted, and also Dickens' dandy-gentleman Rigaud in *Little Dorrit*. His scepticism about moral substantiality is tied to a desire to transmute *all* substance into style, to aestheticise what he sees. In this he parodies the intelligent hypocrisy of those high bourgeois manners he observes and exemplifies. He is both a very rich *rentier* who could afford to occupy a symbolic apex of this world when he considers buying a house in the Boltons, and also a Jewish outsider, belonging and yet homeless. Julius' function in the book, apart from manipulator of the action, is also close to Dostoevski's Grand Inquisitor so far as the idea-play is concerned: it is his role to speak for a *realpolitik* of the emotions, for a devastating cynicism about the human heart and the fragility of its moral attainments and attachments. Of the Grand Inquisitor D. H. Lawrence wrote that his was 'the final and unanswerable criticism of Christ'. Christianity—or, in Rupert's case, a Christianised Platonism—is the ideal, but it is impossible: 'Man can but be true to his own nature. No inspiration whatsoever will ever get him permanently beyond his limits.' The legend of the Grand Inquisitor implies a rediscovery of the fallen nature of man, an item of knowledge, as Lawrence saw it, excluded by the facile perfectibilitarian optimism of the Enlightenment. The Grand Inquisitor accuses Christ of 'tragically over-estimating the stature of man or his ability to bear the agonies of free will'.[7] Just as the Grand Inquisitor's legend forms the crisis and resolution of the running debate between Ivan and Alyosha over the roles of spiritual nihilism and idealism, so Julius' nihilism is opposed to Rupert's idealism.

Julius' psychology is revealed to us piecemeal. We learn at the start that he has been experimenting with germ-warfare, and has given this up not because he views it as immoral but because he is easily bored. Later we find that he spent the war in Belsen, at the same time that we find that Tallis' sister died; not, as Tallis claimed, from polio, but after being raped and killed by a sex maniac. These two facts provide a context for one another. Simone Weil believed that extreme affliction is passed on by all but the saintly. Murdoch is philosemitic, and meant no more by making Julius a Jew than that Satan had been a Jewish invention (Caen, 1978). These sensational disclosures provide, as it were, a partial rationale for Julius' destructiveness: he is a restless, deracinate spiritual force actively involved in the business of transmitting suffering; Tallis, on the other hand, absorbs it.

Julius also shows a yearning for justice in its way as remarkable, and arguably more 'profound', than Rupert's. To Rupert he suggests that the sense of being justly judged would console 'most of all, most of all, most of all', and adds 'If there were a perfectly just judge I would kiss his feet and accept his punishments upon my knees' (226). He likes Simon for saying that Tallis should not have taken Julius' hand when they first met, and later congratulates Simon, glittering-eyed, for having revenged his humiliations by pushing Julius into the swimming-pool. When he watches Tallis' defeat of the louts in the Chinese restaurant he is full of thrilled fascinated interest, radiant with delight, feeding pathologically on the spectacle of violence and cruelty. This *Schadenfreude* he shares with Morgan: 'I adore violence! . . . her eyes bright with interest' (138).

Above all, however, Julius is, as he twice remarks of himself, an artist. 'After all I am an artist' (431) he says, when helping Tallis at last to clear up the appalling mess in his flat. Julius, by contrast, is a fanatically neat man; his exposure of Rupert to Peter can be put down by him to 'just my instinct as an artist, it was entirely impromptu' (408).

*

The gap which lies at the heart of this tragi-comedy is that between the wisdom which is professed and the wisdom which is lived from the heart. It is a gap which Julius as artist is uniquely equipped to unmask, and one which only Tallis—significantly a man who does not rate himself as an intellectual—is able to overcome. Rupert's exposure is the book's largest tribute to the theme but it radiates everywhere. The historical setting helps it. The challenge to bourgeois proprieties offered by the dionysiac ferment of the 1960s prefigures and enables Julius' attack. In the first chapter Rupert suggests of the younger generation that they are really 'consumed by a sort of incoherent love' and that such love must rightfully be used to oppose cynicism. 'Rot', Hilda replies to this. The book explores what the right kind of love to oppose to cynicism might look like, and it is Tallis', if anyone's, not Peter's. Tallis' attempts to expunge fantasy and live in the present are not, unlike Peter's, irresponsible or self-serving.

Given the importance of this quarrel between love and cynicism, it is worth noticing the comic circumspection of the narrative voice. A Sikh tenant in Tallis' house is early mentioned as in dispute at the bus depot over the wearing of his turban. In the penultimate chapter the dispute is over: 'The men had got used to their fellow worker. The Sikh was now happily united with his fellow males in an attempt to sabotage a campaign for women drivers.' A dry impassivity here marks the recognition of the imperfection of earthly things. This can be read either as a systematic small improvement, so that Sikhs, like the homosexual Axel and Simon, will be treated less inequitably; or the emphasis can be placed on the pyrrhic nature of the victory—the defeat of one species of bigotry at the expense of strengthening another. This comic moral realism is echoed in the exchange between Tallis and Julius over Tallis' relations with his father. Julius is learning to love Tallis as the nearest to the 'perfectly just judge' he is likely to find, and asks concernedly: 'Are you on good terms with him?' 'Yes. We shout at one another' (337).

Tallis plays saint or holy fool to Julius' artist. He is shown to us in a double focus, both admirable and absurd. Where the other characters articulate various 'philosophies' of love, it is Tallis who is shown to be, however incompetently, trying to put the thing into practice. 'Love' and 'value' are related securely in him, and arbitrated variously by the others. The characters who know themselves to be but slight creations, who have a humble self-contempt, come off best; the intellectuals worst. Simon considers himself 'flimsy' (434) compared to Axel, but it is Simon's life which is 'filled by love' (40), Axel's by caution. Hilda likewise considers herself to have been 'a very dull wife for such a brilliant man' (321) but, like the feminine Simon, is a practitioner, not a murderously high-minded theoretician. 'What is the purpose of life, Hilda?' asks Morgan and her sister answers 'I think loving people' (56). The depiction of her relationship with her teenage son Peter is superb. She puts up 'humbly and uncomplainingly with any degree of casualness and neglect. Peter knew that it was a metaphysical impossibility that her love for him should diminish by one iota whatever he might or might not do, and this precisely enabled him to dismiss her altogether from his mind' (291);

and criticism is not currently well equipped with terms to praise its truthfulness. Even the dry Axel when challenged to produce a philosophy replies that he wishes 'to do my work and have innocent friendships with gentle intelligent people' (82). 'I have to follow the kind of love that I am capable of' (214) the hopelessly self-deceived Morgan asseverates. This turns out often to a mean a self-serving, careless and witless romanticism.

The point is nicely made in her exchange with Simon in Chapter 16. Morgan speaks first: 'I've made a discovery.' 'Tell me! Or is it a secret?' 'It is possible to love people.' 'Oh. I knew that already actually' (197). The ironies here are multiple. Simon loves Axel and puts up with Axel's unacknowledged jealousy, withdrawals, depressions and bullyings, while Morgan behaves like a malevolent spirit or light-weight adventuress undergoing a nervous breakdown, pursuing a callow and destructive ideal of freedom, and within minutes of her protestation that she is 'learning to love people' betrays Simon casually to Axel as she is later to betray both Rupert and Hilda's confidences to Julius. Julius significantly suggests that Morgan's new creed is roughly 'a broken down version of Rupert's stuff' (404). Both are theoreticians of love, which the book makes clear is the only kind of romanticism worth advancing, but neither can put it fully to work. This is not merely because of their inadequacies; loving is hard to do. 'I think young people *really* don't know how wretched and vulnerable every human heart really is', Morgan, at her sympathetically perceptive best observes of Peter's attack on his parents' *moeurs* (138). The real cost is discussed in Chapter 2 when Simon declares the planet void of any redeeming grace, for which the agony of Marsyas being flayed by Apollo—blood, pain, no love—is the apt emblem. Simon, though an art historian, is first ignorant of and then denies to the flaying of Marsyas its customary Neoplatonic value as an image of divinely inspired ascesis. Axel knows such recondite matters, but it is the ignorant Simon who can practise them, living in a constant condition of 'ecstatic pain' (39) while the puritan and expert Axel is shown to be the more self-regarding. As with Dora and Paul in *The Bell,* an innocent worldling is coupled with an insensitive ascetic, and it is not the ascetic who comes off best.

Rupert, however, presents the most fulsome and mellifluous version of the love-philosophy when he early tells Hilda that:

> . . . love is what tells in the end, Hilda. There are times when one's just got to go on loving somebody helplessly, with blank hope and blank faith. When love just *is* hope and faith in their most denuded form. Then love becomes almost impersonal and loses its attractiveness and its ability to console. But it is just then that it may exert its greatest power. It is just then that it may be able to redeem. Love has its own cunning beyond our conscious wiles.
>
> (26)

This is very much the voice of *The Sovereignty of Good,* and a voice heard at some point in most of the novels. What Rupert is criticised for is not the philosophy but his consistently clumsy inability to live by it. He is persistently shown to us as shy and wooden, in a recognisably English way and, despite warm intentions, he bungles his encounters.

It is not only Julius who repeatedly points this out. Axel teases Rupert when he maliciously says he is most impatient to see his book. 'I expect to be told how to live, my dear fellow. I shall take it as my guide to good behaviour and follow it slavishly' (46). Peter asks whether his father intends to read aloud from his book at the dinner table; Julius satirically pretends to hope that the cast will all have to make 'philosophical speeches just like in the *Symposium,* I should like that' (221). When Rupert says to Morgan: 'Love is the last and secret name of all the virtues' she innocently replies: 'That's pretty. Do you say that in your book?' (94). And such satire has, as it were, a purgative function: wisdom in this book, as in *Phaedrus* and the *Seventh Letter* is ultra-verbal, and simulacra or copies may degenerate in the client's mind once committed to print. Rupert's philosophy is in fact a doctrine of love, as he comes to ponder when under extreme pressure from Julius' manipulations and his own frailty:

> The top of the moral structure was no dream, and he had proved this by exercises in loving attention: loving people, loving art, loving work, loving paving stones and leaves on trees. This had been his happiness. . . . He had written about it in a formal half disguised way, as if it were a secret, in his philosophy book.
>
> (359)

Rupert tries to restore Morgan to wholeness through such an exercise in high Eros, supported by his 'deep age-old confidence in the power of goodness' (359) and the philosophy of loving he has not been able properly to communicate even to Hilda. Julius was right to invoke the *Symposium*: as in that dialogue each character here praises and lives by a different view of love, which is to say, by a different personal history and character.

The gap between love and its working materials is occupied in part by lying, a theme about which the book has much to say. The breakage of the celebration by the swimming-pool occurs when Peter denounces the hypocrisy behind his parents' 'good manners'. He accurately says that his parents' coterie hide the reservations they have about one another in public and betray one another in private. To this Axel ripostes that civilisation is based on *not* saying what you think (135), and when charged with cowardice about concealing his homosexuality accuses Peter in return with concealing behind his rejection of bourgeois values an equally cowardly fear of his own mediocrity. The sheer force of the scene comes in part from Murdoch's success in identifying with every participant in it, and, behind that, her identification both with the case that love is, as Rupert argues, the primary obligation, is what is compulsory, and her countervailing sense of what and how much it is that resists love, of how intractable the materials are on which the force of love is to work or play.

Axel is puritanically truthful, Simon tells instinctive small lies about which he has a bad conscience that Julius can easily exploit. Julius' actions always widen the 'gap'. He exploits Hilda's secret subsidy of Peter, and Rupert's of Morgan, and involves all the major characters in an imbroglio of lying until they are envenomed by it. Even Hilda, inexperienced in inventing plausible falsehoods, has by the end to solicit Julius' help in fabricating untruth.

Not all lying is presented thus. Tallis agonises over whether or not to tell his father the truth about his illness, and lies about his sister's death, just as Julius, aside from his more ambitious fraudulences, fails to disclose where he spent the war. It is Tallis who lives but cannot articulate the philosophy of love. He is early referred to by Julius as an 'unperson', and his lack of egoism makes him both a saviour and a constant mild irritant to the others. A Christ-figure, he provides himself with a latter-day stigma when wounding his palm with a screw-driver, parodies the Passion in walking through London with a hand-cart piled high with Morgan's possessions, which he is renouncing though they are precious to him as mementoes of her, instead of a cross. Morgan, in a clear reference to original Sin, feels that she offended Tallis 'years before she knew him, years before either of them were born' (152). Like Julius, who smells of perfume, and Murdoch's dae-monic characters in general, Tallis *smells*. He suffers visitations from his dead sister and others, and what may be epileptically induced hallucinations about flying. He may have doubles, one of whom Morgan sights (329).

Though he is comically bewildered by Rupert's disquisition on why stealing is wrong—the arguments of a linguistic philosopher—and by Julius'—the sophistry of a utilitarian—he is never shown to be in much doubt about the ethics. He is tolerant and loving to Peter, though contemptuous of his stealing, and correctly predicts that Peter's problems will require a psychiatrist. He is interestingly a Fabian or liberal Christ, working that is to say within the system, assisting the police in general except when on instinct he suddenly decides not to, a perpetrator of multifarious and unend-ing good works, many of them uncompleted. It has been argued that Tallis is, unlike Julius, a saintly apostle of contingency—the disorder into which his house sinks once more in the penultimate chapter[8] despite Julius' minis-trations, being taken as conclusive evidence. That opposition is too sche-matic. Hilda gives the book's authoritative verdict on the matter when she thinks: 'Wherever Tallis is there's always muddle! Then she thought, this is unjust. Wherever there is muddle, there Tallis is' (178). Both Julius and Tallis seek order, it should be said, but of different kinds, at different speeds, and for wholly different ends.

Tallis' inner life is distinguished from that of all the other characters. Simon, for example, while drawn with great sympathy, and shown as quixotically loving, is given to 'immense flights of fantasy' involving his possessive jealousy and fear of losing Axel. It is on such fantasies that Julius is able to practise. Hilda, like Tallis, has little self-image, and when manipulated by Julius answers 'I don't want to imagine anything'—so that Julius has to conspire with more than usual devilishness to coerce her into a *detailed* imagining of the putative adultery. ('How quickly one can lose one's faith and abandon one's standards' thinks Hilda (345) once the idea of searching Rupert's desk has been planted.) Peter is an easier victim: 'I told him, in fact, in a curtailed version, the truth, and his imagination did the rest' (408). Rupert and Morgan are easily gulled by pity, vanity, novelty and fundamental humourlessness into imagining that the other has indeed fallen in love, and take the first stages themselves of falling in love in return as a result. Axel likewise 'imagines it all into existence' (396), imagines that Simon has started an erotic adventure with Julius and 'all the details and everything seemed to fit'.

Tallis is different. Imagination for him, too, is a source of temptation—his Greenford W.E.A. class seem hostilely to enjoy catching him out 'but perhaps it was all imagination' (442). Halfway through the book, when Morgan has rejected him and is behaving with more than usual destructiveness, he tells Julius that correspondence with Morgan helps ease his hurt. 'If one writes letters one can go on hoping.'

> 'Your particular kind of tenacity amazes me,' said Julius. 'I could understand your going round and making a scene and I could understand your switching off altogether and looking for someone else. *This dull holding on and hoping* I find incomprehensible. . . . Perhaps it's a virtue. I suppose there are such things.' [my emphasis]
>
> (401)

In the penultimate chapter Tallis is still and movingly holding on and refusing to imagine less than charitably, or in detail. Morgan never writes to him. 'He did not even wonder if he would see her again. He simply let her continue to occupy his heart.' He struggles much harder than the others to imagine neither less nor more than the truth; and when told by Julius of Rupert and Morgan's supposititious liaison is the only person to say 'That simply cannot be true' (339); and to add, appropriately enough (as Julius is his interlocutor) 'Oh go to hell.' His is in fact that 'blank hope and blank faith' early and vainly invoked (26) by Rupert. It is he that leads Julius to the telephone to instigate his confession.

*

'The incomplete pseudo-object, the work of art, is a lucid commentary upon itself' Murdoch has suggested (sw). I should like to suggest further in what ways this is true here. The burden of what Julius argues to Morgan in the

Tate Gallery is that the unconscious has few types to play with. A saint might perceive the world as full of 'absolute individuals', but, as he has asserted already to Rupert, modern psychology makes the claims of saintliness look dubious, and 'Most so-called saints really interest us because they are artists or because they have been portrayed by artists, or else because they are men of power' (224).

Julius' pessimism about the individual potential for good is partly Murdoch's. A saint might be endowed with the capacity for seeing the world as full of absolute individuals, but an artist is no saint, must in some sense be anti-type to the saint. The defeat of Rupert, of good by evil at the book's close, is only an ambiguous victory for the comic realm of mechanical substitution and repetition. It is partly redeemed by Axel and Simon having the wit to break down and trust one another, though not to warn Rupert and Hilda of Julius' machinations. Murdoch's triumph is to give the harsh, behaviouristic assessment its full rein, and yet to persuade us that these are 'real people' who are simultaneously inward and free, and about whom we care. The conflict is formal as well as moral. The triumph of Julius' view would tend to produce the claustrophobic, centripetal world of Murdoch's closed romances.

Rupert twice uses art as *exemplum* of the reality of value-judgements (130, 222). But intuitions of the negative sublime, in which the experience of value is wholly withheld, abound throughout. The distribution of these moments is interesting. Simon early proclaims the planet as lacking in any redeeming grace except sexual love, but is shown to us as a virtuous pagan who can find innocent sensual pleasure (almost) everywhere. Leonard, a Beckettian God the Father who finds that it has all gone wrong, sees the world as a 'stinking dung-heap' (64) which went wrong from the start. He is given a series of Swiftian jeremiads about the horror, for example, of sex, eating, the coming end of the world, which do much to establish the prevailing tone of *comédie noire*.

Julius is appropriately the dean or impresario of such moments of negative sublime. When Morgan recalls the feeling of revelation which accompanied part of the experience of falling in love with Julius, she speaks of a sense of 'deep truth' revealed:

> It had been like a mystical vision into the heart of reality, as if one were to be promised the secret of the universe and then, with all the sense of significance and finality fully preserved, to be shown a few mouldering chicken bones lying in a dark corner covered with dust and filth.

> (149)

This 'lesson' is of course couched in exactly the terms of Carel's anti-sermon to Marcus, and what Radeechy's black magic turned out partly to consist in. Just as the metaphor comes weirdly to life between the two earlier books, so this vision of trapped avian, and hence spiritual life, is also, later in this book, to come to life.

Before that Morgan and Peter dispute the essential beauty or wickedness of the universe, after Morgan has experienced each in succession. She has a marvellously evoked experience of 'dionysiac biolatry', an experience of idyll, which immediately follows an experience of the most negative asceticism and horror.[9] This contest between two visions of the world immediately precedes Morgan and Peter's 'quarrel': 'Everything is contaminated and muddled and nasty and slimed over and cracked', says Peter, and Morgan opposes to this view first of all the splendour of nature, symbolised by a vetch flower, and then, when Peter protests that he has in mind *human* things, she opposes culture, and sings or recites 'Full Fathom Five' from *The Tempest*.

The love which Peter and Morgan discover for one another and decide to express chastely here is, Morgan suggests, 'outside the machine. This is felicity, blessing, luck, sheer wonderful undeserved luck.' The 'machine' in this book is the name of the world seen deterministically, void of spirit, repetitive, outside hope of real change. 'Human beings are so mechanical, certain relations, certain situations, inevitably make one behave rottenly. This one can do the opposite' (193). Morgan's protestation that a grace wholly outside the machine is possible is one that the plot painfully ironises. By placing her own need for admiration above Peter's more urgent requirements Morgan betrays this moment of affection. The desire to step outside the mechanism, however, runs through the novel. Hilda and Rupert agree that they are both rather 'mechanised' about Peter; both long to 'break down the mechanism' (26). Leonard in the first of his mock-Swiftian disquisitions on the absurdity and horror of humanity discourses on sex as 'the invention of a mere mechanic': low Eros is again the realm of mechanical substitution and repetition itself. The Notting Hill house is also closer to the sources of suffering and evil than Priory Grove. Tallis hopes this will educate Peter:

> Here the causes of human misery, though they were infinitely complex, were shadowily visible and one could see the machine. Tallis had trusted that a glimpse of the machine might make Peter understand something, might make him see that revolt may be itself mechanical, and that human ills need thought and work which are disciplines of the imagination.
>
> (112)

Imagination, too, therefore, is the vehicle of the mechanical, is its vehicle in a sense *par excellence*, and it is in disciplining the imagination that the machine may be altered. Morgan is peculiarly liable to perceiving the world in mechanical terms. 'I must see him as a puppet. I must go through this like a machine' (119), she thinks in an early interview with Tallis; and, in a much later one tells him: 'It's no good, Tallis. You keep talking but I can't hear you. I'm mechanical. I'm just a machine. I look like a human being but I'm really a robot' (284).

The crux of the argument about the mechanical nature of human imagining comes in the disputation between Rupert and Julius:

> 'You make human beings sound like puppets.'
> 'But they *are* puppets, Rupert. And we didn't need modern psychology to tell us that. Your friend Plato knew all about it, when he wrote *The Laws*, after he had given up those dreams of high places which so captivate you.'
>
> (225)

When Rupert receives what purports to be Morgan's ecstatic love letter to him he seeks 'to latch himself onto the machinery of virtue and decent decision' (254). Shortly after this Julius 'produces', as if in a masque, the preliminary love-dance of Rupert and Morgan, after promising Simon, appropriately enough, a 'puppet show' (268). When it is finished he says to Simon 'let them work the machinery themselves' (268).

This is indeed what they do. It is not merely Morgan who declares herself a robot. By the time of the last broken feast Hilda and Rupert's marriage seems on the point of break-down, but Rupert ponders

> There must be some way to halt the destruction, to switch off the machine.
> 'Hilda, I will not let you destroy our marriage.'
> 'I am not destroying it. Rupert, don't you see that these things are completely automatic?'
>
> (378)

This rhetoric helps to give special force to the virtuoso Kafkaesque writing of Book Two's Chapter 10, where Morgan repeatedly experiences 'the horror, the horror of the world' (331) in a quasi-'objective' form. Morgan struggles to liberate a pigeon trapped within the Underground at Piccadilly Circus, associated early with Simon's promiscuous adventures. The bird, though it is nowhere clearly stated, becomes, like the chicken in the unwholesome vision somehow conveyed to her by Julius, a figure for spirit itself, trapped within the machine. We experience Morgan's distress and the bird's confusion together as though in each case spirit were subordinated to matter, 'freedom' to determinism. The Underground, as in *A Word Child*, stands aptly enough for the Underworld; and it is at the point at which Morgan is most restlessly destructive, when the fate of her soul might be said to hang in the balance, that this episode occurs.

Finally, when Julius makes his Iachimo-like voluntary confession to Tallis he says:

> I must say, they have behaved predictably to an extent which is quite staggering. Indeed if any of them had been less than predictable the whole

enterprise would have collapsed at an early stage. They really are puppets, *puppets*.

(408)

Julius explains how he 'set the machine going' by sending off the purloined letters ('letters are such powerful tools': 402), and describes women in particular in behaviouristic terms:

> You know, any woman can be flattered into doing anything. You just can't lay it on too thick. Just flatter them outrageously, it simply doesn't matter how outrageously, and they will lose their minds, like some birds and animals when they're tickled in a certain kind of way.

(406)

Morgan too muses, 'How very peculiar one's mind is. There's no foothold in it, no leverage, no way of changing oneself into a responsible just being. One's lost in one's psyche' (96). The unenlightened mind behaves like a machine, and machines work through a repeating action with component parts which are replaceable. There is much play about the idea of substitution, as there is about the mechanical.

Julius may be the impresario of such substitutions, as of the negative sublime, but Morgan is his deputy. When Morgan and Peter have their odd, convincing love-passage Peter comments: 'You're my mother's sister, but that's what's so marvellous. You're like my mother and yet you're quite different. That makes you perfect' (191). With Morgan he hopes to experience the perfect gratification of his incestuous love of his mother, dulling the Oedipal pain through taking Morgan as mother-substitute. This substitute-incest, like that also implicit but not consummated between Morgan and Rupert, figures, as in *The Time of the Angels*, together with theft as a paradigm form of law-breaking. High Eros might mean perceiving the unutterable particularity of each love-object; the confusions and substitutions of low Eros give us here two proximate incests, between Morgan and her nephew, and Morgan and her brother-in-law. Substitution also has laws which operate within the social group. Julius is able to carry out his imposture with letters since:

> The style of letters in a certain class of society is remarkably similar. This is particularly true of women's letters, even of intellectual women's letters. I've had hundreds of them. That sort of ecstatic self-indulgent running on has an almost impersonal quality.

(405)

Against all this, however, Simon has moved from promiscuous erotic substitution to the attempt to love someone in particular. In the magnificent, surreal scene in his Brook Street flat in which Julius cuts up Morgan's clothes, Morgan turns out to fit Simon's clothes exactly, and afterwards Simon has a nightmare in which his mother appears wearing Morgan's steel-rimmed spectacles, leading him to what appears to be the corpse of his father but is actually Rupert's (167). At one level this predicts Morgan's complicity in Rupert's death. At another it places Julius' claim that 'human beings are essentially finders of substitutes' in the unconscious, from which Simon's dream comes. Simon, who forever sees himself as a small boy, perceives the world as full of parents and parent-surrogates. The ending of the book, in which Axel can divest himself of some mock-paternal authority and distance, is thus also a hopeful one. All the characters, it is worth repeating, are felt from the inside with a sympathy so vivid and precise that the harsh 'outside' and 'mechanical' view has to exist in a balance, or contest. We experience this contest, as readers, in our involvement with the characters' fates. It is as if in this book Murdoch had solved both her formal problem (how to create a realism which does not underestimate the world's darkness and unintelligibility) and her moral problem (how to show human beings as possessing real, limited subjective freedom as well as appearing, as we do to others, predictable) together. For want of any better term, the achievement of such balance might still be praised as 'realism'. It is a superlative achievement.

*

It is a realism perfectly consonant with, and feeding off, the highest artifice. Much of the dialogue between Tallis and Julius acknowledges their awareness of one another as supernatural beings. Julius twice declines to explain the motivation of some particular piece of wickedness since 'You know why' (402, 408). He speaks of 'another big assignment' (431), leaving open whether a job like his research into germ warfare, or a job like his research into Rupert's moral frailty, is intended. 'In the nature of things we'll meet again' he salutes Tallis finally (430), in reference to the spiritual zone they share. This last colloquy is interesting not least because of the apologetics Julius stages. Axel had early referred to Julius as 'a man of principle' (34). The ironies of the phrase reverberate, firstly because the description seems testimony to Axel's obtuseness, and then, much later, because there is a curious sense in which it is half-true. Julius conducts an insolent running monologue of self-justification with agnostic replies from Tallis: 'Possibly', 'Mmm', 'Maybe'.

Tallis leaves two remarks of Julius' entirely unanswered. When Julius asserts that Rupert died not of drowning but of vanity Tallis is silent. And Julius' last remark in the book is 'You concede that I am an instrument of justice?' (431). To this Tallis merely smiles. Tallis concurs in part with Julius' diagnosis of human ills but not with the pleasure Julius derives from showing that it is so. His own authoritative judgement is given, when, two chapters on, 'He grieved blankly over something which seemed, in its disastrous compound of human failure, muddle and sheer chance, so like what it was all like' (443).

Julius, like the artist he professes himself, or like the novelist in particular, has the uncomfortable role of showing how things are, and at the same time of being guiltily complicit in their being so. Murdoch's plots have always tended to test their characters to breaking-point; here the guilt is Julius'. Tallis' calm grieving contrasts with Julius' provocative and guilty *Schadenfreude*, but Julius is a 'man of principle' and an 'instrument of justice' because he attacks spurious *simulacra* of the true unity to whose existence Tallis is ambiguous testimony. It is Julius who tells Morgan that he is 'allergic to reproductions' (236) and given the novel's wit on the subject of copying the joke is a metaphysical as well as a snobbish one. Thus in Chapter 2 of the second book, he also attacks Morgan's 'glossematics' in terms which recall his attack on Rupert's facile High Church Platonism. But the destruction of 'copies'—Rupert's creed (literally torn up, just as Rupert is destroyed), Morgan's fashionable investigations—does not necessarily disconfirm the existence of an 'original' Good. It throws the question, especially as it is Julius who is the mischief-making antagonist, once more open.

The end sees an ironic distribution of appropriate destinies, in the mode of a pastiche Victorian novel. Rupert may or may not be dead of vanity, but Morgan, Peter and Hilda are rewarded or punished by a Californian house with Spanish tiles, carport, and ocean view, and a psychiatrist for Peter. The court is scattered and only Tallis continues as and where he began, in a life of charmless holiness and endless good works. Axel and Simon are rewarded by provincial France on their way to Italy, by a renewal and strengthening of their love for one another, and ironically blessed by 'a very battered Christ who opened long arms and huge hands, receiving, judging' (436). Axel will in future open and give himself more.

Julius, like a Victorian villain, ends in pagan and libertine Paris, looking forward to *L'Incoronazione di Poppea*, an opera that dignifies and prettifies another diabolical anarch—Nero—and which also concerns the pain and the politics of an earlier erotic substitution. Nero capriciously replaces his old wife (Ottavia) with a new one (Poppea), after banishing both her erstwhile husband and his own former wife. Its sweet final duet celebrates, too, the relative triumph of evil.

Notes

1. Bradbury, *Possibilities*, p. 237.
2. Ann Wordsworth, in R. Young (ed.), *Untying the Text* (Boston and London, 1981): 'An Art That Will Not Abandon the Self to Language: Bloom, Tennyson and the Blind World of the Wish', pp. 189–206.
3. Murdoch discussed this structure at Caen (1978) and with Bellamy (1977).

4. Swinden, *Unofficial Selves*, p. 253.

5. Northrop Frye, *A Natural Perspective* (London, 1973) p. 253. Iowa notes show Murdoch hesitating between *Don Giovanni* and *Fidelio* before choosing the former for Chapter 2, and hesitating between *The Abduction from the Seraglio, Fidelio*, and *Figaro* before settling for the second of these for Chapter 6. See also Chapter 1, n.4.

6. Wind, *Pagan Mysteries*, p. 115n.

7. D. H Lawrence, Preface to *The Grand Inquisitor* (trans. Koteliansky) (London, 1930), collected in A. Beal (ed.) *Selected Literary Criticism* (New York, 1961) pp. 223–41.

8. Dipple, *Work,*, p. 184, argues, for example, that despite two moments of moral vigour Tallis' goodness is defined by an attitude of 'generous waiting'.

9. For an account of the alternation of these moods in the annals of 'metaphysical passion', see A. D. Nuttall's *Two Concepts of Allegory* (London, 1967) pp. 120ff., a work which began as a B. Litt. thesis partly supervised by Miss Murdoch.

The Comedy of Contingency in
An Accidental Man

ANGELA HAGUE

Iris Murdoch's desire to write realistic fiction that allows her characters to remain free of the author's tendency to impose pattern and form is a recurrent topic in her statements about her own novels. In an interview with Frank Kermode she discusses the temptation of the novelist to "give in to form," or what she calls "myth," to allow the pattern of the novel to draw the characters "into a sort of spiral, or into a kind of form which ultimately is the form of one's own mind."[1] This is not to say, however, that Murdoch is opposed to the presence of form in her fiction; in a later interview she has said that "I think myself that pattern in a novel is very important. . . . I care very much about pattern, and I want to have a beautiful shape, an apprehensible shape."[2] Murdoch believes that the problem with form, or mythic structures in fiction, is that the pattern of the novel tends to over- whelm the characters, preventing their development as complex and fully realized individuals; form can also "stop one from going more deeply into the contradictions or paradoxes or more painful aspects of the subject mat- ter."[3] She wants to free her characters from the story, to create people with "depth and ordinariness and accidentalness," and to write fiction that, like Dickens's novels, is filled with characters who are able to escape from the constriction of a highly structured plot and to gain an importance and reality of their own. "I sometimes think," she has said, "that if I could have a novel which was made up entirely of peripheral characters, sort of accidental people like Dickens' people, this would be a very much better novel. One might go so far as starting to invent the novel and then abolishing the central characters."[4] The word *accidental*, which reappears in her statements, is important, for Murdoch believes that the realistic novelist should depict the random, contingent dimension of human life; the "form" she distrusts tends to deemphasize and simplify this aspect of reality. She maintains that there is a direct relationship between realism and contingency, and in an interview with Ronald Bryden admitted: "I would like to have much more accident in my work than I've yet managed to put in. That is, I would like to be a much

From *Iris Murdoch's Comic Vision* (Selinsgrove: Susquehanna University Press, 1984), 70–94; © Associated University Presses. Reprinted by permission.

more realistic novelist than I am."[5] Reality, she believes, is fragmented and often inexplicable, and the role of art is to mirror this incompleteness. In "Against Dryness" Murdoch states that "reality is not a given whole. An understanding of this, a respect for the contingent, is essential to imagination as opposed to fantasy. Our sense of form, which is an aspect of our desire for consolation, can be a danger to our sense of reality as a rich receding background."[6] She calls this background "transcendent reality," and describes it as a "sort of continuous background with a life of its own."[7] The realistic novelist should aim for as complete a rendering as is possible of the unexplainable, contingent dimension of reality and human nature, and should avoid the error of the Symbolists, who feared "history, real beings, and real change, whatever is contingent, messy, boundless, infinitely particular, and endlessly still to be explained. . . ."[8] The novelist's job is to portray the world as "aimless, chancy, and huge," and it is an error for the artist to simplify reality by attempting a rational, patterned rendering of this world.[9] In *The Sovereignty of Good over Other Concepts* Murdoch describes this godless, random world:

> I can see no evidence to suggest that human life is not something self-contained. There are properly many patterns and purposes within life, but there is no general and as it were externally guaranteed pattern or purpose of the kind for which philosophers and theologians used to search. We are what we seem to be, transient mortal creatures subject to necessity and chance. That is to say that there is, in my view, no God in the traditional sense of that term. . . . We are simply here.[10]

Murdoch, who believes that there is a direct relationship among comedy, contingency, and realism in fiction, has written a comic novel that embodies her vision of a random and godless world. *An Accidental Man*, a brittle comedy of manners with over twenty-four characters, contains four deaths, two attempted suicides, and characters suffering from mental retardation, schizophrenia, and brain damage. The novel is Murdoch's attempt to write fiction with a Dickensian sweep of characters and to create a world that expresses her belief in the comic nature of contingency. *An Accidental Man*, which shows Murdoch's comic skills at their best, successfully combines comedy and horror in a way that intensifies both.

At the end of the novel Matthew Gibson Grey meditates on how his brother Austin has successfully appropriated and "contaminated" Mavis Argyll, concluding that "it had all been, like so many other things in the story, accidental."[11] Like his uncle, Garth Gibson Grey is troubled by his vision of a random world ruled by contingency: "The contingent details of choice disturbed him. Everything that was offered him was too particular, not significant enough, though at the same time he realized with dazzling clarity that all decent things which human beings do are hole and corner.

That was indeed, as he had told himself earlier, the point" (p. 161).[12] Charlotte Ledgard, about to commit suicide, has a similar vision of a universe ruled by chance and sees a world of "chaos upon which everything rested and out of which it was made" (p. 306). Even the uncontemplative Gracie Tisbourne is frightened by "a sense of the world being quite without order and of other things looking through" (p. 408); and Ludwig Leferrier, trying to decide what he should do about avoiding the draft, sense that "human life perches always on the brink of dissolution, and that makes all achievement empty" (p. 371). The lives of several of the characters are irrevocably altered by a bizarre series of accidents, among them Mitzi Ricardo's broken ankle, which abruptly ends her career as an athlete: "Her life had been wrecked by a momentary absurdity which it should be possible to delete" (p. 33). The deaths of Rosalind Monkley, Henrietta Sayce, and Dorina Gibson Grey are all accidental, as are Norman Monkey's fall and the resulting brain damage. It should be noted, however, that this chaotic, accidental world does not always result in tragedy, for that would endow it with a predictability that would contradict its essential nature; events such as Mavis's new spiritual awareness and Gracie's inheritance of the family fortune are also a result of chance.

Several images in the novel illustrate the accidental, inexplicable world in which the characters live. Throughout the novel Dorina is puzzled by the sentence, *"Pliez les genoux, pliez les genoux, c'est impossible de trop pliez les genoux,"* thinking that it may possibly be of religious significance. Just before her death, however, she remembers that her skiing instructor, not a holy man, had said these words to her, and the phrase's lack of profound significance exemplifies the nonsensicality and meaninglessness of phenomena in *An Accidental Man*. "So that was all that was, another senseless fragment of ownerless memory drifting about like a dead leaf" (p. 361). Several times in the novel people walk by each other without seeing or acknowledging one another, or miss meeting by moments. London's labyrinthine streets become symbolic of the ignorance and blindness of the characters as they pass and miss one another, and, in the instance of Rosalind Monkley, of accidental death itself. The two scenes of violence that haunt Garth and Matthew, appropriately called "street traumas" by Frank Baldanza, both take place on streets, one in New York and one in Moscow, and the streets of London become symbolic of the mazelike, unpredictable world in which the characters must attempt to function.[13] At the beginning of the book Matthew and Ludwig pass in the street, oblivious to one another and unaware that they will later meet and develop an important relationship. Dorina's accidental death could have been prevented had chance not prevented her from making contact with Charlotte or Austin, or if Ludwig had acknowledged seeing her on the street. Similarly, Austin's search for Dorina is *almost* successful: "Austin's intuitions were good, but temporally confused. He was often upon her track or in places which she visited on the next day. He too walked along the Serpentine, but too late. He went to the Tate Gallery, but too early. Once they were both in the same cinema at the same time, but arrived and left at different moments" (p. 359). The implication is that the characters are traveling in a maze they cannot see or understand and, as a result, are powerless to take any kind of effective action. "There's nothing to be done," says Austin. "One can't see the network" (p. 381). One of the lessons that Matthew, a more sympathetic version of Murdoch's earlier power figures, must learn is that the size and complexity of reality make control and manipulation impossible; man is not God:

> When a man has reflected much he is tempted to imagine himself as the prime author of change. Perhaps in such a mood God actually succeeded in creating the world. But for man such moods are times of illusion. What we have deeply imagined we feign to control, often with what seem to be the best of motives. But the reality is huge and dark which lies beyond the lighted area of our intentions.
>
> (P. 411)

For Murdoch, human nature and reality itself are irrational, unstructured, and unpredictable, and people who attempt to impose structures or manipulate others are acting in opposition to the nature of reality. Her belief that fiction should express the density of reality and that characters should not be overwhelmed by the story or author has its corollary in the errors the power figures in her novels make in seeking a simplication and false control of their surroundings.

Murdoch's opinion that reality is too complex for human beings to understand or control is expressed in the frustrated attempts of her characters to find consistent patterns or causal relationships in the world around them. Northrop Frye, who believes that the ironic mode, and satire in particular, often make use of this view of reality, defines satire as "the collision between a selection of standards from experience and the feeling that experience is bigger than any set of beliefs about it."[14] The satirist, according to Frye, reveals both the futility of dictating what course of action human beings should take and the uselessness of any attempt to order or formulate a coherent scheme of what man in actuality does. Garth Gibson Grey searches for some kind of logical order and rationality in the world, but is unable to discover the "system."

> Because a child could step into the road and die there was a certain way in which it was necessary to live. The connections were there, a secret logic in the world as relentlessly necessary as a mathematical system. . . . These deaths were merely signs, accidental signs even. They were not starting points or end

points. What lay before him was the system itself. . . . Absolute contradiction seemed at the heart of things and yet the system was there, the secret logic of the world, its only logic, its only sense.

(Pp. 218–19)

Mavis Argyll, speaking of her sister Dorina, echoes Garth's fear that, although some sort of secret rational order exists, it is impossible for human beings to see it: "Sometimes I think it's like a puzzle and she can see and yet not quite see," says Mavis, refusing to define "it" (p. 220). Matthew, discussing with Ludwig the difficulties of achieving unselfish, unpremeditated goodness, says that the great actions of the century, such as fighting tyranny, are no longer significant: "It's more like gambling, it's roulette." It is impossible to say whether these actions have any positive effect on human life in the long run, for only "in the great web of cause and effect" that is hidden from man can this be discerned (p. 270). He mentions Gödel's theorem as an example of a system that finally must break down because it cannot prove or disprove its propositions, and disagrees with Ludwig's optimistic belief that "there must be a way through." This world of hidden meanings, unprovable propositions, and unpredictable outcomes is also, as could be expected, godless. Garth, who no longer believes in the concept of a personal God, reflects on the "rhetoric of the casually absent god" (p. 218), while Matthew, who prays not to God but to "whatever great and powerful heart might yet throb in the universe with some consciousness of good" (p. 291), thinks of his fate as arranged by "whatever deep mythological forces" control the destinies of men.

The thematic content that has been discussed so far in *An Accidental Man* would not appear to be particularly amusing. The overall tone of the novel is, nevertheless, comic, and the numerous deaths and accidents that befall the characters are for the most part viewed from a comic perspective. Frye's theory of comedy helps explain how Murdoch is able to treat this kind of dark, pessimistic subject matter in a humorous fashion, for she uses the structures of both ironic and regular comedy that Frye describes in his theory of modes. According to Frye, the theme of typical comedy (as opposed to comedy that contains elements of the ironic or romantic modes) is the integration of society and the acceptance of the comic figure. The plot structure of most modern comedy closely resembles that of Greek New Comedy, which generally presents a romantic relationship between two young people hindered by an opposing force, usually paternal. Some sort of discovery about either the hero or heroine solves the problem concerning their union, and a new society comes into being around the hero and his bride. This new society is usually controlled by youth, for the parental blocking figure has been vanquished, and the event is frequently celebrated with a party or festive ritual. As comedy moves toward the ironic mode, however, it begins to take on the darker, more pessimistic tone and structure of irony, and in its most ironic phase allows the society that has been causing problems for the hero to remain undefeated, or permits the hero, having failed to transform his society, to leave it behind. Ironic comedy also contains the comedy of manners, which Frye defines as "the portrayal of a chattering-monkey society devoted to snobbery and slander," and characteristics of the demonic world, including the expulsion of the *pharmakos*. Murdoch uses all of these elements of comedy in *An Accidental Man*, and manipulates the various comic structures for her narrative purposes.

Murdoch comes close, in *An Accidental Man*, to achieving her desire to invent a novel and then to abolish the main characters, for it is certainly a novel without a central character and conspicuously lacks any kind of hero in the traditional sense of the term. Two figures, however, can be seen to correspond to Frye's description of the comic hero. Austin Gibson Grey and Ludwig Leferrier represent, often ironically, the heroes of both the typical and ironic comedy modes that Murdoch uses to structure the novel. It is Austin who resembles in many ways the hero of the typical comic action by emerging victorious over the forces around him, while Ludwig corresponds to the hero of ironic comedy, who, in Frye's scheme, chooses to leave an unreformed society behind him. Austin, a far from sympathetic character whose actions are frequently despicable, is last seen physically and emotionally transformed into a healthy, happy individual who has used all his reversals for personal gain; ironically, this transformation is partially a result of losing his wife rather than winning a bride. Murdoch also inverts many of the conventions of the typical comic action in her treatment of Ludwig's relationship with Gracie Tisbourne. The typical comic figure usually must fight for his bride, overcoming parental or societal objections to the union, but for Ludwig the problem is that everything is simply too *easy*. The book begins with Gracie's acceptance of his proposal and the delight of her parents, events quickly followed by his receiving a teaching appointment at Oxford. Instead of Gracie's inheritance coming about so that the heroine can be made respectable or acceptable and the marriage can be performed, as in traditional comedy, her windfall occurs after her engagement and is simply one more aspect of the couple's idyllic situation. The blocking *senex* figure is instead Ludwig's father and the government of the United States: his father wants him to terminate his engagement and return home to gain conscientious objector status so that he can avoid fighting in Vietnam. Instead of the novel's ending with the expected wedding of Gracie and Ludwig, he decides to leave his bride-to-be and a rosy future in England, opting for a return to the United States and the prison term that awaits him. The newly married couple at the end is instead Garth and Gracie, and the party that concludes the story is an ironic version of the "festival" that Frye speaks of as the typical ending of the comic action. Murdoch inverts the structure of typical comedy and uses elements of ironic comedy in her treatment of the fortunes of Austin and Ludwig, and by doing so creates an extremely complex comic structure that defeats the reader's generic expectations. Murdoch also reverses the comic convention of the triumph of youth over age in her portraits of Ludwig and Austin. It is the middle-aged Austin rather than the twenty-two-year-old Ludwig who is successful and rejuvenated at the end of the story; Ludwig, on the other hand, bows to the wishes of his father. The deaths of the two young children in the novel, Henrietta Sayce and Rosalind Monkley, are another aspect of this, for in this world young people appear to be more vulnerable to the vicissitudes of fortune than their elders. In another sense, however, youth is in control throughout the novel, and there is no movement from one kind of society to another; in fact, one comic element in *An Accidental Man* is the fact that many of the young people are more sophisticated, articulate, and intelligent than their elders. Clara and George Tisbourne, both comically in awe of their two children, illustrate this, as do the personalities of Patrick and Gracie.

Another characteristic of ironic comedy is the presence of the *pharmakos*, an individual who must be driven out of the society to insure its continued existence and vitality. Dorina Gibson Grey is the most obvious scapegoat character in all of Murdoch's fiction. Dorina, who sees herself as hounded and pursued by others, observes that "it was as if something were closing in for the kill" (p. 98), and several of the characters believe that they benefit by her death. Matthew describes Dorina as a "hunted creature," a "captive," and Austin, because of his paranoid fears, wishes to keep his wife "immobilized and spellbound" in Mavis's home. Many of the characters feel that Dorina needs to be dealt with in some way, and Mavis and Matthew in particular wish her to leave Valmorana so that they can be free to resume their affair. Dorina is also described as having close affinities with the occult, an aspect of her personality that is treated comically at one point in the novel: "There had been strange incidents. 'I am afraid your sister attracts poltergeists,' one headmistress had complained severely to Mavis, who had her own ghosts to contend with" (p. 57). The schizophrenic Dorina's delusions are not treated comically, however, and the scenes in her hotel room before her death are a chilling depiction of a mentally ill person attempting to remain sane.

Mavis, Garth, and Austin all feel that Dorina's death has been, in a sense, a positive event that has had beneficial effects on their personal lives. Mavis tells Matthew that "I cannot help feeling that she somehow died for us, for you and me, taking herself away, clearing herself away, so that our world should be easier and simpler" (p. 400). Mavis later meditates that "she has died for me," and says that "Dorina's departure had released her into some sort of vast beyond" (p. 423). Dorina's death causes Garth to make a vital contact with his past, which in turn enables him again to feel love for his father: "Her death had this use for him, that a stream flowed again between himself and the past and after being dry-eyed for many years he was able to weep again." The result of this is a renewed interest in himself and the rebirth of affectionate feelings for Austin; the narrator says that "love for his father possessed his body like a memory" (p. 374). Significantly, the policeman arrives at this moment to return his lost novel, for it is almost as if Garth's creative potential is restored by Dorina's death. Austin, who describes his wife's death as a "felicitous solution," rejoices that her death has isolated her from the influences of other people and has insured that she cannot hurt him. In fact, Austin's rejuvenation is apparently due, to a degree, to the death of his wife, as Matthew clearly realizes: "Something or other had, in however ghastly a sense, done Austin 'good.' Perhaps it was simply Dorina's death" (p. 432). Dorina is a character who, partially because of her mental instability and lack of egocentricity, must be cast out of the society of the novel, a society that can accommodate only such characters as Mavis, Austin, and Garth; the strong survival instincts of these individuals guarantee their ability to endure and recover from catastrophes. Dorina's death has positive effects on each of these characters and corresponds to the "point of ritual death" that Frye describes as a typical event of ironic comedy, and both her expulsion from society and her connection with the occult show her to be a character of that mode.

An early indication of the tone of *An Accidental Man* is evident when Charlotte Ledgard telephones her sister to report that their mother is dying. "Oh God. We're dining with the Arbuthnots," replies Clara (p. 37). At the end of the novel, though extremely upset over Henrietta Sayce's death, her thoughts return to money and matchmaking as she grieves: "I used to think sometimes she might make a wife for Patrick when she grew up, they were so fond of each other, and there's all that money on Penny's side, and now she's dead, oh dear, dear, dear—" (p. 412). The death of Alison Ledgard is one of the most sustained comic scenes in Murdoch's fiction, a scene in which the nurse's primping and Clara's worry about a possible "legal snag" over the inheritance take precedence over the fact of death itself. The doctor's lack of interest in his patient and the clergyman's forced and cliché-filled death prayer add to the comedy; Dr. Seldon makes a point of advising the family that there is no need to call him in the event of Alison's death, and Enstone appears to be more involved with ping-pong at the Youth Club. The comic technique used in this passage is obviously Freud's idea of the "economy of sympathy," a process by which the emphasis is taken away from the painful aspects of a situation and attention is redirected to an area less painful. Charlotte alone appears to be sensitive to the reality of her mother's death, and the narrator chooses to place the pathetic and sorrowful dimensions of the event in the background. Dying is treated comically not because it is intrinsically funny, but because of the selfishness and greed of the living juxtaposed to the finality of death.

Alison's death and funeral are later used for comic purposes by other characters in the novel. In a letter to Gracie, Patrick refers to the "funeral games. I hope you enjoy them. Poor old Grandma. Everyone will be rejoicing, won't they, especially Aunt Char. What news of the carve-up?" (p. 73). Gracie's reply to her brother, which begins "Grandma's funeral was a riot, I wish you'd been there" (p. 78), later casually characterizes her father as taking the funeral in a "literary sense." She also mentions that her Aunt Charlotte looks twenty years younger and describes the festivities that followed the funeral in this manner:

> You see, everyone stood around for a while trying to be solemn, and then we heard a burst of gay laughter from the kitchen where Papa and Sir Charles had opened a bottle of champagne. Then we all converged on the kitchen and there were drinks all round, and people were sitting on the kitchen table and draped round the hall stairs with glasses in their hands and corks were popping, it was quite a wake.
>
> (P. 79)

Gracie, who rarely allows surrounding disasters to discomfit her, also describes Norman Monkley's fall down Austin's stairs, which results in permanent brain damage, as "another jolly disaster" (p. 245). Not surprisingly in a novel in which characters view death and disaster with such jovial equanimity, Norman's partial "recovery" is treated comically, and both Austin's phony concern for Norman and Mrs. Monkley's appreciation of it become ironically humorous in light of what the reader knows about the true facts of the "accident." The narrator concludes this section of the novel with a statement that aptly exemplifies the tone of *An Accidental Man*: "The hospital staff now thought that Norman would never fully recover. So that was all very satisfactory" (p. 319).

Patrick's reaction to the death of Rosalind Monkley is similar:

> So Austin has run over a little girl. Good for him. He has certainly maximized happiness in the Tisbourne family. Ma was incoherent with delight about it when she telephoned and I could just imagine her face, pulled into that false sadness with glee looking through. And don't tell me you don't feel exactly the same. I would be moderately bucked myself if I hadn't got other troubles. As it is, I wake up in the morning and feel at once that at least *something* nice has happened.
>
> (P. 180)

Patrick Tisbourne actually emerges as a fairly sympathetic character in the novel, for he openly acknowledges the feelings the other characters attempt to hide. While Margaret Scanlon's description of him as the "sober moral arbiter" of the novel is rather exaggerated, his unabashedly truthful analyses of people and events do have a moral dimension.[15] The Tisbournes, however, are not alone in their enjoyment of the troubles of others. The fact that many of the characters in *An Accidental Man* wholeheartedly enjoy the misfortunes of other people is a recurring comic motif, and the pleasure is usually intensified when the "victims" are close friends or family members. Mitzi glories in Austin's marital difficulties, and Mavis finds pleasure in Dorina's problems with Austin. Mrs. Monkley's tragedies are, for Garth, "a bit exciting. It was life-giving, even pleasurable" (p. 206); in the same way Matthew finds Ludwig's troubles "thoroughly exhilarating." In a scene reminiscent of the group assembled around Georgie Hands's hospital bed in *A Severed Head*, Mitzi informs Charlotte that her visitors were "thrilled" by her suicide attempt. Patrick Tisbourne's statements in his letters make him the most truthful and objective of the characters.

Characters do not limit themselves to a simple enjoyment of other people's catastrophes; rather, they often utilize them for their own purposes. Andrew Hilton uses the suicide attempt of a pupil as an excuse to begin a sexual relationship, telling Oliver Sayce in a letter that "my ablest pupil has just attempted suicide. I must go and surround him with affection" (p. 327). In the same way, the hoped-for renewal of the relationship between Matthew and Mavis, which fails miserably over lunch and drinks, suddenly blooms in an automobile after both have paid a visit to the disconsolate Mrs. Monkley. The narrator's refusal to treat any human problem with sustained sympathy, an important aspect of the novel that deepens its comic tone, is also evident in the scenes between Matthew and Charlotte, and Charlotte and Mitzi. Charlotte is treated dismisively by Matthew when she tells of her lifelong love for him, and the exact phrases of their conversation are repeated in the in the parallel scene in which Charlotte attempts to leave Mitzi, a repetition that reduces the importance of the characters' emotions and in the process renders them comic. Scenes that are potentially emotionally explosive, rather than being presented as uniquely important events, are trivialized by being made to seem stereotyped and cliché-filled. There are few subjects in *An Accidental Man* that are not comically reduced or treated ironically, a humorous treatment of subject matter that is increased by the lack of narrative information in many scenes, particularly in the epistolary chapters.

One of the most important comic dimensions of *An Accidental Man* is the attitude of the narrator: the absence of narrative comment and information at certain points in the novel becomes a comic device. The tone is one of detachment and distance from many of the horrible events described, and the narrator's gradually expanding vision of people and situations helps create the comic perspective of the narrative. Chapters consisting solely of letters written from one character to another and chapters of untagged dialogue also serve to eliminate the presence of a narrating voice. Murdoch has stated her wish to expel herself from her fiction, to avoid imposing "the form of one's own mind" on the characters, and *An Accidental Man* is one of her most successful attempts at eliminating authorial presence. Individuals are frequently seen and heard from the outside, for the narrator does not reveal the reactions or thoughts of the characters in several important dramatic scenes, and the reader is called upon to contribute the information. Again, Freud gives an insight into why this lack of narrative is funny: his theory of the "principle of economy" in jokes helps explain why forcing the reader or listener to arrive at a conclusion or understanding without a full explanation is often a humorous technique. This is not to say that the narrator is always absent, however, for in a scene in which Charlotte and Mavis attempt to persuade Dorina to leave Valmorana the narrator creates a comic counterpoint between the polite social conversations of the characters and the far different reality of their thoughts (pp. 145–48), a technique used again in the luncheon scene between Matthew and Mavis.

Several of the novel's most comic scenes are rendered dramatically through dialogue only; the narrator does not provide the additional information the reader generally expects from omniscient narration. In the final confrontation between Austin and Matthew, the comedy is a result of the reader's prior knowledge of Matthew's personality, a knowledge that enables the reader to guess Matthew's real thoughts as he makes the short replies to his recently rejuvenated brother. Austin, speaking of the brain-damaged Norman Monkley, does most of the talking, and Matthew's complete disgust with his brother's transformation is brilliantly presented through indirection and irony:

> "I went to see the Monkleys last week. Norman was doing some sort of basket work. He's quite a sweet character now."
> "Good."
> "I must fly. I've got to get over to the flat, and I said I'd cook supper for Mavis. She'll be exhausted. She's been spending today carting the char's idiot child to an institution."
> "Mavis is very kind."
> "Yes, isn't she. You know, her kindness to me has been an absolute revelation. I felt such a miserable wreck and she's quite put me on my feet again. I must say I had a rotten time. But now I feel like a re-constituted Humpty Dumpty."
> "She's good at helping."
> "You can say that again. You know, she's awfully like Dorina in a way, she's got that concentrated sweetness, but without any of the feyness and fear. I don't think Mavis is afraid of anything."
> "No, indeed,"
> "Poor old Dorina was just a sort of half person really, a maimed creature, she had to die, like certain kinds of cripples have to. They can't last."
> "Maybe."
> "That idiot child will probably die in its teens, the doctor told Mavis. A good thing too. Mavis didn't tell the mother, of course."
> "Naturally—"
> "Mavis has certainly helped me to see the world in perspective."
> "I'm glad."

(P. 410)

Austin's first appearance in the novel is presented in much the same way, but in this instance Murdoch's technical feat is more impressive because neither of the characters in the scene has appeared before. The reader begins to identify with Austin and to realize, without help from the narrator, his reaction to his dismissal:

> "Recession. Yes," said Austin Gibson Grey. He was not sure what recession meant, but he knew what Mr. Bransome meant.
> "It is a matter of computerization."
> "Indeed."
> "There is nothing personal involved."
> "Quite."
> "The management consultants who were here last month—"
> "I thought they were interior decorators."
> "Possibly they were so described."
> "They were."
> "It was a matter of being tactful."
> "I see."
> "Recommended a thoroughgoing streamlining of staff ratios."
> "Ah, yes."
> "You appreciate that we have been losing money."
> "I do."
> "Our situation, I say in confidence, is difficult."
> "I am sorry."
> "We shall pay you of course for the entire month."
> "Thank you."
> "But I trust you will feel free to leave at any time."
> "How kind."
>
> (P. 16)

The cocktail-party chapters are handled in a similar fashion. Murdoch presents pages of untagged one-liners that create what Frye so aptly calls the "chattering-monkey society" of ironic comedy, leaving the reader to try to ascertain the identities of the speakers and to piece together the relationships among the characters. By this time, however, the reader knows more about the events of the novel than any of the characters. For example, in the first of these chapters (pp. 130–36) the reader's earlier knowledge of Oliver Sayce's homosexuality causes his first encounter with Andrew Hilton to have a comic dimension dependent on this knowledge, just as Mavis's questioning of Charlotte about Matthew is amusing because the reader has been informed of the reason for her interest. Murdoch also uses these chapters to reduce important events that were treated seriously in earlier episodes to comically trivial cocktail-party conversation. Charlotte, whose unhappiness has been sympathetically treated for the most part, is turned into a figure of fun:

"Isn't that Charlotte Ledgard?"
"I thought she'd run away to sea."
"She only ran as far as Bailey's Hotel."

(P. 132)

The long-delayed meeting between Matthew and Austin, which the reader has expected to occupy an important place in the narrative, is reduced to five lines:

"Oh hello, Austin."
"Hello, Matthew."
"Your job must be very interesting too, Mr. Enstone."
"How about a drink sometime soon, Austin?"
"Sorry, Matthew, I'm just leaving town."

(P. 134)

The party chapters and epistolary sections are an important comical dimension of the novel, for Murdoch uses them to advance the narrative through fragmentary bits of information that are often necessary for a complete understanding of what is happening; her belief that "reality is not a given whole" is expressed in her narrative technique. The reader is given fragmented insights into the characters and situations, but is almost always in the position of knowing more than the characters, a position that creates a comic irony directly related to the lack of direct information from the narrator. The disappearance of the narrator in certain sections of the novel parallels the beliefs of the characters in the absence of god; it is as if Murdoch wishes to create a novelistic world in which the reader must search for his own patterns and conclusions without the guiding presence of the author. The narrator's refusal to pass judgments or to give information about the thoughts of characters, despite the fact that he has shown himself to be omniscient, results in a coldly detached tone that refuses to grant a fundamental importance to any act. Margaret Scanlon believes that the novel is flawed because the reader is denied an explanation of Ludwig's decision to leave England, and she says that "we are not sufficiently involved in his mind to perceive the gradual enlargement of vision that impells the return home."[16] This, however, is a deliberate stratagem on Murdoch's part: the failure to give the reader a complete account of Ludwig's motives is one aspect of the comic perspective of the narrator, which partially depends upon his distance and detachment from the events of the narrative. Because of this it is not surprising that the reader, like Ludwig's parents, is suddenly notified of his decision to return to America by a telegram at the conclusion of an epistolary chapter: "FATHER PLEASE CANCEL YOUR SAILING I AM COMING HOME LUDWIG" (p. 401).

At times the narrator seems to disappear from *An Accidental Man*, and this lack of narrative presence is most evident in the epistolary chapters, which consist solely of letters written from one character to another, chapters that make up over ten percent of the novel. Like the chapters of dialogue, these sections create a voyeuristic situation for the reader, in which he is privileged to read correspondence and to overhear conversations. Voyeurism, a recurrent theme throughout Murdoch's fiction, is a very important motif in *An Accidental Man*, and the characters have a noticeable penchant for eavesdropping and reading other people's letters. Matthew listens outside Austin's door, Austin overhears his son lecturing Ludwig, and Dorina stumbles in on her husband about to make love to Mitzi Ricardo. In the same way Austin reads Dorina's letter to Ludwig, Norman steals Matthew's letter to Austin, and Charlotte discovers Betty's note to Matthew.

As in the dialogue chapters, comically ironic effects are created because the reader knows more about the entire situation than do the individual letter writers. In light of the reader's knowledge of Patrick's homosexuality, Hester Odmore's hope that Patrick will be a "steadying influence" on her son is comic, as is Matthew's entreaty to the unrepentant Austin not to be "filled with grief" and blame himself for Rosalind's death. Clara, unaware that her sister has attempted suicide, writes to Hester that "Charlotte seems reasonably okay, in fact she has gone away on holiday. We are doing our best to cheer her along" in a letter that is darkly comic (p. 322). It has been noted that Murdoch is interested in the way people use language to lie and distort the truth, and Murdoch's letter writers in *An Accidental Man* are adept at protective verbal manipulation. Austin's first letter to Dorina, filled with outright lies about how he lost his job, what Mitzi charges for rent, and his first meeting with Matthew, is one of the most comical letters in the novel. Clara Tisbourne's letter to Hester Odmore about Gracie's condition after her break-up with Ludwig, in which she describes her daughter as "quite restored and gay," becomes extremely humorous in light of the content of her next letter to Dr. Seldon: "She still refuses to eat and lies all day on her bed crying and talks a good deal about suicide" (p. 397). This kind of comic juxtaposition is used throughout, for Murdoch will often switch abruptly from a scene of horror, such as Rosalind Monkley's death or Norman's fall, to a series of comic letters, changes in tone that disorient the reader and call into question the seriousness of the events of the novel. Murdoch, who has said that the artist must aim for a depiction of "death without a consolation," denies the reader the consolation of a consistently serious attitude toward the novel's terrible events.

The epistolary chapters also give Murdoch a chance to expand the boundaries of her fictive world, to include, as she has stated she wishes to do, more and more peripheral characters. The reader becomes increasingly interested in the sexual adventures of various individuals, many of whom are not involved in the main action of the book. In these chapters the reader sees Patrick conquer Ralph Odmore's objections to a homosexual relationship,

Karen Arbuthnot plan and succeed in marrying Sebastian Odmore, and Andrew Hilton and Oliver Sayce begin and develop their love affair. All these liaisons are humorous because of their indirect presentation through letters; the reader is given a sense of an almost limitless potential in the novel, an ever-expanding view of persons and interrelationships that corresponds to Murdoch's desire to write fiction that depicts "reality as a rich receding background," a "continuous background with a life of its own." The widening framework of the novel contributes to its comic dimensions by creating a constantly changing perspective: as the narrator pulls back from a direct presentation of events, as in the case of the automobile accident or Norman's fall, to the reactions of peripheral and uninvolved characters, the importance of the events is reduced through distancing and in the process is rendered comic. For example, Rosalind Monkley's death, which is first presented dramatically and is meant to have an emotional impact on the reader, is followed by a chapter of letters in which the incident is relegated to a P.S. in Karen Arbuthnot's humorous letter to Sebastian Odmore: "Did you hear that Austin Gibson Grey ran over a child? I am so sorry for that man. I think he is in love with Gracie, incidentally. What a planet" (p. 181). The death of a child becomes less and less important as the reader moves into the worlds of minor characters, what Frank Baldanza calls the "shadow novel" in *An Accidental Man*.[17] Murdoch again transforms the serious into the comical when Austin overhears his son's conversation with Ludwig, for when the reader hears a portion of Garth's lecture for the second time, this time from Austin's point of view, the perspective is changed and Garth appears pompous and ridiculous.

Austin Gibson Grey has several of the characteristics of the comic hero, including a talent for survival, resilience, and the ability to manipulate the people around him. Austin is the self-acknowledged accidental man of the book's title; "I am an accidental man," he tells Mavis, who tries to comfort him by saying that we are all accidental people. "With me it's gone on and on," replies Austin (p. 424). It is true that although events transpire to place Austin in unfortunate situations, his callousness and resilience allow him, as Mavis observes, to turn all his accidents to account. Austin, one of the most invidious characters in Murdoch's fiction, nevertheless has a sense of irony and detachment from his own life, and his sometimes ironic perceptions of himself cause the reader to temper the disapprobation his actions and attitudes merit. Murdoch's portrayal of Austin has a decidedly comic dimension that shows her once again choosing to present human failings in a humorous light, a choice that parallels her comic treatment of the power figures in the later novels. Though Scanlon calls Austin a "monster" and Mavis admits that he is a "vampire," he is merely the most exaggerated example of human egotism and solipsism in *An Accidental Man*, and the statement at the end of the novel that "Austin is like all of us only more so" is appropriate in the context of the novel's world (p. 440).

Comic characters are often endowed with an egotistical nature that the action of the comedy will either correct or vindicate. Although Austin realizes his inability to "rise upon . . . humiliations to higher things" in the moral realm, his egotism is his means of survival, as Mitzi learns (p. 18):

Austin helped Mitzi by a revelation of how it was possible to live simply by egoism. Austin, with nothing particular to boast of, never seemed to doubt his own absolute importance. Just because he was himself the world owed him everything, and even though the world paid him very little, he remained a sturdy and vociferous creditor. Misery could not crush Austin. Simply being Austin enabled him to carry on.

(P. 34)

Austin, more self-consciously bent on his own survival than any other character in the book, realizes that appealing to Matthew for help from Norman's blackmail would break his "springs of survival," and the narrator observes that Austin is aware that often "a man can see himself becoming more callous because he has to survive" (p. 157). This growing callousness to events is evident in his letter to Dorina about the death of Rosalind Monkley: "I am *all right* and I will survive and recover, I have had worse blows than this" (p. 179), and he later tells Mavis that "I've got to survive—that's what my will's been for—" (p. 383).[18]

One characteristic of Austin's ability to survive is his refusal to allow the tragedies of others to touch him. After Norman's accident he falls into a sound sleep; his reaction to his wife's death is similar. His first thoughts about Alison Ledgard's death are also predictable: "So the old woman was gone. Good. Charlotte would be rich and would lend him money" (p. 50). In fact, in keeping with Austin's propensity for turning unfortunate happenings to personal gain, his search for his missing wife becomes such a pleasurable experience that he often forgets her entirely. Dorina's death is for Austin a "felicitous solution," which he uses as a catalyst for his own rejuvenation. At the conclusion of the novel the reader witnesses the figurative "rebirth of the hero" that several comic theoreticians discuss, and, in fact, Austin's acknowledgment of his "accidental" existence and talent for overcoming misfortune make Langer's description of the comic action as the "upset and recovery of the protagonist's equilibrium, his contest with the world and his triumph by wit, luck, personal power, or even humorous, or ironical, or philosophical acceptance of mischance" a fitting one for *An Accidental Man*.[19] Austin's ironical acceptance of his own plight also gives him a much-needed attractive quality; his sense of humor is particularly evident in the comic scenes in which Norman Monkley attempts to blackmail him into reading and criticizing his novel.

One of his more negative traits is his skill in manipulating the people around him. Mitzi and Dorina are especially dominated by him, and he succeeds in finally vanquishing the specter of his brother, in the process, as Scanlon observes, turning Mavis into a replica of Dorina, a feat that "contaminates" her in Matthew's eyes and ruins all possibilities for their future relationship. The final scene of the novel, in which Austin is finally able to move his fingers, underscores his final victory over the forces that have plagued him, for his inability to use his hand since his childhood "accident" has been symbolic throughout the novel of his problems in dealing with the world. His new physical flexibility parallels the rebirth of his personality, brought about, as previously noted, by the misfortunes of other people.

The final section of *An Accidental Man*, with its emphasis on Austin's rejuvenation and acceptance by society, with the pairings of couples and the resulting pregnancies of Ann Colindale, Gracie, and Karen, and with the cocktail-party setting, would seem to be an example of the typical ending of comedy discussed by Northrop Frye. However, the novel ends on the same darkly comic note that has been its tone throughout, and because several factors cause this "festive party" ending to be less than celebratory, Frye's description of the conclusion of ironic comedy is much more applicable here. For a number of characters, the action of the novel has brought about a realization of personal failure. Matthew, sailing to America with Ludwig, realizes that "he would never be a hero. . . . He would be until the end of his life a man looking forward to his next drink. He looked at his watch and drifted down to the bar" (p. 436). Garth's marriage to Gracie is another admission of failure; like Matthew, he has searched and failed to find some sort of moral pattern. Though the reader does not see the process by which Garth is transformed from a philosophically oriented social worker to a sleek, successful novelist and party-giver, it is obvious he has decided to settle for the comfortable, shallow existence represented by Gracie and her social set. Garth's answers to Gracie's questions before the party reveal him to be satisfied and happy with his new life-style, and his apparent discovery of Gracie's secret nickname, "Moggie," is humorously noted by the narrator: it would appear that Garth is willing and eager to share what Gracie has earlier called her "talent for happiness." The acceptance of failure by Matthew and Garth can be contrasted with the positive transformations of Austin and Clara Tisbourne, both of whom are described as looking younger in the final pages of the novel. The fact that both these individuals, unsympathetically presented throughout the narrative, have apparently survived unscathed and used the horror around them for personal betterment is described by the narrator from an externally objective point of view. "Clara was now wearing her hair straight and rather short. She looked radiantly juvenile. So did Austin, his copious golden locks flowing down onto his collar. He never wore glasses now. His contact lenses were a great success" (p. 437).

The final party section of *An Accidental Man* is characterized by the same dark, ominous tone that was present throughout the novel. Presided over by

Mary Monkley, now the Gibson Grey's cleaning woman, this section contains the information that Ludwig Leferrier has been sent to prison in America, a fact that is casually mentioned by one party-goer and quickly dropped. Just as valuable and meaningful information and events were reduced to triviality and absurdity in earlier sections of the novel, so Ludwig's fate, the real moral dilemma of the story, is treated as less important than Gracie's arrangement of cushions on the sofa. In fact, Ludwig's problem is not even stated correctly by the guest, who, when asked why he is in prison, answers, "Drugs or something" (p. 439). The society depicted at the conclusion of the novel is one in which the external, social aspects of existence take precedence over morality and truth. In four lines of dialogue Murdoch expresses the brittle tone and hypocrisy of the upper-middle-class liberal milieu she has created in *An Accidental Man*:

> "Clara will soon be Lady Tisbourne."
> "Mollie will soon be Lady Arbuthnot."
> "Aren't we all getting grand."
> "Anyway, we're still socialists."

(P. 440)

She shows, in the differing descriptions of Patrick Tisbourne's reactions to Charlotte's new living arrangement, how the truth and unique importance of human relationships are distorted and rendered ridiculous by outsiders. Charlotte's earlier realization that a knowledge of the truth about reality leads not to happiness but to "some final bitter wit" can be seen as important here, for the novel ends on a bitterly comic note that is a result of both its form and content. In this final sequence, unlike the earlier chapters of dialogue and letters, the reader becomes less and less sure who is speaking; the disembodied voices create an ominous atmosphere from which the narrator *and* major characters seem to have departed, leaving the reader alone to eavesdrop on the chattering of strangers. Frye's theory that the most ironic phase of comedy is one in which a humorous society triumphs or remains undefeated best describes the situation at the end of *An Accidental Man*, for the society that is in control in the final pages of the novel has accepted its "accidental man," expelled its *pharmakos*, and remains devoted to snobbery and slander.

Notes

1. Frank Kermode, "The House of Fiction: Interviews with Seven English Novelists," *Partisan Review* 30 (1963): 64.
2. Ronald Bryden, "Talking to Iris Murdoch," *The Listener*, 4 April 1968, p. 434.
3. Kermode, "House of Fiction," p. 63.
4. Rose, "An Interview," p. 11.

5. Bryden, "Talking to Iris Murdoch," p. 434.

6. Murdoch, "Against Dryness," p. 20.

7. Murdoch, "On 'God' and 'Good,' " p. 54.

8. Iris Murdoch, "The Sublime and the Beautiful Revisited," *Yale Review* 49 (1959): 260.

9. Murdoch, *The Sovereignty of Good over Other Concepts*, p. 32.

10. Ibid., pp. 3–4.

11. Murdoch, *An Accidental Man*, p. 433. Hereafter all page references to this book will be indicated parenthetically.

12. Though Garth is obviously speaking for Murdoch here, the more "decent" aspects of "hole and corner" acts are not emphasized in the novel. One of Garth's weaknesses is that he, unlike Jake Donaghue in *Under the Net*, fails to come to terms with contingency.

13. Baldanza, *Iris Murdoch*, p. 167.

14. Frye, *Anatomy*, p. 229.

15. Margaret Scanlon, "The Machinery of Pain: Romantic Suffering in Three Works of Iris Murdoch," *Renascence* 29 (1977): 71. Scanlon correctly observes that Patrick's insights are repeatedly dramatized throughout the novel.

16. Scanlon, "The Machinery of Pain," p. 77.

17. Baldanza, *Iris Murdoch*, p. 167.

18. This scene begins comically because the reader makes the assumption that Mavis and Austin are discussing Dorina's death; only as the scene progresses does it become obvious that Austin, in another display of obsessed egotism, is discussing his injured hand.

19. Langer, *Feeling and Form*, p. 331.

Circularity versus Progress in the Religious Life: A Study of *The Bell* and *Henry and Cato*

ELIZABETH DIPPLE

Between *The Bell* (1958) and *Henry and Cato* (1976), Murdoch wrote thirteen novels and two plays, not to mention extensive work in philosophy and dramatic versions of two of her novels, and there can be no doubt that significant development took place. Echoing Murdoch's own statements in various interviews to the effect that novel-writing is a craft at which the practitioner becomes more skilled with practice, one can validly assume that *Henry and Cato* is the better book. Certainly it is a much denser, more complex work which accomplishes its extensive tasks unobtrusively, and with apparent ease achieves the mysterious sense of endless reverberation which has consistently characterized Murdoch's style since *An Accidental Man* (1971). By comparison, *The Bell* is thinner and its skeleton shows; every device in that novel contributes tightly to the end in view and speaks to its specific purpose, making the book feel more narrowly contained and obviously controlled than the later one.

I have chosen to compare the two works for a number of reasons, some better than others. First of all, *The Bell* is Murdoch's first approach to the style which I believe will define her reputation as one of the foremost novelists writing in English in the twentieth century. Its coherence centres on the spontaneous activity of the characters rather than on a too tightly expressed ideology, although in fact there are so many ideological points of view expressed, all of them oddly convincing during their expression, that discriminations are complex and exceedingly (even excessively) interesting to make. The reader feels absorbed in much more than the well-spun plot and is persistently hard at work, as he must always be in later Murdoch. The circularity of *The Bell*'s structure, in which Michael Meade in his middle age repeats a pattern of behaviour which in his youth condemned him to years of guilt and unhappiness, is much more predictive of the dramatic and terrible *déjà vu* of *A Word Child* (1975); I have nevertheless chosen to set

From *Iris Murdoch: Work for the Spirit* (Chicago: University of Chicago Press, 1982), 243–64; © Elizabeth Dipple. Reprinted by permission.

Henry and Cato against this early work (it is Murdoch's fourth novel) even though the structure is quite different, primarily because both novels' most important thematic concerns are with the characters' basic apprehensions of religion. Although Murdoch's work has always inclined towards religious scrutiny even when apparently dealing with an all too secular milieu, the inclination to concentrate on religion as a major subject was present very early and has been predominant in the last few novels.

I think, as the title of this study shows, that Murdoch is primarily a religious writer, and that the easiest and most pointed way of making this inclination evident is to examine how she works within a religious framework which is obvious and unconcealed, rather than oblique and indirect as in many of the novels. By pitting *The Bell* against *Henry and Cato* . . . it should be possible to see not only the nature of Murdoch's development as an artist from her early period to the most recent great novels, but also the extended range of her thinking on a subject with which the current historical period is ill at ease.

Critics have described Murdoch as inexorably falling into an opposite of two basic character types as a way of defining many of her structures— the aspiring saint versus the would-be artist—but it is frequently more accurate to talk about a person immersed in the sacred as opposed to one completely subject to the profane. *The Bell* and *Henry and Cato*, conveniently for discussion, make parallel use of these types, but they are less obtrusive than several other comparable elements in the two novels, and one can see the mileage Murdoch gains from the contrast without having to concentrate also on that other major subject of hers, the unworthiness of the contemporary artist and the paradoxes of art. Of course Dora in *The Bell* and Henry in *Henry and Cato* are artists *manqués*, and are principally interested in art in a failed professional way, but they are not practitioners, and interest in art is for them a version of religious attention in a world in which the outward, lingering signs of Christianity hold no particular interest for them. Opposed to them are Michael Meade and Cato Forbes, both men with a religious vocation who define their lives in terms of their allegiance to the Church and to Christ. Both of these latter two also have homosexual inclinations which they sadly and unsuccessfully fight and which they place in an either/or relationship to their Christianity.

In both novels Murdoch explores the labyrinth of sexuality and spirituality whose subtle interactions are so confusing and often so damaging. Her choice of homosexuality in both books is interesting in that is is the mode of sexuality which has been questioned and largely disapproved of in the Christian tradition, and about which much guilt can accumulate. Both novels feature a character who comments on the problem, and both of these commentators are deeply involved in ideas of the spiritual life. James Tayper Pace in *The Bell* disapproves of homosexuality simply and outrightly, and pointlessly drops anti-homosexual remarks as in his uncharitable references to Nick Fawley, who he claims looks like a 'pansy'; when an embarrassed Toby Gashe goes to him to confess his very slight flirtation with Michael, James is shocked and has no machinery for understanding or forgiving the beleaguered and only slightly erring Michael. In his sermon on the good, he sees the whole issue, indeed the whole of moral life, as very simple:

> We should consider not what delights us or what disgusts us, morally speak-ing, but what is forbidden. And this we know, more than we are often ready to admit. We know it from God's Word and from His Church with a certainty as great as our belief. Truthfulness is enjoined, the relief of suffering is enjoined, adultery is forbidden, sodomy is forbidden . . . sodomy is not disgusting, it is just forbidden.
>
> (p. 133)

In this sermon, James is probably consciously attacking Dora's sexual care-lessness, and reflecting on that of Nick Fawley and, unconsciously, Michael. His reversion to the Law is certainly not a ringing example of Christianity's putative allegiance to mercy, and his entire sermon is an ambiguously handled statement. On the one hand, his idea of a disciplined following of an external good as opposed to directing energy to the infinite delights of egotism is very much a Murdochian statement, and his handling of it has the confusing double ring of accuracy and reductiveness. His later analysis of Michael's misdemeanour—and from the point of view of his limited knowledge of Michael's past and present behaviour it is hardly more than that—obviates the continuation of Michael's spiritual aspirations. This kind of negative judgement, inherent in established Christianity and of which James is so pure a spokesman, cannot be seen as other than destructive to both the secular and the spiritual life. Poor Nick Fawley, in angrily catechizing Toby about his relations with Michael and Dora, describes the virtuous James as the 'only available saint' (p. 262), but his statement reflects only his own inclination towards guilt and a guilty relationship to Christianity as opposed to James's simple, untemptable nature, not any noteworthy truth about the real thrust of the novel.

Very unlike James in theological temper is the Roman Catholic priest, Brendan Craddock, in *Henry and Cato*. Whereas James is obtuse, Brendan quickly perceives the nature of the relationship between his fellow priest, Cato, and the clever delinquent boy called Beautiful Joe. Brendan is a theologically more sophisticated character; moreover, he reflects a real change in Murdoch's apprehension of Christianity and the possibilities of the reli-gious life. He does not assume that Cato's homosexual longings are blamewor-thy or unusual; he focuses rather on Cato's naive egotistic belief that he is the only person in the world who can 'save' Beautiful Joe. For Brendan the only important issue is Cato's hurtful or helpful behaviour in respect to Joe, and he castigates his colleague's lack of humility and failure to believe in the functioning of a separate providential agent. As he sees it, the state of being in love is automatically a powerful egotistical one, in which major substitutions take place. Brendan is one of Murdoch's characters of the good, and a voice to be listened to; the direct and passionate truth and irreversibility of his arguments reflect both the quality of those arguments and the texture of the character himself. Unlike James Tayper Pace in *The Bell*, Brendan Craddock speaks at great length but does not sermonize, and rather than merely reflecting an abstract theoretical system, his words bear the force of a personality which lives out to its spiritually necessary end the content of his arguments.

Brendan's intelligent passion in outlining the real and necessary in the traditional language of Christianity depends on a sophisticated sense of the higher spiritual reaches of his Catholicism, so that for him the breaking of questionable Levitican and Pauline rules like those forbidding homosexuality is not at all important, as it had been for the more naive James. Like the Abbess in *The Bell*, Brendan concentrates the force of his argument on the nature of the spiritual life taken at its highest, but unlike the Abbess he is not protected by the cloister or by years of unworldliness—and above all he is perceived as a real character with real depth. The danger he sees in Cato's behaviour has to do not only with Cato's pride in his ability to reform Beautiful Joe and make him happy, but most significantly with the confusion of images and the dangerous paths of substitution Cato's mind automatically falls into. In both Cato's speculative daydreaming and his awful hallucinations while Joe's prisoner, Brendan's fears turn out to be quite right: the face of the Redeemer becomes the face of Beautiful Joe, and the spiritual erotic energy directed during his seminary and priestly years towards Christ is now entirely concentrated on Joe. Cato's spiritual vagaries receive, through Brendan's intelligence and generosity, every chance that advice or well-meaning, with their attendant insufficiencies, can deliver. Cato is, moreover, set against the background of a Christian organization—the Roman Church—which in its internal workings has seen the spiritual history of many Catos. He is balanced in the fiction by the secular Henry, whose fervent, unexamined desire to destroy an established historical past apparently contrasts sharply to the atavistic conversion which had led Cato to the Christian Church in the first place. In simpler outline, *The Bell* takes up some of the same points, with one crucial difference: the apprehension of Christianity is more confused, the religious community cannot agree among themselves and the multiplicity of points of view in this general confusion leads to a task laid rather too heavily on the reader—the task of discriminating among arguments which all at first appear acceptable. Michael Meade in his longing for piety is differentiated from his secular balance, Dora Greenfield, but he is also without powerful personal support (the Abbess, although endowed with real spirituality, talks to him too seldom, too briefly and at the wrong times) or powerful, subtle arguments directed to his aid, of the sort that Cato has if he could only begin, as Brendan puts it, to 'try at least to use [them] now in relation to yourself' (p. 366).

Every argument Michael knows, develops or hears applies to him: his conviction that the good are powerless, the Abbess's contention that all failures are failures in love and that the way is always forward but never back, James's conviction that the moral life can and should be simple, his own sermon which argues that the human being must know himself and work with the material given him. The multiplicity of routes is intrinsically confusing and reflects the diversity of points of view among those living in or on the fringes of the religious community at Imber. Within the community, some members who want to shoot pigeons and squirrels are opposed by vegetarians offended by the slaughter of the innocents. Some of these latter even disapprove of Peter Topglass ringing birds and Dora picking wildflowers. The community divides into factions over arguments about man's labour within nature, which complicates the problem of buying or rejecting a mechanical cultivator. That they are all, except naive James, deeply unsettled becomes obvious at the climax of the book, and it seems evident that Murdoch is deliberately delivering a picture of the difficulties and probable impossibility of setting up a utopian religious community for those who, as the Abbess describes it, are in search of a non-cloistered working life endowed with spiritual significance:

> although it is possible, and indeed demanded of us, that all and any occupation be given a sacramental meaning, this is now for the majority of people almost intolerably difficult; and for some of such people 'disturbed and hunted by God', as she put it, who cannot find a work which satisfies them in the ordinary world, a life half retired, and a work made simple and significant by its dedicated setting, is what is needed. Our duty, the Abbess said, is not necessarily to seek the highest regardless of the realities of our spiritual life as it in fact is, but to seek that place, that task, those people, which will make our spiritual life most constantly grow and flourish; and in this search, said the Abbess, we must make use of a divine cunning. 'As wise as serpents, as harmless as doves.'
>
> (pp. 82–3)

In contrast to the failures of Michael's group, the community which genuinely works is the one within the convent walls, where the wise Abbess and her cloistered nuns evidently live in simplicity, joy and devotion. In the few contacts the uncloistered characters have with them, they are pictured as filled with gaiety and wisdom, entirely contented, like creatures from another world. When a sister, Mother Clare, strips to her odd nunnish underwear to rescue Catherine and Dora from the lake, she looks distinctly peculiar, almost otherworldly, a condition that her vows dedicated her to.

The distance between her world and secular Michael's is vast. Bowing under the guilty burden of his failures, he expresses the problem of the gap between spiritual aspiration and human defeat after a conversation with the Abbess:

> How well she knew his heart. But her exhortations seemed to him a marvel rather than a practical inspiration. He was too tarnished an instrument to do the work that needed doing. Love. He shook his head. Perhaps only those who had given up the world had the right to use that word.
>
> (p. 238)

The practical, workaday secular-religious community, although it tries very hard, does not seem capable of the high ideals the Abbess urges, and the strain of loving one's neighbours too often shows. In that community, Nick is an outsider, Dora is disapproved of, sermons contradict each other directly, moral arguments uncharitably arise.

The real problem among Michael's community involves their inability to deal with other than the perfect and ideal; their one point of unity lies in the admiration they all feel for Catherine Fawley and the symbolic association they all, but particularly James, make between her and the new convent bell, both shortly to be installed inside the cloistered walls. The attachment of Catherine's personality to the bell is carefully worked out to encompass the concluding ironies: the bell as the voice of love and a symbol of purity had, in its conventual history, always been gainsaid by the labyrinthine power of human sexual love. Thus the medieval story of its mysterious flight into the lake because of the unchastity of one nun parallels the new bell's unceremonious tumble into the water as a result of Nick's ministrations. Catherine, who has identified the bell's symbolism with her religious desires, rushes into the lake in a suicide attempt, overwhelmed by guilt over her comparative unchastity in loving Michael. The violent, obsessive quality of her action suggests not only a deep mental instability, but also a negative violence within Christianity itself unless conceived very clearly in non-idealistic terms.

The London journalist, Noel Spens, cheers up erring, profane Dora by lecturing her against the would-be piety of a community like Imber:

> I can't stand complacent swine who go around judging other people and making them feel cheap. If *they* want to wallow in a sense of unworthiness, let them; but when they interfere with their neighbours one ought positively to *fight* them!
>
> (p. 187)

Noel is, of course, arguing from a point of view most unsympathetic to the community: he does not believe in God, but sounds rather like the 'sincere' man of British empiricism. The dangers of Christianity therefore send him into paroxysms of rage which are not intended to represent Murdoch's posture so much as another very real possibility in interpreting the peculiar and dangerous quality of religious belief in general. Certainly the reader is expected to see the hopeless problems of human community, and more specifically of the religious life, and Noel is one of the means to this end.

Dora keeps insisting through the course of the book that Catherine could not *want* to lock herself in the prison of the convent, but Dora does not, until after all the drama is over, know anything at all about religion (she gave up Christianity, we are amused to be told, when she discovered that she could repeat the Lord's Prayer quickly but not slowly). Nick and Catherine Fawley, unnervingly alike in appearance, both have a strong religious inclination, and for both this aspect is, as Freudian psychoanalysis has been telling us for years it must be, suspiciously close to their sexuality. The implication may be that success in separating these modes of intensity can occur either by being purely a sexual being, as Dora is, or purely committed to the sacred, as the nuns are and Catherine wishes to be. Catherine is able to repress the temptation of her love for Michael until the collapse of the bell ceremony, at which point her obsessional guilt neurosis surfaces with grotesque power. The rigid practice of repression which both she and Michael attempt in their very different sexualities is obviously unhealthy and absolutely destructive, and it is interesting to notice that both lives are crushed by what, in justice, are little more than peccadilloes—but peccadilloes subject to real, destructive Christian judgement. Nick as a schoolboy had originally been driven by the power of an itinerant evangelist's sermon to report to his headmaster his little affair with Michael, who was then his teacher, thus ending the latter's dream of becoming a priest; a cynical and embittered Nick as virtuous sermonizer drives Toby to confess the business with Michael to James Tayper Pace; Catherine is driven by the collapse of the bridge and the ruin of the bell ceremony, which she interprets as a divine judgement on the horrendous unchasity of her love for Michael. This sorry catalogue reduces the possibilities and definitions of the Christian life with chilly efficiency, so that Noel can easily and even justly write up his very witty, funny and devastating newspaper account which completely denigrates the whole religious experiment at Imber.

Murdoch uses this sexual material partly as sensationalist stuff which can bolster the argument of atheistic rationalists like Noel, and partly to show how easily more profound content can be caught up and destroyed by the strongly negative and basically superficial idea of the religious life that both the egotistically pious and the proudly rationalist hold—the idea that Christianity is perceived by its rules and behavioural exterior rather than in the hard-won life of inner discipline. Dependence on the exaggerated image of something like Catherine's purity is wrong in the light of simple human frailty, where one is never secure in any idea of belief: 'At any moment one can be removed from a state of guileless serenity and plunged into its opposite, without any intermediate condition, so high about us do the waters rise of our own and other people's imperfection' (p. 161). Michael and Catherine are both ashamed of their imperfections because they feel they must interfere with the rigid and ideal patterns they have set for themselves and, in Catherine's case, the self-image that has been accepted. Both want to live tight lives in which their special destinies will be flawlessly lived out: the reader already knows of Michael's flaws and failures; Catherine's fall is a sensational surprise which underlines the errors they share in their conception of the spiritual life.

That conception, ironically, comes from the wisdom of the Abbess. It is not judgmental or negative, and always emphasizes the need to escape the past and attempt to live in a loving present with a sense of forward movement. But the Abbess is like an abstract exhortatory text, untouched by the world in which it exists and having only the authority of its detached wisdom. In this respect, her words are analogous to the literal text of Julian of Norwich's *Revelations of Divine Love*, a book central as a background to this novel and which Murdoch repeatedly refers to in her other works. Catherine has made it evident that her desire to become a contemplative was influenced by Julian's history and writing, and Chapter 12 of *The Bell*, which immediately follows Michael's 'mistake' in kissing Toby, opens with Catherine earnestly reading aloud from the *Revelations'* beautiful passages which show the anchoress's 'simple understanding of the reality of God's love' (p. 167). Julian's assurance that God will make all things well in spite of marred life in the world is quoted through one of her Showings of God: *'That which is impossible to thee is not impossible to me: I shall make all things well'* (p. 161). Unfortunately, this theology of God's power and man's impotence does not transfer to the anxious characters, who cannot give up their struggle with self or subdue their hyper-kinetic egos under God; instead they either fall into guilt through basically egotistic shame and failure or cause real destruction, as Michael does in brooding neurotically on himself and not heeding Nick's signals for help.

Nick is like many characters in Murdoch novels who savagely echo and pervert Julian of Norwich's famous phrase: 'All shall be well, and all shall be well, and all manner of thing shall be well.' The perversion is automatic, for the lines represent a terrible distance between the speaker and the God who in our period can scarcely be known. Nick sees himself as finished and shows his suicidal inclinations when he asks that the brake be released so that the lorry he is working on will run over him, and gives his version: 'All shall be well and all shall be well and all manner of bloody thing shall be well' (p. 209), and indeed, for contemporary man his twisting of the words appears to have a kind of direct truth. Before Nick's suicide, a seeking, hopeful Michael knows that all might still be well if he could break through his shame and the disastrous confusion of things and act simply towards Nick. His complete inability to do so, coupled with the foul timing of events in the world, shows how remote the state of grace is from personalities diseased by neurosis.

When Nick is dead, Catherine mad, the community broken up and Michael utterly destroyed by his inadequate love of Nick, the religious idea is clearly stated as the central recognition of the book:

> [Michael] thought of religion as something far away, something into which he had never really penetrated at all. He vaguely remembered that he had had emotions, experiences, hopes; but real faith in God was something utterly remote from all that. He understood that at last, and felt, almost coldly, the remoteness. The pattern which he had seen in his life had existed only in his own romantic imagination. At the human level there was no pattern. 'For as the heavens are higher than the earth, so are my ways higher than your ways, and my thoughts than your thoughts.' And as he felt bitterly the grimness of these words, he put it to himself: there is a God, but I do not believe in Him.
>
> (p. 312)

Michael, like most Christians, had associated his interpretation of life with the idea of a necessary pattern, a visible and comprehensible providential order whose design is automatically consoling and meaningful. This longing for order is a built-in component in western culture to which existential thought as well as conventional Christianity is devoted: Sartre, one of Murdoch's early subjects of study, subscribed to this longing and recognized its power. The horror of Michael's experience denies such coherence and comfort, and emphasizes what Murdoch sees persistently through her work as the unbridgeable space between human images of God as a pattern-setter and the ineffable nature of whatever, if anything, is out of there in the divine distance. Michael's necessary lesson stresses the unknowability of God and bitterly asserts that the ways of God are higher and wholly other than that which human faith and desire for knowledge can fruitfully deal with. Michael's attempt to fit his life to a pattern has been wrong, pointless, destructive—and when he says 'there is a God, but I do not believe in Him', he is saying that his need to live a coherent life is eternally separated from the immense human need for large and mighty symbols. This particular alienation can be seen as Murdoch's definition of the ravages of Romanticism.

When Julian of Norwich's radiant belief in an absolute benignity even amid the pain of life is set side by side with Michael's recognition that God's ways are higher than man's, there is little contradiction; but a real savouring of the meaning of Julian's ecstatic belief that 'All shall be well and all shall be well and all manner of thing shall be well' involves a pointed discipline. All shall not be well in a world governed by the theories of personality that dominate our period, and for the mystic's words to have any value, major steps in a direction contrary to ours would be necessary. All cannot be well in a world in which separation from reality is inevitable because concentration on self obscures the necessary quality of transcendence in religious experience. Murdoch's people are world-immanent characters who often and bitterly acknowledge this limitation, but who feel trapped in a world where their undisciplined spiritual energy has no object of attention. The necessary quality of religious experience does, however, have possible outlets in the secular world, and interestingly, the most apparently profane and spiritually undeveloped character in the book, Dora Greenfield, is given most immediate access to them. Confronted with the bell, a beautiful object in which the power of viable religion and artistic production coincide, Dora can dimly perceive the quality of holy reality which the medieval bell-founder had perceived as he sculpted the images from the life of Christ. Much more consciously Dora knows this transcendence in art as she looks at her favourite paintings in the National Gallery, seeing them as real and perfect, as 'something real outside herself, which spoke to her kindly and yet in sovereign tones, something superior and good whose presence destroyed the dreary trance-like solipsisms of her earlier mood' (p. 192).

Art apparently has the power to draw the self out of the self which the Christianity imaged in the Imber community lacks. Its members cannot even properly perceive the specifically theological data of Julian's words, as Murdoch illustrates art's greater ability than theology's to call out religious feeling in the contemporary world. The brief, luminous glimpses of reality art gives are, as she later argues in *The Sovereignty of Good*, a sort of contemporary substitute for prayer which is not a workable source of grace for people who confuse religion and power, the idea of God with the idea of self.

Keeping pace with and helping to define the religious failures in the novel are the various sexualities—Catherine's and Michael's repressions, Nick's destructive revenge, Toby's initiations, the Stafford's obscurely troubled marriage, Dora's promiscuity and, perhaps most interestingly of all, Paul Greenfield's demonic possessiveness. A pale secular shadow in the religious community, Paul is not extensively developed and in certain ways remains a caricature; but like many other characters in the novel he too is trying in a perverted way to fabricate an ideal, purposive life through a futile combination of his sterilely elegant collection of art objects and bibelots which he perceives only as his possessions and his sexual tyranny over a wayward Dora. His poisonous, selfish anger and inability to see either art or another person clearly ruin the marriage, and his attempt to juggle his profession, the scholarly life and his recalcitrant and misunderstood sexuality contribute to the novel's total aura of chaos in community and the individual soul.

*

Michael Meade's grieving conclusion near the end of *The Bell*, 'There is a God but I do not believe in him', is basically a statement of utter and irremediable separation of the divine from the mortal: 'For as the heavens are higher than the earth, so are my ways higher than your ways, and my thoughts than your thoughts' (p. 312). The same idea will be wordlessly present in *Henry and Cato* where the kestrel, sighted by both Henry and Cato on different occasions, soars above the Ladbroke Grove wasteland and is specifically but ironically identified as a symbol for the Holy Ghost. When Cato, whose belief in God has been replaced by a dream of redemption and love with Beautiful Joe, stuffs his filthy cassock (his own consciously symbolic mark of himself as priest) into the rubbish tip, the kestrel swoops in a powerfully symbolic gesture:

> Then he saw the kestrel. The brown bird was hovering, a still portent, not very high up, right in the centre of the waste, so intent yet so aloof, its tail drawn down, its wings silently beating as in a cold immobile passion. Cato stood looking up. There was no one else around upon the desert space where already, after the rain, upon the torn and lumpy ground, spring was making grass and little plants to grow. The kestrel was perfectly still, an image of contemplation, the warm blue afternoon spread out behind it, vibrating with colour and light. Cato looked at it, aware suddenly of nothing else. Then as he looked, holding his breath, the bird swooped. It came down, with almost slow casual ease, to the ground, then rose again and flew away over Cato's head. As he turned, shading his eyes, he could see the tiny dark form in its beak, the little doomed training tail.
>
> 'My Lord and my God', said Cato aloud. Then he laughed and set off again in the direction of the Mission.
>
> (p. 186)

Cato's laughter, following his ironic quotation of St Augustine's infinitely repeated brief prayer, 'My Lord and my God', is the laughter of a career dangerously set free from discipline and prepared to pursue a *vita nuova* of egotism. The swoop of the bird on its victim presents a nice parallel to Cato's original conversion, but what his mind cannot yet comprehend is the final doom of the religious life—the terror, darkness and death he is yet to experience, which will become his great teachers. Murdoch carefully points out that Cato's ecstatic early perception of the Trinity, his sense of having stepped out into the light and looked at the sun itself, is a misapprehension of the spiritual life which must be corrected in the course of events.

The spiritually much more advanced Brendan Craddock, one of Murdoch's characters of the good, differs radically from Cato's limited perception of the Christian problem. Writing with full awareness of the dark night of the soul to a distraught Cato, he says:

> We have to suffer for God in the intellect, go on and on taking the strain. Of course we can never be altogether in the truth, given the distance between man and God how could we be? Our truth is at best a shadowy reflection, yet we must never stop trying to understand. . . . There is a mystical life of the

church to which we must subdue ourselves even in our doubts. Do not puzzle
your mind with images and ideas which you know can be only the merest
glimmerings of Godhead. Stay. Sit. You cannot escape from God.

(p. 161)

Later, in conversation, Brendan will argue that Christ represents a principle
of change rather than of settled theology, and he will finally leave everything
in his English life and intellectual order to go to India alone, without
theology or traditional images, in order to follow the furthest reaches of the
religious life and to enter an area of obedience where even speculation is
disallowed. His final statement fearlessly accepts the limitations of human
knowledge.

The point is, one will never get to the end of it, never get to the bottom of
it, never, never, never. And that never, never, never is what you must take
for your hope and your shield and your most glorious promise. Everything
that we concoct about God is an illusion.

(p. 339)

Brendan, like Michael Meade in *The Bell*, perceives the distance between
man and God, but unlike Michael he is not driven to despair by it. Brendan
faces no conflict between the blank face of reality and our rich desire for
images, and we can see him as a steadily advancing character, changing and
moving as the demands of the religious life impel him onwards. A telling
distinction between *The Bell* and *Henry and Cato* comes from Murdoch's
development of Brendan Craddock as a powerful character with an eloquent
ability to recount the dangers and disciplines of the religious life. Contrasted
to the briefly glimpsed Abbess of *The Bell*, he is the spokesman for the aloof
pressure of the spiritual life, and his convincing portrayal reminds both
Cato and the reader that that life is supremely important, not the bitter
impossibility Michael Meade had seen it to be. Throughout *Henry and Cato*
Murdoch confronts religious problems with a firmness not seen in earlier
religious novels like *The Bell* and *The Unicorn*, and her luminous writing on
the subject of spiritual experiences is a daunting and brilliant achievement—
something courageously taken on and movingly absolute, whether she is
talking about Cato's first wonderful apprehension of the Trinity, the darkness
of his defeat after Joe's death, or Brendan's spiritual knowledge.

Cato and Michael Meade are far distant from Brendan and very much
alike: both are caught in the conflict between messy personal desires and the
unrewarding, even impossible demands of a strangely alien transcendence.
The birds evoked in both books establish a connection both literal and
symbolic between the natural world and the spiritual, and the hovering
kestrel high above the wasteland of the grim present effectively illustrates the
distance and separation so strongly felt by the spiritually restless characters. It

is impossible not to notice the parallel between the alien transcendence of the divine and the highest reaches of art in *Henry and Cato*, as again Murdoch insists on her sense of reality and the artist's obedience to it. Again, she has set this novel against several works of art, most importantly against the German expressionist Max Beckmann's large triptych entitled 'Departure' in the Museum of Modern Art in New York.

This painting is most specifically connected to Henry, whose spiritual energies expend themselves on the secular and are split between his demonic desire to destroy his ancestral home, Laxlinden, and his very real love of art. The triptych possesses great spiritual significance, and Henry identifies the King of the central panel as the kingfisher—another Christian symbol. In his book, *Max Beckmann* (New York: Abrams, 1977), Stephan Lackner quotes Lilly von Schnitzler's letter of explanation which purports to be Beckmann's own interpretation of the picture:

> Life is what you see right and left. Life is torture, pain of every kind—physical and mental—men and women are subjected to it equally. On the right wing you can see yourself trying to find your way in the darkness, lighting the hall and staircase with a miserable lamp, dragging along tied to you, as a part of yourself, the corpse of your memories, of your wrongs and failures, the murder everyone commits at some time of his life—you can never free yourself from your past, you have to carry that corpse while Life plays the drum.
>
> And in the center?
>
> The King and Queen, Man and Woman, are taken to another shore by a boatsman whom they do not know, he wears a mask, it is the mysterious figure taking us to a mysterious land. . . . The King and Queen have freed themselves of the tortures of life—they have overcome them. The Queen carries the greatest treasure—Freedom—as a child in her lap. Freedom is the one thing that matters—it is the departure, the new start.
>
> (p. 116)

The framing images of appalling suffering exist in sharp contrast to the luminous sea and sky of the central picture of boatman, king, queen and child—a secular reproduction of the Christian holy family, and a reflection of transcendent achievement.

The problem for Henry—and indeed for all the characters in the novel—is how to cross the borders of suffering to attain this transcendent image. Henry is a student of Beckmann, and has been fiddling around on a book on him as part of his attempt to get tenure at a bad little college in Sperriton, Illinois, where he has been teaching art history and in the process has had to learn some. The proximity of this fictional dull little town to St Louis, where Beckmann spent the last few years of his life, no doubt gives his project its novelistic *raison d'être*, but Henry as a character brilliantly models his life on his apprehension of Beckmann's style and career. He perceives himself as ill-treated, tentative, suffering, and in his insecurity he identifies with the strong masculine symbolism of this most assertive of painters. Equalled only by Rembrandt in the number of self-portraits he produced, Beckmann is a model for Henry, who constantly looks at himself in the mirror, mentally creating hard, romantic adjectives to describe himself: 'foxlike Henry', 'assuaged drunken Henry', 'harlequin Henry' (the latter a direct reference to a self-portrait by Beckmann). His enormous egotism is firmly sustained through this powerful stylistic device. Throughout the book he refers to the images of suffering on the side panels of the triptych, but the reader is increasingly convinced, especially because of the terms of Cato's ordeal, that Henry's suffering is neurotic, a barrier thrown up by a personality which has largely imagined its pain. As his mother, Gerda, says to him in the only real conversation they have, her own struggle with her marriage made her choose between her husband and her demanding child; the result was a special joy in her elder, kinder child, Sandy:

> I couldn't deal with both you and him. Sandy was all right, I think he sort of understood, and anyway he was independent. I hoped you'd be. You weren't. You were demanding then, you were terribly hostile. A child's hostility can hurt too. I couldn't reach you. I had my own fight, and my own tears. It was partly just a matter of energy. . . . Sandy was the only thing that gave my life any pure sense and any pure joy, but I never talked to Sandy. I never communicated with Sandy. I never told him what I've just told you. I never touched him or kissed him after he was twelve.
>
> (pp. 301–2)

We first see Henry on a plane above the Atlantic delighting in the death of his brother, Alexander, the Sandy of Gerda's plaintive account. The elder son and heir to the Marshalson estate, Alexander is one of the puzzles of the novel. Neurotic, untrustworthy Henry gives no reason for hating him, except that Alexander apparently fitted into the Marshalson picture more readily than seething Henry and was obviously everybody's favourite. Alexander's interest in boats, cars and little else separated his sensibility from Henry's, but the ghost of the dead brother is strangely anonymous—and very much like the masked helmsman of the boat in the Beckmann triptych. He is a mysterious presence, separate from the action and yet necessary and ominously present. His ghostly recurrence in everyone's mind keeps making itself felt, yet his anonymity is never broken. For Henry he is a probably false object of envy and hatred; Gerda, who idealized him and mourns absolutely for this tall, red-haired son she never talked intimately with or touched as an adult, dreams of him as a great redemptive figure cut off from her forever and taken away on his yacht. Lucius recalls him only as a large, comfortable, indifferent presence, and Stephanie, who never met him, fantasizes the romance that could never have been. We discover late, after Henry and Colette's wedding, that the bird-headed servant, Rhoda, had had an affair with him and that he gave her the heirloom ring, the Marshalson Rose. But our most important piece of information comes from the priest, Brendan Craddock, whose authority the reader is very willing to accept. His account of a drunken Alexander, suffering and inwardly tormented, is a surprising detail after the neutral descriptions of his bland personality, bland room, bland flat in London. Whatever this man might have been in life, his death becomes a large symbolic issue haunting the novel.

The second half of the novel is entitled 'The Great Teacher', and the teacher is death. Murdoch, obviously interpreting the helmsman in the Beckmann triptych as death, is not interested in romantic readings of happy families sailing into the serene blue of the horizon; but in her heavily ironic denouement she depicts the newly married Henry and Colette on a punt in the lake, contemplating Colette's new pregnancy, a mimetic image of the Fisher King and Queen. The space between them and the transcendent serenity of the painting is as enormous as the distance between shattered Cato and the Christ he had once worshipped, and their apparent continuation in a viable world comes only from strong denials of reality from both Colette and Henry. Colette, when imprisoned in the darkness by dangerously criminal Beautiful Joe, had realized in her terror that her romantic childhood dream of marrying Henry—a dream with which she had been persecuting him and poor dazed Stephanie—has utterly gone, replaced by a darker, more adult recognition:

> She thought, I *ran* to Henry, I had to. And she saw his dark glowing eyes looking at her, and she wished for physical desire to distract her from her misery and terror, but it would not come. And she felt with a sadness that she had lost him, not because he did not want her, but because she did not any more want him. In this darkness Henry gave no light, he was just a young girl's empty dream.
>
> (p. 258)

Her subsequent intuition of guilty Cato as a soul in hell and her own remorse over Joe's death lie at the heart of the novel, and the quasi-cheerful note of future happiness, children and a calm life continuing the tradition of beautiful Laxlinden Hall is off-key indeed.

Henry's compromise is in many ways greater than Colette's, and involves a more complete recognition than hers. His egotism is not easily broken into, and indeed he survives in a comfortable world by retreating into that egotism. After the disaster of Cato and Joe, Henry reluctantly seeks out Cato at Brendan Craddock's flat. He is astonished and appalled by Cato's sneering reference to Henry as a tourist in the situation and by the bitterness of his new moral line:

> One realizes that there are no barriers, there never were any barriers, what one thought were barriers were simply frivolous selfish complacent illusions and

vanities. All that so-called morality is simply smirking at yourself in a mirror and thinking how good you are. Morality is nothing but self-esteem, nothing else, simply affectations of virtue and spiritual charm. And when self-esteem is gone there's nothing left but fury, fury of unbridled egoism. . . . I just hope and pray for you—may you never see what I see now, never know what I know now, never be where I am now!

(p. 295)

Henry flees from Cato to the consolation of art, and sits before Titian's 'Death of Actaeon'. As he looks at that great painting, he ponders how horror can be transformed into beauty, and even assumes that perhaps great artists do not know the horror of reality. Frantically he repeats Cato's prayer that he never see or know the dark fury that Cato's failures and actions have unleashed. The passage is extremely important:

Something frightful and beastly and terrible has been turned into one of the most beautiful things in the world. How is this possible? Is it a lie, or what? Did Titian know that really human life was awful, awful, that it was nothing but a slaughterhouse? Did Max know, when he painted witty cleverly composed scenes of torture? Maybe they knew, thought Henry, but I certainly don't and I don't want to. And he thought of Cato now with a horrified pity which was a sort of disgust, and he gazed into the far depths of the great picture and he prayed for himself—May I never see what he sees, never know what he knows, never be where he is, so help me God!

(p. 296)

One suddenly recognizes Henry's essential superficiality as he gazes at great art, his choice to see the beauty and ignore the pain. Thinking of Beckmann and Titian much earlier in the novel he had questioned why these artists were so arresting, why he loved Beckmann so; clearly he now has an answer which he chooses consciously and fervently to shut out from his life, repeating the words of Cato's prayer that he never see, know or be in the horror of pain and death the artists so absolutely depict. Choosing ease and consolation, he cannot begin to confront the profound question of how death and pain can be transformed into beauty. He buys his restoration of Laxlinden and his marriage to Colette by this compromise, and he remains wistfully aware of his limitations:

As a spiritual being I'm done for. The pity I felt for Stephanie was probably the only spiritual experience that I ever had. . . . Yes, I'm done for, thought Henry. Now I shall never live simply and bereft as I ought to live. I have chosen a mediocre destiny. . . . I have failed, but I don't care. I shall be happy. I never expected it, I never wanted it or sought for it, but it's happened. Apparently I am doomed to be a happy man, and I shall do my damnedest to make it last.

(pp. 326–7)

Henry's recognition of failure in a higher task is oddly parallel to Cato's spiritual bleakness and to Lucius Lamb's dying knowledge, as well as to the feelings of defeat that encompass every character in this novel. This exciting, fast-moving book, with the wry illusion of happy marriage and new starts in its denouement, reflects Murdoch at her grimmest. Except for Brendan Craddock, the characters operate consistently at a level of failed ambition and personal defeat. All of them are ambitious to succeed at an idealistic level, and to a greater or lesser extent the course of action shows them a vision of the bleak truth behind these ambitions. Cato's final knowledge that morality and the spiritual life he had lived are merely cosmetic gives us a good place to begin, as does Brendan's much truer definition of the spiritual life and its identity with death. Brendan's point of view has been fully discussed in Chapter II, but it is important to connect his insights to the central idea of this novel about the Great Teacher:

> Death is what instructs us most of all, and then only when it is present. When it is absent it is totally forgotten. Those who can live with death can live in the truth, only this is almost unendurable. It is not the drama of death that teaches—when you are there facing it there is no drama. That's why it's so hard to write tragedy. Death is the great destroyer of all images and all stories, and human beings will do anything rather than envisage it. Their last resource is to rely on suffering, to try to cheat death by suffering instead. And suffering we know breeds images, it breeds the most beautiful images of all.
>
> (p. 336)

Cato's ambition and image of himself as a priest were indeed limited, and as Brendan correctly points out to him, he had scarcely begun the endless journey the spiritual life involves. In the novel we see a Cato whose vanity and egotism centre on his near-homosexual relationship with Beautiful Joe. Even vain Henry is astounded by the egotism in Cato's letter asking for money to support the two of them, and the reader tires of Cato's endless litany acclaiming himself as the only means of Joe's salvation. Cato's loss of faith occurs obscurely, in conjunction with his increased interest in Joe, and shows the limit of his commitment to the rigours of the religious life. Until his imprisonment he looks as Henry will look at the end of the book—compromised, but perhaps heading for a personal, longed-for happiness. His sorry failure inevitably casts its shadow on the false image of happiness in the novel's ironic closure.

Murdoch's virulent undoing of his false ideal and her general attack on happiness are vital in considering reader response to this powerful book. Although *Henry and Cato* is a serious novel about the rigours of the mystic way and Cato's egotistic fall into the delights and horrors of the secular renunciation of that way, Murdoch is also closely attuned to an audience impatient of or indifferent to the religious life and more likely to delight in Henry and Colette's doggedly happy marriage than respond to Cato's punishment or to Brendan going forward into the final stages of the saintly *via negativa*. Like Henry himself, novel audiences have a strong resistance to the knowledge of reality in its hardest forms; we huddle as he does before great art, praying not to know the horror that might be at its centre. The ironies of the marriage can certainly console, and Colette and Henry are generously conceived by Murdoch. Colette's identification with punts and fish reminds us of the Beckmann triptych, and certainly she rescues Henry from his romantic perception of himself as suffering and demonically destructive like the characters on the two side panels of the painting. Even more, Colette's utterly courageous rush to save Cato, combined with her frantic attempt to be brave before Beautiful Joe's demands, align her in a small but substantial way with the good. Her romantic vision of the saving power of her virginity, her image of herself as the lady of Laxlinden and her witch-like curses on the Stephanie/Henry engagement show her deep attachment to fantasy, but because novel readers are always on the borders of fantasy, we are more likely to go along with her girlish foibles than damn her false images.

Henry is another case entirely. In his first conversation with Cato, he explains that he is writing a book on Max Beckmann called *Screaming or Yawning*, a title based on an early Beckmann drawing (p. 66); this title gives the reader a good pair of responses to Henry's impossible behaviour: his criminal destructiveness in trying to destroy Laxlinden as well as his mother's and Lucius's lives, his constant romantic readings of and self-association with Beckmann's paintings, his sustained hatred of the dead Alexander, his perverse falling in love with Stephanie Whitehouse because of his triumph in being alive while Alexander is dead. Neurotic and self-obsessed, he leaps about Laxlinden and London in an orgy of rotten behaviour which indeed drives the reader to both screams and yawns. His excessive brooding on himself carefully shields him from perceiving outside reality, and he sees nothing clearly—not Beckmann, not Stephanie, not Cato, not his mother, not Lucius; everything is screened through his heavy curtains of romanticism and hatred. In this quality Henry resembles Austin Gibson Grey in *An Accidental Man* and is another example of Murdoch's Everyman, who is in truth so close to us as readers.

Henry sees himself as a hero (identifying with the great H's including Hamlet, Hannibal and Hitler, as well as with Beckmann's self-portraits), but is too anxious and uncertain of himself to define his intentions very well. Principally he sees himself as a kind of social saint, who will destroy the paternal legacy of the Laxlinden estate, distribute his enormous fortune to the poor and return to a humble American backwater where he and Stephanie will drink many martinis with his American parent surrogates, Bella and Russell. This ill thought out plan is merely window-dressing to his real motivations, and through Henry the reader is strongly compelled to see the futility and fraudulence of the intellectual life among the characters in this novel. Several of them sustain the myth that they are working on books, the substance of which they fail to enact. Henry cannot understand the basis of Beckmann's art, even though he knows a great deal about him and 'loves' him; Lucius Lamb long ago gave up everything except the fiction of writing a book on Marxist thought as he settled into the sparse luxuries of life with Gerda; John Forbes spends his sabbatical writing lecture notes and reading rather than writing a book on the Quaker history of his ancestors. Apart from these failed works, large projects like Henry's socialism and Cato's priesthood fall through. Except for the consistency displayed by Brendan Craddock's moral position, all disciplines seem intractably difficult. Henry's lucky emergence into the world of external happiness is unearned, but by the end of the book he knows this fact and himself much better than before the frenzy of the action overtook him on page three of the novel. Moreover, the audience, without idealizing him, is able to respond with a certain degree of relief to the small changes that have taken place.

The women in *Henry and Cato* are markedly different in quality from the men. None is engaged in an ambitious intellectual or spiritual project or knows much about painting and art history. The American Bella, whom we know only by Henry's report, is a college professor but not notably intellectual; Gerda, who lives daily with a seventeeth-century Flemish tapestry and a good collection of paintings and furniture, is evidently unversed in their provenance; Colette deliberately withdraws from her college because she eschews the intellectual life; Stephanie is wonderfully ignorant and totally vulgar. Yet the image of woman aggrandized as goddess and redeemer is one of the most powerful and interesting in the book—and again it is emphasized by a series of references to works of art. Although these women function without conscious knowledge of theories or absolutes, they play a consistent symbolic role, most often illustrated by the Laxlinden tapestry depicting Athena hauling Achilles up by the hair. Both Colette in her efforts to marry Henry and Gerda in her prevention of his marriage to Stephanie play similar roles of powerful woman over inadequate man, and Henry in the National Gallery ruminates on the power of goddesses:

> It was certainly dangerous to tangle with goddesses. Athena was a fearful authoritarian and very austere even with her favourites. Hera was thoroughly vindictive. Artemis and Aphrodite were killers. What poor thin semiconscious beings mortal men were after all, so easily maddened, so readily destroyed by forces whose fearful strength remained forever beyond their powers of conception. Surely these forces were real, the human mind a mere shadow, a toy.
>
> (p. 96)

These human female powers prowling courageously through the novel-Colette, Gerda, Stephanie, even Dame Patricia Raven and the absent Bella-provide centres of control on the ordinary human level which are, as always in Murdoch, echoed by more profound and mythic ideas. Colette graduates from Athena to the Redeemer's face (for Cato) and the Fisher Queen (for Henry); Gerda is both Athena and, for Lucius Lamb, a Calypso who has kept him from his great work and reduced him to secret haikus; Stephanie plays a voluptuous Aphrodite.

Henry's cogitation on the goddesses takes place before Titian's large and beautiful painting in the National Gallery in London called 'The Death of Actaeon', bought by the Gallery after a large fund-raising drive at just about the time Murdoch was composing this novel. This impressive painting is, after Beckmann, the most important art object in the book; it is also described through Henry's consciousness:

> The immortal goddess, with curving apple cheek, her bow uplifted, bounds with graceful ruthless indifference across the foreground, while further back, in an underworld of brooding light, the doll-like figure of Actaeon falls stiffly to the onslaught of the dogs. A stream flashes. A distant horseman passes. The woods, the air, are of a russet brown so intense and frightening as to persuade one that the tragedy is taking place in total silence. Henry felt such intense pleasure as he looked at the picture, he felt so purely happy that he wanted to howl aloud with delight.
>
> (p. 96)

His joy in the work is the reader's one access to sympathy for him, and in this passage we have a fine example of Murdoch's painterly eye and splendid capacity to catch briefly and completely the tonal achievement of a great work of art. In symbolic terms, the passage contrasts Diana's sacred undefiled hunt, powerfully in the foreground, with the horrible suffering and death of Actaeon, torn apart by the hounds of his own mind. This image of Diana, unlike the other goddesses invoked, is not connected to literal women in the novel even though the symbolism of the goddess subtly links to the general plot idea. Just as the Beckmann triptych connects to the secular suffering and successes of Henry's part in the plot, the Titian reflects most fruitfully on the essentially religious tale of Cato's suffering. Even so, however, 'The Death of Actaeon' provides the reader with the novel's central symbol.

Titian's dramatic reversal of the myth puts Diana's otherworldly, chaste hunt in the foreground rather than either balancing it with Actaeon's death or substituting the more common image of the goddess and her nymphs bathing. Diana's purposiveness in the hunt here vitally overshadows Actaeon being devoured by the hounds, with the result that the viewer is forced to rethink the myth. In Titian's version, the divine concentrates on its activity, indifferent to the human suffering and horror which is obscurely linked to it by a human causal means: Actaeon has incorrectly stumbled on and seen the divine Diana bathing, and as a result of this vision must be torn apart by his dogs. Titian's contrast between the overbalancing fleeting image of the divine and the less central brown suffering of the human is enormous, and an excellent image for this novel, where at a deep, infrastructural level the absolute nature of reality (the divine) is so much more important than the Actaeon-like centre of its double tales of false suffering and human failure. Murdoch's trick of so often diverting the reader from this deep level is counterbalanced by the strength and intensity of the conversations about or references to reality and the religious life when they infrequently occur, and only the tendency of the novel reader to escape (all of us) makes so many readers fasten onto the ironic novelistic notion of happy closure in marriage as ameliorative.

The important fact which connects us to the symbolic message of the Titian painting is, however, that the novel ends where it had begun, with Cato walking into the dark rain with an object in his mackintosh pocket. The turn from gun to crucifix illustrates the dominant progress of the book, from violence to quiet, from emotional turbulences of all sorts to happiness or serious theological summing-up. The aesthetic elegance of the Spanish ivory crucifix with which Cato exits endows it with a certain value even apart from its having belonged to the spiritually advanced Brendan. It replaces both the humbler wooden crucifix (an ostentatious sign of Cato's false humility as a swinging priest?) and the gun with which the book opens, and adds to the primacy of the idea of the 'divine' to which the Diana allegory points.

In the progress of the novel, however, the gun appears to be central, inasmuch as it motivates a great deal of the action and leads to the first and major split between Cato and his beloved Beautiful Joe. For all its dramatic placement, however, it is only one of several talismanic objects of violence which become so important: the gun itself, Joe's knife, the section of piping Cato manages to unscrew in his black prison. These objects represent not only the level of social violence and threat from which all twentieth-century people suffer, but also a continuous counter-current against which old, traditional ideas fight. As instruments of physical violence, they align thematically with Henry's desire to commit a 'murder' (p. 59), a 'crime' (p. 86), a 'destruction' (p. 125) against Laxlinden, his dead brother and father and his childhood. In deeply ironic terms they are pitted against the impotent figures of Christianity, as Joe's knife lies on the table like a holy image on an altar, or as, stained with Henry's blood, it becomes a nasty counterforce to the crucifix.

Murdoch's evocation of darkness, raw fear and both casual and horribly spontaneous violence is among the best things in this excellent novel, which in process takes on something of the quality of a Graham Greene or Joyce Carol Oates production—something rare in Murdoch and, I suspect, not particularly intentional. Probably the best explanation in terms of design is not in the inclination towards sensationalism which earlier marred some of her novels, but the connection with the major idea of this novel expressed in the title of its second half, 'The Great Teacher'. The sacramentalized instruments of violence cause the death of Beautiful Joe at the hands of an hysterical Cato, and Brendan describes his death most clearly as a version of the redemptive death which is at the centre of traditional Christianity: 'We live by redemptive death. Anyone can stand in for Christ. . . . Death is what instructs us most of all, and then only when it is present . . .' (p. 336). Joe's death certainly jells the action in its new pattern, where the egotistic characters have faced reality and been turned from their frenzied activity into new silence. The first half of the book, 'Rites of Passage', has set up this shift with an elaboration of rapid activity in which words like freedom and love have been hurled about in a farrago of emotion. Joe's death utterly changes Cato, as well as Henry and Colette, but it is not the only great teacher: we remember that the death of Alexander Marshalson has hovered behind the novel, and touchingly, Lucius Lamb is given final temporary prominence.

A much more minor character than Lucius, Cato's early spiritual advisor, Father Milsom, had written to Cato: 'Your task is love and love is your teacher' (p. 162). Illusions of love, divine and human, prove useless in this novel, but Brendan, and finally Lucius, see the love that Father Milsom evoked as identical with death. Lucius throughout the novel has meant to love Gerda properly and intended to marry her, but he perpetually escapes commitment and lives as easily and comfortably as he can. Like and yet so unlike Henry, Lucius slips into the easiest, most comfortable mode of life, allowing his talents to slip away unused. His haikus, to which his supposedly enormous poetic talent has been reduced, reflect his resentments—against Gerda whom he has loved so imperfectly, and old age, which has him relentlessly in its grip. In addition Henry, the new master, threatens his parsimonious comfort and becomes the enemy. As the denouement approaches, a now redundant Lucius has a stroke, collapses and takes up his notepad for a final haiku:

> So many dawns I was blind to
> Now the illumination of night
> Comes to me too late, O great teacher.
> (p. 330)

Although the poem is obviously scrawled just a few moments before death, Lucius's end is not reported until the last page of the novel, when Brendan reports briefly but poignantly that as a young man Lucius had written a good poem called 'The Great Teacher'. He cannot recall its substance, but the shadow of some great lost human talent joins with the salient imagery to suggest to the reader that this novel is about the waste of human knowledge and talent, something wilfully and dreadfully thrown away by careless hands.

At a crucial point, Beautiful Joe enunciates an important principle to

Cato: 'And a funny thing, do you know, it's awfully easy to frighten anybody. Not everybody knows how easy it is, but it's dead easy . . . Dead easy. Do it even with a knife . . .' (pp. 41–2). Joe's success at frightening Cato, Henry and Colette is ample proof of his boast, but the reader is cunningly led to believe that talent, aspiration, love and goodness are all too easily undone by the easy ability of any casual forces of the world to join with individual human weakness and fear to undo our loftiest and doubtless our best aspirations. Joe's insistence on fear reminds us of Dickens's Magwitch in *Great Expectations*, who uses the same techniques on a seven-year-old boy on the marshes, and one of the heart-sickening ways Murdoch's novel drives home its proof of human inadequacy has to do with such analogies and with the fact that Beautiful Joe is all too painfully correct when he estimates the childish fragility of humankind.

Iris Murdoch's Conflicting Ethical Demands: Separation versus Passivity in *The Sacred and Profane Love Machine*

Dorothy A. Winsor

Iris Murdoch's novels have intrigued critics partly because a persistently puzzling quality has lurked beneath their deceptively traditional surfaces. A reader frequently comes away from her novels with a sense of having not quite grasped what is going on in them. The ready availability of Murdoch's philosophical essays has tended to shape analysis of what she is doing. Confronted by the baffling quality of her novels, critics have often extracted moral principles from her essays and used these principles to analyze the rights and wrongs of her characters' behavior and the moral import of the form in which the novels are couched.[1] Although the study of Murdoch's essays has helped readers identify the fantasy-absorbed behavior she sees as destructive and therefore immoral, it has not led to a clear understanding of the behavior she evidently intends to be seen as admirable. I believe that this is because, without seeming to be aware of any inconsistency, Murdoch endorses in her novels behavior which is a form of the self-absorption she condemns in her essays. I believe that at the root of this confusion lies a picture of people as necessarily solipsistic, a view which we all at some time share and by which Murdoch is, like all of us, both attracted and repelled. Her essays voice only the rejection of solipsism, but her novels are more complicated. I wish to examine the ethical standards implied in her novels as opposed to those argued in her essays, and then to show how these opposing standards—and the world view upon which they depend—shape her work. Instead of trying to survey all of Murdoch's many novels, I will discuss in depth one of her most successful: *The Sacred and Profane Love Machine* (1974).

As both novelist and philosopher, Murdoch is concerned with the human tendency to see the world through the distortion of fantasy. "We are not isolated free choosers, monarchs of all we survey," she writes, "but benighted creatures sunk in a reality whose nature we are constantly and overwhelmingly tempted to deform by fantasy."[2] In the resulting false vision,

From *Modern Language Quarterly* 44, no. 4 (December 1983): 394–409; © University of Washington. Reprinted by permission of the author and publisher.

things appear as the viewer wishes them to be, and other people become only means of fulfilling desires. A character—or a person—thus violates the real needs and rights of others, failing to arrive at "the extremely difficult realisation that something other than oneself is real," which Murdoch variously calls love, freedom, and morality.[3]

The confusion of fantasy with the exterior world may be compared to the way all people think when they are very young children. The infant has not yet clearly differentiated himself from the outside world and commonly sees others as extensions of himself.[4] Although this state of merger is attractive for the child because it means that agents of gratification are under his control, experience gradually teaches him the limits of both his power and his being. In the ethic Murdoch argues in her essays, the recognition of his separate state is a moral as well as a developmental task, for if he is separate, then so are others, and their separateness implies that his needs are not to be satisfied at their expense. Failure to achieve this recognition of separateness leads to the damaging actions of a character like Julius King in *A Fairly Honourable Defeat* (1970), who feels free to manipulate Rupert and Morgan into a fake romance for his own amusement. In *The Nice and the Good* (1968), on the other hand, one sees John Ducane's growing recognition of the separate state of others; at the beginning of the novel he keeps Jessica Bird tied to him to the extent that she is literally blind to the outside world, and at the end he recognizes and denounces his own egotism.[5]

Yet, implicit in Murdoch's novels is an ethical standard that contradicts the demand for separation she simultaneously makes: the novels often seem to treat the merged world of childhood as inescapable and operate entirely within its solipsism. Because one cannot accept a world apart from oneself, behavior that should reflect separation becomes instead substitution of an active, powerful move toward merger for a more passive form of it. In this childish world, self and world are perceived as one and maintained as such against all threats through fantasies of incorporation. The cliché that identifies the world as an eat-or-be-eaten one is absolutely accurate; in order to maintain the desired fusion, one incorporates others or is oneself incorporated. In accordance with this view, the ultimate moral division in Murdoch's novels is not between merging and separating, for all is merged, but between those who allow themselves to be absorbed and those who absorb others. Implied in the novels is the view that goodness comes through allowing or even promoting destruction of oneself in order to prevent oneself from destroying others.

Murdoch's ambiguous attitude toward supposedly "separated" behavior is epitomized in her treatment of sex, probably because sex itself epitomizes the way we relate to others. Ideally, sex replaces incorporation of another with the union of two recognizably separate people. Within the merged world the novels imply, however, such separation is impossible, and intercourse becomes a sadomasochistic power exchange in which one character intrudes upon another in an attempt at personal control, an acting out of fantasies of control dating, as we have seen, to childhood. Thus, in the world of Murdoch's novels, sex becomes a disguised extension of solipsism instead of a transformation of it. In the world Murdoch portrays, separation is all but impossible, and characters are judged as moral not because they recognize a separate reality, but because they refuse to exercise power over those who are inescapably linked to them.

This ethical ambiguity is one source of both strength and weakness in Murdoch's fiction. It gives a real sense of the difficulties involved in escaping solipsism, yet it also creates confusion. Murdoch's novels reflect the moral dilemma of her essays in ways she does not, perhaps, intend, and testify to the powerful pull of solipsism even for the author herself.

The characters in *The Sacred and Profane Love Machine* operate within these double demands for separation and self-extinction. The novel is the story of psychologist Blaise Gavender's marriage and affair, loves he himself thinks of as "sacred" and "profane."[6] Blaise, his wife, Harriet, and their fifteen-year-old son, David, lead an affectionate conventional life in the London suburb where Blaise practices therapy. Nine years before the novel begins, however, Blaise met and fell in love with Emily McHugh, an energetic, lower-class young woman whose sadomasochistic sexual predilections matched Blaise's own. He has since maintained Emily and their son, Luca, in a run-down London apartment which he visits with decreasing frequency, though the sexual tie between them remains strong.

Although the novel is the story of Blaise, it opens with a portrayal of David Gavender in the throes of an adolescent identity crisis that sets the theme for much of the novel. Murdoch commonly uses adolescents as minor characters in her work, perhaps because the identity crisis traditional to adolescence symbolizes her central concern: the vacillation between adult separation and childlike merger with parental figures. Because it deals with issues first raised in early childhood, *The Sacred and Profane Love Machine* is as much about love between children and parents as it is about love between adults. Vacillation between parent/child merger and adult/adult love is experienced not only by David, but by the adults who attempt to define themselves as separate individuals but inevitably participate in a more malign, powerful form of merging.

David's dissatisfaction with childish lack of boundaries is indicated by his fear "of never being able to be a real person at all. He felt obscenely amorphous, globular, a creature in metamorphosis . . ." (p. 4). As the novel progresses, his need for separation is gradually revealed as caused by, focused upon, and finally resolved through the necessary move away from relating to others by means of merger toward relating to them by means of sex. This development is not treated positively, however, for it is clearly associated with inevitable violence.

The highway that is being built across the meadows near David's home symbolizes his emerging sexuality. The road is gradually constructed as the book progresses and is open at the end. While Blaise and Harriet regard the road as a civilized despoiler of nature, David rather likes it. After learning of his father's double life, however, he visits the still unused highway, lies down upon it, and is aware both of his life as "spoilt" by his father's sexual guilt and of an "automatic, sexual desire" (p. 201). The spoiling of his life is described in terms that might also be used to describe the effect of the highway upon the countryside: "How irrevocably spoilt, down to its minutest detail, his world was now. Even the countryside was spoilt, the animals, the birds, the flowers" (p. 201). In the iconography to which Murdoch's title refers, "profane" bodily love is represented by a richly attired woman pictured against a city, while "sacred" love of God is a naked woman pictured against a natural background.[7] For David, too, sexuality—whether Blaise's or his own—is an adult, "civilized" force, which will destroy forever his "natural" childish happiness. In the inevitably merged world of Murdoch's novels, sexuality will lead, not out of incorporative relationships, but back to them in a form that is less passive, and therefore less innocent, than the incorporation one experiences in childhood.

David's happiness has been built in part upon belief in a God who knows him totally, and both his growth to adulthood and his emerging sexuality are linked to the loss of that faith and to the knowledge that "no one from now on forever would know . . . what it was really like to be him" (p. 201). He is aware, that is, of his separateness, and this awareness leads him to experience desire for both "violence" (p. 202) and sex. In the world of Murdoch's novels, sex and violence are often equated, because both are attempts at personal domination.

David's sexual initiation takes place through Constance Pinn, who has been Emily's charwoman and is now her roommate. Pinn sleeps with David after he refuses to go to Germany with his mother, thereby breaking with her and with the innocent merging of childhood. Pinn's touching him "produced an instantaneous and very complex change in David's being. At one moment he was hanging in space. . . . He was disincarnate and scattered in terrible regions. At the next moment his body had assembled promptly and compactly round about him . . ." (pp. 325–26). David feels himself to be without clear boundaries because he has not yet found a substitute for merger with his parents; he achieves a limited separate identity in his body through sex. In place of "sacred" presexual love, which would involve God or his parents merging with him and knowing him absolutely, there is Pinn, who stands outside him and so can see him absolutely: "He had never been so absolutely looked at before" (p. 327). For David, the "profane" sex results in at least temporary salvation, but circumstances surrounding it suggest an inevitably violent quality which will ultimately lead him to destructive behavior. Pinn, for instance, clearly manipulates others—always a bad sign in Murdoch's work. Moreover, just before he is approached by Pinn, David passes the highway which has finally opened, as if to mark his transition to sexuality. Upon the road is a dead hare (p. 322). David's "natural" innocence is dead, and the fates of the book's adults bode no good for him.

The adult characters echo, with varying degrees of success, David's attempts to recognize reality separate from himself and his fantasies. I have said that it is relatively easy to recognize characters who are behaving badly in Murdoch's novels. This is because they fail to meet either of her two ethical standards: they cannot see the world apart from their own minds, and in the resulting state of merger they seek power rather than passivity. Blaise, for instance, has allowed fantasies to shape his perception of and behavior toward the external world. He had entertained sexual fantasies of an apparently sadomasochistic nature long before he met Emily, and his acceptance of those fantasies prepared him for his match with her. "When moments of decision arrive," says Murdoch in an essay, "we see and are attracted by the world we have already (partly) made."[8] Blaise and Emily's life together was thus "a solidifying dream" (p. 70), a concretizing of fantasy. In his work, too, Blaise sees the world through fantasies. He himself is familiar with the temptations Murdoch sees as inherent in psychoanalysis, and he refers to "the enchanted, enchanting, curiously self-determining world of psychoanalytical theory" (p. 17).[9] In contrast to Harriet, for whom Blaise's patients remain "objects of reverence and mystery" (p. 15), Blaise sees them as utterly predictable, for he sees them through the ready-made patterns of psychoanalysis.

Blaise, then, is a fantasizer. This is not a role with which he is altogether comfortable, as his mourning for his lost innocence and his desire to leave his present occupation and enter medical school indicate; but, as Murdoch shows, Blaise's past life has effects that operate with machinelike inevitability no matter how he tries to control them.[10] This is because he has failed to achieve the separation Murdoch describes in her essays. There she explains that if one has clearly recognized and attended to external reality, then one can see where truth and obligation lie and act upon them, but if one's perception has been obscured by the fantasy of what one wishes to see, then one is not able to act with love and justice by wishing to.[11] Blaise's harmful actions thus proceed quite undramatically from his tendency to believe that reality is what he wishes it to be. He is unable, that is, to separate internal and external worlds.

Blaise behaves badly, however, not only because he fails to separate but also because he fails to submit to those to whom he is linked. In the merged world of this book, he is in a position of power and can actively impose his fantasies upon others. His patients, for instance, actually seem to conform to the patterns through which he sees them. When he ceases to "treat" them, most of them cease to be neurotic. During his deception of Harriet, he clearly felt power over her and loved her for it; he feared telling her about his infidelity because he would be, in the words of his neighbor Monty Small, "losing the initiative" (p. 129). Blaise's attempt at reform is unsuccessful partly because he finds it possible to grip "the situation in his own way" (p. 142) even when he confesses and claims to submit to Harriet. His submission is not true passivity, not true virtue.

In Blaise, then, the demands for separation and self-extinction converge and suggest similar judgments. Contradictions between these standards become increasingly evident, however, when one considers other characters who show varying degrees of "virtue." Emily, for instance, is at moments treated sympathetically, not because she attempts to see her duty and break from Blaise, but because she is his victim. She is accorded less approval, not as she indulges to a greater degree in fantasy, but as she attempts to a greater degree to control Blaise. She appears at her best early in the novel in her helpless love for her son. When the book opens, moreover, she keeps a messy house and maintains a disorderly personal appearance, both of which are often good signs in Murdoch, for they are used to symbolize lack of control over the world. Emily is treated sympathetically, however, only so long as she passively suffers. When Blaise confesses to Harriet and apparently returns to her, Emily's appearance smartens and her housekeeping improves—signs of her readiness for battle. Emily wants to control the world and not be controlled. In contrast to Harriet, who cannot manage violence, Emily feels that "a little violence will make me real again" (p. 88), "like people who go to an airport with a machine gun and just shoot everyone within sight" (p. 92). Because wishes can attain reality when internal and external worlds merge, it is not surprising that Harriet actually is shot in an airport and that Emily feels "as if, in some quite guiltless and proper way, she herself had eliminated her rival" (p. 351). Emily has been forced into self-sacrifice and feels deprived by it. She is, she says, "hollow" (p. 180), and she becomes destructive in her effort to be filled, to absorb others rather than be absorbed herself.

The contradictory nature of Murdoch's ethical standards plays a large role in her treatment of Harriet. At the opening of the novel, Harriet is presented as existing in the unformed, merged manner of children.[12] As with Emily, Harriet's inability to impose patterns is reflected in her messy housekeeping. Moreover, she lives through others, as though she were one with them. She wants, for instance, to be "behind" Blaise "looking at the world through [his] eyes"; she has, she says, "no other being, no other vision" (p. 26). She herself is "empty, floppy, disjointed, . . . and this was for her really a form of being happy" (p. 12). When events force her to look at her life differently, however, she concludes that she "never grew up" (p. 272). She was, she says, "just a piece of ectoplasm" who only by the force of events becomes "a person, an individual, something with edges" (p. 272). That is, she establishes boundaries; she separates. One would expect Murdoch to treat this as a good action, and in a way she does, suggesting that in her merged state Harriet is faintly menacing. Blaise feels that Harriet, with her small family, suffers from "a sheer excess of undistributed love, like having too much milk in the breasts" (pp. 15–16). Harriet, the nurturer, has too much nurturing to give, and thus there is a suspicion of grasping in the love she extends. She herself "knew that she led a selfish life because all her otherness was so much a part of herself" (p. 12); the immersion of herself in others may also be seen as a demand on others that they immerse themselves in her. The merged state natural to children is dangerous in the adult Harriet. She must grow up, just as David must; she must separate.

Within the novel, however, Murdoch implies that for Harriet such an act of separation is destructive because it inevitably leads her to attempt to reestablish merger through exercising control over others. It is in her original merged state that Harriet has a vision of reality as symbolized by a tree in a painting by Giorgione she sees in the National Gallery:

> There it was in the middle of clarity, in the middle of bright darkness, in the middle of limpid sultry yellow air, in the middle of nowhere at all with distant clouds creeping by behind it, linking the two saints yet also separating them and also being itself and nothing to do with them at all, a ridiculously frail, poetical vibrating motionless tree which was also a special particular tree on a special particular evening. . . .
>
> (p. 49)

The tree is significant both in itself and as a link between two other parts of reality. It is both separate from and joined to others. Harriet's apprehension of the possibility for such a double existence is a sign of her innocent state. But it is a double existence she cannot attain. Once she separates, she can be good only by isolating herself and ultimately by dying, thus preventing herself from harming others. The characterization of Harriet reveals the profound doubts about separation which lie at the heart of much of Murdoch's work.

As with David, the force that destroys Harriet's "innocence" (p. 271), her untroubled merged existence, is sex. After Harriet receives Blaise's first letter, telling her of Emily and Luca, she compares herself to "an 'Annunciation' by Tintoretto in which the Virgin sits in a wrecked skeleton stable into which the Holy Ghost has entered as a tempestuous, destructive force" (p. 144). Like the Virgin, she is touched by an act of sex, though in the value structure of this book, she remains potentially holy since the act is sexless for her. Because Blaise's revelation has given her power over him, she reacts as almost all people in Murdoch's novels react: she makes Blaise feel "her will . . . the strength he had made in her by this ordeal" (pp. 150–51). Moreover, she becomes preoccupied with herself in a way she had not been before. Before, she "saw the world, not her mind. Now, however, her emotions and her ideas preoccupied her. . . . She was aware that her whole mental being had altered . . ." (p. 194). Instead of feeding others at Hood House, she feasts upon the situation and attempts "to swallow Emily whole" (p. 190). What makes Harriet's behavior less innocent in the later part of the novel is not that she indulges in greater fantasy, but that she seeks to control where she once was passive.

That her attempt at controlling Blaise is ineffective is apparently a sign of her innocence and his corruption. Edgar Demarnay, an Oxford scholar who is visiting Monty Small, tells Harriet the truth about the results of her behavior. By forgiving Blaise and tolerating the situation, Edgar says, Harriet has put Blaise "in a position where he cannot stop lying" (p. 213). Unable to shape the results of Blaise's actions, Harriet has only prevented him from seeing them. She "was not in control after all," she realizes, "nobody was in control . . ." (p. 127). Past actions have consequences which people cannot stop. The "sheer awfulness of the situation had an impetus of its own" (p. 217).

Edgar's ability to perceive the truth results from the kind of person he is. Like Harriet and David, Edgar feels that he lacks structure and separate definition. "You've got a sort of hardness in you, a centre," he tells Monty. "I'm soft all the way through. . . . Maybe I'm retarded, yes, that's it, retarded" (p. 43). Edgar's "retardation" places him in the realm of eternal childhood, with connotations of merged existence rather than sexuality, and Edgar has apparently eschewed sex with a puritan sense of guilt (p. 43). One suspects that his chastity is a precondition of his truthful vision.

One sign of his presexual and thus nonthreatening state is his habitual mode of loving, which is always from afar: "his love for women was unrequited and his love for men undeclared" (p. 362). The situation is exemplified in his feelings for the Smalls. He is visiting Monty because he is in love with Monty and was in love with Sophie, Monty's recently deceased wife. He had been content, however, to love Sophie and not possess her. Unrequited love, he says, "is a contradiction. If it's true love, it somehow contains its object" (p. 118). Freedom from desire for possession of the loved one exemplifies a willingness to recognize the other as separate, which is moral according to Murdoch's essays; the belief that love contains its own object, however, could also be seen as a denial of one's separateness from the loved one, an affirmation of innocent merging, which seems to be good in the context of her novels. Edgar's love for Monty has been undeclared (though not unrecognized) and ends in his being rejected, and thus alone and powerless.

A further sign of Edgar's lack of menace is his rather foolish appearance. Like Harriet in her "innocent" state, Edgar is a plump eater and drinker, substituting consumption of food and alcohol for the absorption of others with which love seems to be equated. Edgar is typical of one variety of good fools in Murdoch's novels, in which innocence often looks weak and foolish because competence in ordering the world is by definition aggressive.

Edgar's truth-telling reveals to Harriet something of her actual powerlessness, but it does not tell her how she ought to act. She makes a second attempt to become a new person when her powerlessness is revealed again by Blaise's second letter, in which he tells her that he has decided to live with Emily. Again, she feels destroyed. "Like a cloistered jungle native suddenly infected by the viruses of civilization, she keeled over" (p. 270). Just as sexuality analogous to the "civilized" road destroyed David's "natural" happiness, so revelations of "civilized" sexuality intrude upon and corrupt Harriet's "natural" preadult state. Like David, she has an adolescent sense of just starting out in the world, "as if she were young and in anguish" (p. 271). This time, Harriet rejects Blaise and actively seeks to fulfill her "powerful loving nature" (p. 271) in someone else.

Harriet turns successively to Monty, Edgar, and Blaise's fictive patient, Magnus Bowles, in vain attempts to find someone to love, but her attempts are inevitably aggressive. Monty experiences her arrival as an "invasion" (p. 256) and sees her search through Blaise's files for Magnus's address as "a violation, a kind of violence" (p. 312). She finally flees to Germany, taking only Luca with her, as even David fails to come to her. There, stripped of her past life and waiting in an airport, she contemplates herself and sees truly at last. Blaise is the only one who needs her love, and she will eventually return to him. The "only escape from this," she thinks, "is a kind of violence of which I am not capable" (p. 340). Only, she has "grown up" and will no longer be able to live innocently through others. In living for Blaise, she will be "alone" (p. 340). Harriet is a separate being at last, and living with this fact will mean unhappiness and the constant temptation to seize power over Emily and Blaise. "There is," she thinks sadly, "no great calm space elsewhere . . . where a tree stands between two saints and raises its pure significant head into a golden sky" (p. 340). She cannot be both joined and separate. She cannot meet both demands. In a sudden odd intrusion of the outer world, Harriet dies in a terrorist attack in the airport waiting room, shielding Luca with her body in a last maternal gesture. For Harriet, the wages of virtue is death, an ultimate blotting out of self.

The confusion of ethical demands is evident in Murdoch's treatment of Monty Small as well as Harriet. Monty's occupation as novelist is, like Blaise's as psychologist, that of a fiction-maker.[13] The similarity in their occupations indicates that Blaise and Monty may be "cognate" characters. Murdoch often uses such pairs in her work, showing them as inevitably linked and rivalrous, with one character harmed as the other succeeds. Success at the expense of another is unavoidable because, in the world Murdoch portrays, it is impossible for a character to assert himself without harming those linked to him. Frequently, the paired characters are siblings or cousins, further emphasizing their identified status. Between Blaise and Monty, as between many of these characters, there is a sense of rivalry or power struggle, right down to Blaise's desire to shift the boundaries between their properties and buy Monty's orchard. In light of the significance of boundaries in this book, one can say that Blaise wishes to intrude upon Monty and control him. Monty has, however, built his defenses through his fictions.

His chief creation is Milo Fane, an adolescent, fantasized image of

Monty himself (p. 33), originally created as a defense against Monty's mother. As a child, Monty had decided that "he would not let his mother kill him . . . by the sheer intensity of her love, like a huge sow rolling over on its young" (p. 111). To love, in this book equals to kill, to absorb, to smother. His mother is an "eater-up," a "taker-over" (p. 30). So Monty created Milo, "a remorseless killer" (p. 112), in whom Monty could survive in this kill-or-be-killed world, inspiring "terror" in his mother and giving him "an unholy sense of power" (p. 112). Milo is plainly a product of a childish view of the self and the mother as one. His nature suggests that Monty might have been more virtuous to allow himself to be "destroyed" as Harriet did.

Now, however, Monty wishes to shed his fictitious self and come to terms with a reality separate from himself, just as Murdoch's essays say he should. In a desire parallel to Blaise's to enter medical school, Monty wishes to cease writing and become a schoolteacher, whose simple compulsory duties would, he thinks, force him to actions not shaped by his own fantasies. He has apparently been working toward his desire for change for some time, but his immediate need for it has been created by Sophie's death. In the past, Monty had apparently achieved a sense of the possibility of goodness through his love for Sophie, who was "hopelessly foreign" (p. 8), "alien, unjustifiable, unassimilable" (p. 206). She was, in other words, a completely separate being whom he nonetheless loved. But the possibility for good in their marriage was always thwarted by his jealousy, a sign that he both desired to possess her totally and allowed sex to ruin their relationship. In the end, he could not bear her separateness from him and choked her to death as she lay dying of cancer. He killed her, he later says, because he could no longer stand her "*consciousness*" (p. 302). Monty killed Sophie because she was too separate.

He had hoped that Sophie's death would somehow "enlighten him in a sort of spiritual orgasm" (p. 35). Instead, it leaves him with only the "horror of her absence" (p. 35) and an "awful separateness" (p. 30), which, in the merged world of this book, he equates with destruction (p. 30). What he expects from her death contrasts with what he anticipates from a mundane teaching position: "This was no spiritual orgasm, but it looked a good deal more like the way" (p. 36). Even in this highly metaphoric form, "orgasm" is opposed to goodness. The teaching position, which is contrasted with sexual fulfillment, is evidently intended to prevent Monty from acting upon the destructive impulses almost inevitably present in a separated being in Murdoch's novels. It is as though Monty knows that if he separates he will, unless he takes care, be dangerous.

Monty prepares himself to take the position by isolating himself, and thus protecting others, and by meditation, in which he attempts "to get rid of the ego" (p. 124) and merge with the cosmos. For Monty, meditation ultimately would lead to a place "where the fretful struggle of self and other is eternally laid at rest" (p. 204). As Harriet's goodness necessitates her death, Monty's idea of virtue implies a state of "eternal rest." Monty has refused to let himself be lost in his mother, but the alternative he seeks is loss of himself in meditation.

Edgar's intervention finally makes a change in Monty, who feels himself to be, with Edgar, "almost human" (p. 364). Yet Monty's change, in Murdoch's terms, cannot be for the better, because he cannot simultaneously join the rest of the world and keep from hurting it. Confessing to Edgar enables Monty to stop suffering, but in Monty's case suffering and isolation had led to goodness. When suffering ceases, Monty no longer mourns Sophie but feels that she is "part of him forever" (p. 331). He tells Harriet that Magnus Bowles committed suicide, and then feels an exhilarating albeit false sense of freedom (p. 314). To Edgar, he had called himself lame and blind, images that in the Murdoch world imply goodness because they imply humility and castration, but after Edgar leaves, he feels he has had a leg or eye operation (p. 314). He again makes contact with the outside world, answering letters and his phone. His contact with the outer world leads, however, to the regeneration of the sexuality which had apparently wrecked his love for Sophie—he makes love to Kiki St. Loy—and the return of his aggressive Milo self—he goes to Italy to stay with Richard Nailsworth, an actor who played Milo (pp. 247–48). And he tells Edgar that he "may even produce another Milo story" (p. 366).

The Sacred and Profane Love Machine, then, exemplifies a tension present in all of Murdoch's novels, which suggests that in them she achieves a more complex picture than in her essays of the difficulties involved in relating to other people. In her novels, she portrays a world in which people must separate or harm others who become elements in their fantasies, but in which few true alternatives to merger exist. On rare occasions Murdoch conceives of situations in which characters are actually able to separate without menace; and when that happens some of the most joyous moments in her novels result. In *Under the Net* (1954), for instance, Jake Donaghue and Jean Pierre Breteuil, the novelist he translates, are paired characters similar to Monty and Blaise; when Jean Pierre finally writes a good novel, Jake is not harmed but is rather freed to write well too. Again, in *The Nice and the Good* (1968) John Ducane and Mary Clothier actually love one another as separate people. The effect is that of breaking free from an enclosure and emerging into the fresh air. The reader feels suddenly that events have settled into place, and the tension resulting from contradictory ethical demands vanishes. But these moments are infrequent. For the most part, virtue in her novels consists not of separating but of recognizing one's inescapable connection to others and one's power over them and in taking measures to protect others by blotting out the self even to death if necessary.

This implied belief in the ineluctability of solipsism is one of the elements giving Murdoch's work a powerful, disturbing quality, for it is a belief we all have shared and struggled to surrender, just as Murdoch's essays say we should. The belief persists in her novels, however, and largely shapes them. It is evident, for instance, in the form of those novels such as *The Italian Girl* (1964) or *The Unicorn* (1963) which Murdoch herself calls "closed."[14] In those novels, all sense of the outer world is lost, and fantasy and myth predominate. In them, the characters' fantasies are given reality and "externalized" into the "outer" world of the book so that the "exterior" world Murdoch creates, against which characters are to measure their delusions, actually serves to confirm these same delusions. The demand for self-suppression which Murdoch derives from this belief is also evident in most of her novels. It is true, for example, of Bradley Pearson in *The Black Prince* (1973) and of Ludwig Leferrier in *An Accidental Man* (1971), both of whom evidently achieve goodness by going to prison, or of Ann Peronett in *An Unofficial Rose* (1962), for whom goodness requires that she renounce love and wait for her unfaithful husband to return. The moral view Murdoch voices in her essays is not sufficiently helpful in understanding her masochistic notion of goodness, which depends upon a belief in one's inevitable menace to others and which in turn derives from a belief in one's inevitable link to them. These twin beliefs are implied in Murdoch's fiction, and recognition of them is important to understanding her novels.

Notes

1. Studies that use Murdoch's philosophy to judge the morality of her characters are almost too numerous to mention, but the following are examples: Frederick J. Hoffman, "The Miracle of Contingency: The Novels of Iris Murdoch," *Shenandoah*, 17 (Autumn 1965), 49–56 Dorothy Jones, "Love and Morality in Iris Murdoch's *The Bell*," *Meanjin Quarterly* 26 (1967), 85–90; Ann Culley, "Theory and Practice: Characterization in the Novels of Iris Murdoch," *MFS*, 15 (1969–70), 335–45; Daniel Majdiak, "Romanticism in the Aesthetics of Iris Murdoch," *TSLL*, 14 (1972), 359–75; and Zohreh T. Sullivan, "The Contracting Universe of Iris Murdoch's Gothic Novels," *MFS* 23 (1977–78), 557–69.

2. "Against Dryness: A Polemical Sketch," *Encounter*, 16 (January 1961). 20.

3. "The Sublime and the Good," *ChiR*, 13 (Autumn 1959), 51. For further explanation of Murdoch's ideas, see her "The Sublime and the Beautiful Revisited," *YR*, 49 (December 1959), 247–71; "The Darkness of Practical Reason," *Encounter*, 27 (July 1966), 46–50; and "On 'God' and 'Good,' " in *The Anatomy of Knowledge*, ed. Marjorie Grene (London: Routledge & Kegan Paul, 1969), pp. 233–58.

4. The most authoritative work on separation and individuation is being done by Margaret Mahler. See Margaret Mahler, Fred Pine, and Anni Bergman, *The Psychological Birth of the Human Infant* (New York: Basic Books, 1975).

5. New York: Viking Press, 1968, pp. 239, 328–29.

6. New York: Viking Press, 1974, p. 349.

7. See Betty M. Foley, "Iris Murdoch's Use of Works of Art as Analogies of Moral Themes," Diss. Wayne State University, 1979, pp. 118–19.

8. "The Darkness of Practical Reason," p. 49.

9. For Murdoch's opinion of psychoanalysis, see "On 'God' and 'Good,' " esp. p. 251.

10. In her review of Simone Weil's *Notebooks*, Murdoch states that Weil believed that

we are "at the mercy of mechanical forces" until we "become good" ("Knowing the Void," *Spectator*, November 2, 1956, p. 613). The title of *The Sacred and Profane Love Machine* echoes this language as its content echoes the idea.

11. See "On 'God' and 'Good,'" p. 241, and Murdoch's "The Idea of Perfection," *YR* 53 (March 1964), 375.

12. Harriet almost matches the idea of goodness Murdoch expounds in "On 'God' and 'Good' ": "Goodness appears to be both rare and hard to picture. It is perhaps most convincingly met with in simple people—inarticulate, unselfish mothers of large families . . ." (p. 238). This is an oddly masochistic notion of goodness, here present even in the essays. Moreover, as I point out, Harriet's family is small, a fact that makes her menacing because it puts her in a position to consume rather than be consumed.

13. Murdoch's condemnation of novelists suggests that she is doubtful about her own activities. Fiction-makers may be seen as inevitable distorters of reality.

14. W. K. Rose, "An Interview with Iris Murdoch," *Shenandoah*, 19 (Winter 1968), 12.

Released from Bands: Iris Murdoch's
Two Prosperos in *The Sea, the Sea*

LINDSEY TUCKER

Readers familiar with the work of Iris Murdoch quickly recognize her 1978 novel *The Sea, The Sea* as one of her so-called "gothic" works, similar in atmosphere and theme to *The Unicorn, The Flight from the Enchanter, The Time of the Angels*, and *Bruno's Dream*. It contains, in other words, certain characters and motifs we have come to expect: an isolated, rather sinister setting, an enchanter figure, a figure or figures under his/her spell, and a plot comprising elements of the bizarre, the grotesque, the mysterious, and the demonic.[1] More specifically, we find Charles Arrowby, the protagonist of *The Sea, The Sea*, to be yet another of Murdoch's "posturing Courtly Lovers,"[2] represented in other works by such figures as Effingham Cooper in *The Unicorn*, Martin Lynch-Gibbon in *A Severed Head*, John Rainborough in *The Flight from the Enchanter*, and Bradley Pearson in *The Black Prince*—male figures who follow a pattern described by William F. Hall as moving from a "world of form, pattern, and convention, into one of contingency."[3] There is also another familiar and important Murdoch figure in this work, namely, the saint, a character who normally resides in the background, a wise, selfless individual who remains for the most part uninvolved. Another recurrent feature of Murdoch's works is an abundance of Shakespearean allusion; this feature is also present in *The Sea, The Sea*, in which *The Tempest* is used in a number of ways, some less obvious than others, to reinforce meaning and structure.[4]

Nevertheless, *The Sea, The Sea* also represents something of a departure for Murdoch, because it manifests a more complex and focused treatment of two of Murdoch's more compelling concerns. The first of these involves the usually neutral saintly figure who, in this work, is elevated to a role of more importance. This figure, Charles's cousin James, is involved in the action, not for reasons of ego, but because of his need to act in accordance with the teachings of his adopted religion, Buddhism. Indeed, this religious element is of paramount importance to the novel, and brings us to the second of Murdoch's concerns, namely, an increased emphasis on Buddhism as a source of behavioral attitudes, spiritual enlightenment, and ultimate liberation in

From *Contemporary Literature* 27, no. 3 (1986): 378–95; © The University of Wisconsin Press. Reprinted by permission.

a world that has lost its religious consciousness. Murdoch has integrated Buddhist philosophy into previous works, especially *The Nice and the Good, An Accidental Man*, and *Bruno's Dream*,[5] but in this novel the ultimate meaning seems to rely heavily on our understanding of Buddhism, especially Buddhism as practiced in Tibet.[6]

I have mentioned Murdoch's use of *The Tempest* in *The Sea, The Sea*, and I do not wish to imply that the play is of less importance than the religious element. Rather I would like to suggest that both are mutually supportive. *The Tempest* is about the nature of dreams and reality, but it is also about the surrendering of magic. Buddhism likewise concerns itself with the nature of dreams and reality, but it deals extensively with the surrender of magic and with preparation for death. Consequently, *The Sea, The Sea* purports to be the diary/memoirs/autobiography of the retired theater director Charles Arrowby (obviously a Prospero figure), but as it becomes a novel about his experiences on a primitive English seacoast, another Prospero figure, his cousin James, emerges. What Murdoch gives us then in *The Sea, The Sea* is no simple reworking of *The Tempest*, but, through the prism of Buddhist teachings and Shakespeare's perhaps wisest play, a powerful statement about the surrender of magic, the practice of dying, and the making of art.

Charles Arrowby, born in Stratford-on-Avon, has devoted his life to Shakespeare. Unlike Shakespeare, however, Charles is not truly creative. As a playwright he is mediocre, his plays nothing more than "magical delusions," "fireworks."[7] He is also unsuccessful as an actor, the role of Prospero being— not coincidentally—the only "substantial" one he has ever played. What he is successful at is directing. "I always took . . . an almost childish, almost excessive delight," he tells us, "in the technical trickery of the theatre" (p. 29). But we discover also that his abilities lie in one particular type of directing. He says, for example, that for him the theater is "an attack on mankind carried on by magic: to victimize an audience every night" (p. 33). This seems a strange attitude, we may think, but it soon becomes clear to us that Charles loves directing because he loves power. The theater, he goes on to say, is a "place of obsession," and while the genius of Shakespeare was able to change obsession "into something spiritual" (p. 34), Charles enjoys having an audience of victims. He also prides himself on his ability to manipulate his actors, whom he works like demons (p. 34), and adds, "I fostered my reputation for ruthlessness, it was extremely useful" (p. 37).

As the actual "novel" begins, however, this tyrannical director has retired to a seaside house and is resolved upon learning to be good. Here he begins a diary to recount his days. His jottings are a rather tedious outlining of his favorite meals, his swimming activities, and his house improvements. Perhaps, he thinks, he will call his journal "memoirs," and, paraphrasing Prospero as he thinks about his retirement, asks, "Have I abjured that magic, drowned my book?" (p. 39). The answer is that he has not, and before long he begins his own brand of magic with the summoning of Lizzie, an old lover, to his retreat.

Besides our obvious Prospero figure, a number of Charles's colleagues and friends, Lizzie especially, but also Gilbert, Rosina, and Perry, have affinities with the characters of *The Tempest*. Lizzie, for example, is an Ariel figure, and is described as a "wispish enchanting rather infantile sprite" (p. 50). Charles not only takes credit for having "made" her, but has also played Prospero to her Ariel, and has a strong proprietary sense about her. Since their love affair has ended with pain for her, Lizzie, like Ariel, is under a kind of bondage to Charles, although for different and less admirable reasons, since Lizzie's bondage derives from Charles's enormous egotism. He loves her because he has created her and because, unlike other women, Lizzie has imposed no "moral bonds" (p. 51) on him and she flatters his ego. However, by toying with Lizzie again, Charles demolishes her living situation with Gilbert Opian, sending both out to his seacoast retreat, Lizzie into more bondage, and Gilbert—who admits to having "the soul of a slave"— into servitude as Charles's " 'house-serf' " (p. 241). Not only does Gilbert clean and cook for Charles, but he especially joys in cutting and carrying wood, performing, in other words, those chores done by Caliban. Gilbert has some idea about the nature of bondage to people. " 'Being in love,' " he says, " 'that's another slavery. . . . You make another person into God. That can't be right' " (p. 245).

An altogether different kind of relationship exists between Charles and another actress and former lover, Rosina, who resembles the witchlike Sycorax, Caliban's mother. Rosina, whose marriage has been destroyed by Charles (Charles seems compelled to break up marriages but has never married any of the wives), functions as a witch/demon figure during Charles's retirement, having also come to understand a good deal about the sources of Charles's power as a director. " 'You have been a sorcerer,' " she tells him. " 'Women loved you for your power, your magic' " (p. 108). But she also recognizes his sorcery as " 'facile' " (p. 108). Determined that Lizzie shall never have Charles, she appears on the scene, declares herself a " 'demon,' " and sets out to " 'haunt' " him (p. 104). Her bondage to Charles depends not on love but on hate, which "has its own magic" (p. 107).

Besides this more obvious allusive material, however, there is yet another way in which Murdoch uses *The Tempest* to explore states of enchantment. In this novel she takes the more unusual tack of creating a character who is both the enchanter and the enchanted. The reason for this dual role becomes clearer when we ponder the phenomenon of Charles's sea serpent. This serpent, which Charles has seen almost immediately after his arrival at his seacoast house, rising out of a calm sea "like a black snake" possessing a "long thickening body with a ridgy spiny back" (p. 19), marks not only the beginning of his enchantment, but also the true beginning of the novel. Prospero observes at one point in *The Tempest* (III. iii. 88–90) that "My high charms work,/And these, mine enemies, are all knit up / In their distractions."[8] Despite Prospero's so-called powers, the characters themselves are responsible for their own fantasies, and their "distractions" have their origins in the consciousnesses of the characters and represent individual projections and wish-fulfillments.

In like manner, Charles is also a victim of his own mind's creations.[9] In his old London world of form, where everything was under his control, where, in psychological terms, ego consciousness dominated, where he could ignore the trickery of the mind, all went well for him. But when, early in his retire-ment, he undergoes his strange vision of the serpent rising from the sea, he is given a signal that the unconscious is emergent, that a "sea change" has, in fact, taken place. Charles tries to rationalize his vision, of course, attribut-ing it to an old experiment with LSD, a trip that proved so unpleasant for him that he is still unable to write about it except to say that it concerned "entrails" (p. 21). Yet his description of the LSD venture is not unconnected to his sea serpent vision. Charles describes his drug trip as "something mor-ally, spiritually horrible, as if one's stinking inside had emerged and become the universe: a surging emanation of dark halfformed spiritual evil" (p. 21). The use of the word *inside* is important, for the emergence of the unconscious can be described as a kind of turning of everything inside out. To put it another way, Charles's psychic condition is being projected onto his surround-ings, which now take on the coloration of his mind. Both the vision and his earlier drug trip involve the same kind of revelation, one that is repeated when Charles, apparently in need of pondering his serpent vision under more neutral circumstances, finds himself, during a return to London, perusing Titian's painting of Perseus and Andromeda. Not too surprisingly, he is made violently ill, and it is at this junction that James appears on the scene to perform his first rescue of his disturbed cousin. Taking Charles home to his flat, he tells him, " 'we cannot just walk into the cavern and look around. Most of what we think we know about our minds is pseudo-knowledge' " (p. 175).

Because of Charles's egocentricity and his arrogant assumptions about himself and the world he thinks he controls, we do not pay particular attention to James. We do note a kind of sibling rivalry—all on Charles's part—since James, like Charles, is an only child and a person whom Charles tends to view as "an elder brother, not a younger cousin" (p. 56). A letter from James early in the story and the promise of a visit set Charles off to recount his relationship with James, a relationship that is most noteworthy for its lack of importance. "It is not that James has ever been much of an actor in my life," says Charles, "nor do I anticipate that he will ever now become one" (p. 56). Yet every reference to their childhood denies this assertion. James, the son of the more interesting parents, Abel and Estelle (their names, connoting innocence and light, are significant too since they suggest, in Buddhist terms, that James has better *karma*), was early marked as different, possessing, as Charles puts it, "a beastly invulnerability" (p. 57). James has also shown extraordinary promise as a student of languages and philosophy, but has taken up the rather strange occupation of professional soldier. Yet James's Tibetan adventures and his conversion to Buddhism tend to mollify Charles's ruthless ambition, an ambition Charles sees as a direct result of his fear of James.

Still, it is obvious that while Charles can interpret the sketchy events of James's life as failures that allow him to feel less intimidated by his cousin, he remains under James's influence and is always recalling something James has said. Thus while he tells the reader on one hand that he sees his cousin as a pedant and a bore, he also recalls pertinent things that James has said, for example, about ending one's life in caves and about the world being full of gods (p. 69), observations that Charles would do well to ponder.

I have suggested that James functions as a second Prospero figure, and while it is clear that Charles is really the enchanted figure, playing a kind of parodic Ferdinand to Hartley's Miranda, James is an altogether different sort of magician. Like Prospero, he has devoted his life to "secret studies" (I. iii). He has also experienced bad turns of fortune. He too has been exiled, has been forced to leave his beloved Tibet after its usurpation by the Chinese. And he has retired under a cloud of some sort, a bit of news that Charles takes delight in. Yet, as he tells Charles, he does not " 'lack occupations' " (p. 179). What he means by this statement is never made explicit, but we might take him to mean that he intends to assume a role in Charles's life. Indeed, his appearance in the art gallery is portentous, accompanied by Japanese *hyoshigi*—in reality the hammering of workmen in the art gallery. These drums, Charles tells us, are used in the theater to announce doom. Furthermore, James emerges through "curiously brownish murky air," which immediately conveys a sense of his mystery (p. 171). In fact, James is always associated with the mysterious. He is described as having an "occluded" face (p. 145), a face that is "muddy," "dark" (p. 174). His arrival at the seacoast house is "an unnerving portent" (p. 321)

Although Charles tends to down-play it, the reader cannot help but be aware of James's magnetism, the unusual way in which people respond to his presence. Elizabeth Dipple seems to view James's mystery and magnetism as sinister, as evidence of a lust for power, but I see this quality of James as a manifestation of spiritual energy. Nor do I think that at this point in James's life "power is his disease," as Dipple claims.[10] Charles naturally resents his charisma, and yet James doesn't appear to me to use this quality to manipulate people. For example, there seems to be some kind of bond between James and Hartley's son Titus. In the first place, James seems to have some outside knowledge about the boy and is keenly interested in him, even before the main drama of Charles's "rescue" of Hartley gets underway. Furthermore, Titus is especially responsive to James when the two meet, and Titus later says, " 'Perhaps I saw him in a dream' " (p. 328), a rather baffling reference until linked with the Buddhist conception of previous lives, previous dream states.

James's arrival affects the others in strange ways too. He has a particularly calming effect on Ben, Hartley's husband. Their attraction can be explained on the basis of similar military careers, but beyond that fact, James seems to have extensive knowledge of Ben's past and a great respect for the man that is transmitted to Ben and described by James as " 'if something passed between us,' " " 'some vein of honor . . . touched' " (pp. 351–52). James is also Lizzie's comforter and confidant.

Early in the novel Charles tells us that he is not a churchgoer. Indeed, while not antagonistic to Christianity, he seems to regard it as an adolescent pursuit that people outgrow with the coming of adulthood. James, as a convert to Buddhism, is patronized for his aberration, yet we cannot take Charles's quick dismissal of religion at face value, for the religious question does not go away. Furthermore, it is James's Buddhism that determines the means by which we are to interpret the action, and it is Buddhism that illuminates some of the mystery inherent in those actions.

To return to Charles for a moment, it is clear that, while dispensing with conventional religious constraints, Charles does not free himself from the numinous energy expressed in a god figure. Instead, he thrusts that numinosity onto objects or people. For example, he speaks of Shakespeare as his god (p. 29); he talks of his Uncle Abel and his Aunt Estelle as gods in his early life (p. 23). More important, and central to the novel, is his apotheosis of Hartley, who becomes for him a religion, "something holy" (p. 129) "my end and my beginning, she is alpha and omega" (p. 77). She is also compared in a number of places to an angel, a paradise. Hartley is, of course, to use Tillich's phrase, Charles's "ultimate concern"—where the heart lies—or so he imagines. Unfortunately, Charles's worship of Hartley is all projection, a worship based on his own enormous egotism, as the understanding and practice of Buddhist teachings soon make clear.

James's Buddhism not only illuminates Charles's problem, but suggests ways out of it, ways all the characters, including James, need to learn in order to win their respective freedom. We might do well to recall here Prospero's famous speech about the "baseless fabric" of the play he has had just been staging:

> The cloud-capped tow'rs, the gorgeous palaces,
> The solemn temples, the great globe itself,
> Yea, all which it inherit, shall dissolve,
> And, like this insubstantial pageant faded,
> Leave not a rack behind. We are such stuff
> As dreams are made on, and our little life
> Is rounded with a sleep.
>
> (IV. i. 152–58)

Furthermore, the views expressed in this passage are similar to the Buddhist belief about the nature of the phenomenal universe, the *sangsara*, in which individual consciousness exists in a state of ignorance about realities, where *maya*, defined in *The Tibetan Book of the Dead* as a "magical show," deludes the unenlightened.[11] As the Buddha is supposed to have said, "The phenomena of life may be likened unto a dream, a phantasm, a bubble, a shadow, the glistening dew, or lightning flash."[12]

Everyone in the novel is trapped in a world of dreams, but surely no one more than Charles—Gilbert calls him the " 'king of shadows' " (p. 93). As the "rapacious magician" (p. 45) of the London stage, he had long confused illusion with reality. Worse, his so-called retirement has turned his fantasy-governed inner world outward, and Hartley, a figure of his dream world, becomes his reality. The illusions he once thought he controlled on stage now control him.

All the characters are able to see the nature of Charles's dream world. When he complains to Lizzie, " 'I wonder if you know what it's like when you have to *guard* somebody . . . to sort of renew them as if you were God,' " she demurs with another question: " 'Even if it's all—not true—like in a dream?' " " 'It can't be a dream,' " Charles assures her, " 'pure love makes it true' " (p. 361). But of course his love is not pure and he is still playing god. Rosina has much to say as well: " 'you're living in a dream world, a rather nasty one' " (p. 315). Even Hartley tries to get him to see this fact. " 'We're in a dream place,' " she tells him, " 'it isn't part of the real world' " (p. 280). " 'You love me,' " Charles says, and she replies, " 'in an unreal way, in a dream, in a might-have-been. . . . we're dreaming.' " While she admits that one can love in a dream, she also insists, " 'it is a dream. It's made of lies' " (p. 329).

James, as one might expect, has a lot to say on the subject of dreams. Attempting to get his cousin to use common, i.e., moral, sense, he observes about Charles's obsession over Hartley: " 'You've made it into a story, and stories are false.' " And he explains:

> Let us call it a dream. Of course we live in dreams and by dreams, and even in a disciplined spiritual life, in some ways especially there, it is hard to distinguish dream from reality.
>
> (p. 335).

Associated with dreams is the problem of magic, for tricks are the concern and accomplishment of both cousins, although in substance and in intent, their magic is quite different. Charles loves the theater because of its trickery, yet its trick aspect is what bothers Perry, Rosina's former husband, about it. He tells Charles, " 'Everything, everything, the saddest, the most sacred, even the funniest, is turned into a vulgar trick' " (p. 165).

James has an altogether different brand of "tricks," but the difference is that he understands their meaning and their consequences. There are a few instances when, just as he is about to depart from Charles's seacoast house—and, in fact, from life itself—he discusses tricks in relation to his mysterious rescue of Charles. " 'All sorts of people can do them,' " he says, " 'they can be jolly tiring but—you know they have nothing to do with—with— . . . nothing to do with anything important, like goodness' " (pp. 446–47). What James does reveal is the fateful effect of such tricks as well as his own bondage to *sangsara*. He has taken his beloved Sherpa friend over a frigid mountain pass, assuming that because of his own highly developed mental powers, his ability to concentrate heat and thereby raise body temperature, he will be able to sustain them both on their perilous journey. He assumes too much, however, and the guide dies. " 'It was my vanity that killed him,' " James says, and concludes significantly, " 'The payment for a fault is automatic' " (p. 447).

Payments for faults, the "web of causality" that Murdoch often, indeed, primarily elaborates upon in all her fiction, is also addressed in major ways by the teaching of Buddhism, for the belief in *karma*—the consequences of actions incurred both in this life and in past lives—emphasizes the individual's responsibility to be aware of his actions.[13] Charles's ignorance of his real connection to people binds him more closely to the wheel, to life wandering on the *sangsara*, and therefore his *karma* seems more problematical than James's. For example, another belief of Buddhism concerns the existence of what are known as the six *lokas* or poisons of the *sangsara*. These are pride, jealousy, sloth, anger, greed, and lust, all of which Charles expresses or suffers from in one way or another.[14]

Perhaps the most important way in which *The Sea, The Sea* relies on the teachings of Buddhism involves the problem of dying. According to Buddhist teaching, man is born and born again into a world of wandering (*sangsara*) through successive existences, until he is enlightened enough to attain his liberation.[15] But only the *yogi* (the saint) is able to break free from the creations of the *maya*-governed mind and see the light that characterizes the Supreme State of the Void, or *nirvana*, and unite with it. As one Buddhist text expresses it, "When thou hast understood the dissolution of all the 'fabrications' thou shalt understand that which is not fabricated."[16]

Especially significant, then, given the Buddhist concept of life-after-death, is that after-death state known as *bardo*. This period lasts for forty-nine days and involves three separate stages. The first *bardo*, or *chikhai*, is the moment of death when the dying person is closest to the "Clear Light." If the individual is wise, and if his life has possessed good *karma,* he may be enabled to free himself at this point from the wheel and achieve liberation. If he fails to do so, however, he enters the next state, the *chönyid bardo*, wherein he receives a sense of having died and of no longer having a body. With this realization comes the new desire to enter a body, which the dead person now seeks in accordance with his "karmic predilection." The third

state, or *sidpa bardo*, involves a transitional time directly preceding rebirth. [17]
I mention this material in detail because *bardo* is referred to in a number of
places in *The Sea, The Sea* and Murdoch appears to be using the *bardo*
stages metaphorically to structure Charles's new, but transitory, illumination
following the illness he undergoes after Hartley has returned to Ben and
James has returned to London. [18] The use of such stages in this portion of the
book helps to explain some of its more puzzling features.

It is important for us to remember at this point that both *The Tempest* and
Buddhism deal to a great extent with retirement and liberation. Retirement
involves, in Buddhist terms, the surrender of attachments (since desire is a
product of ignorance). For Murdoch, the kind of attachments that Charles
has indulged in are obviously obsessive. But to surrender attachments is not
appealing to Charles who, in discussing the subject with James, offers the
usual Western response to the nature of oriental withdrawal: " 'All this
giving up of attachments doesn't sound to me like salvation and freedom, it
sounds like death.' " But James counters his argument with the view of a
Western philosopher: " 'Socrates said we must practise dying' " (p. 445).

This practice of dying, the surrendering of sangsaric attachments, is
described in an evocative way in the following Buddhist text:

> But all those good and holy men,
> What time they see Death's messengers,
> Behave not thoughtless, but give heed
> To what the Noble Doctrine says;
> And in attachment frighted see
> Of birth and death the fertile source,
> And from attachment free themselves,
> Thus birth and death extinguishing.
> Secure and happy ones are they,
> *Released from all this fleeting show*;
> Exempted from all sin and fear,
> All misery have they overcome. [19]

The above passage, with its emphasis on the illusory nature of all earthly
experience and the freedom from various bondages, is not unlike the famous
epilogue of *The Tempest* where Prospero addresses his audience:

> Now my charms are all o'er thrown,
> And what strength I have's mine own,
> Which is most faint. Now 'tis true
> I must be here confined by you,
> Or sent to Naples. Let me not,
> Since I have my dukedom got
> And pardoned the deceiver, dwell
> In this bare island by your spell;

> But release me from my bands
> With the help of your good hands.
> . . . .
>   Now I want
> to enchant;
> And my ending is despair
> Unless I be relieved by prayer,
> Which pierces so that it assaults
> Mercy itself and frees all faults.
> As you from crimes would pardoned be,
> Let your indulgence set me free.
>   (Epilogue, 1–10, 13–20)

Here in these two passages are gathered together all the thematic concerns of Murdoch's book: the illusion of the phenomenal world, the abjuration of magic, the limits of personal power, the forgiveness of sin, the freedom from bondage to the world of illusion, and, not the least important, the problem of the creation of art.

James, like Prospero, desires to be loosed from bands. Anguished by the loss of his Sherpa friend, he, as a practicing and enlightened Buddhist, can help himself acquire good *karma* by helping others, and this, it would seem, has become his occupation as well as a necessary step in learning the art of dying. He has already freed himself from desire and from the kind of attachments by which Charles and his friends have been enslaved. But the surrender of attachments does not mean for James that he is aloof from the others. What it does mean is that he has conquered, to some extent, three manifestations of sangsaric existence: ignorance, desire, and action, and because he is somewhat free, he is better able to help the others.[20]

Lizzie, reunited with Gilbert, is cognizant of some of James's ideas about the nature of love. Her freedom from her obsession over Charles is evident in her urging Charles to give up "mean possessive passions and scheming" (p. 462), in other words, desire and action. Rosina, reunited with Perry, tells Charles with her usual acerbity, " 'I can't imagine why I got so attached to you. I think it was your own illusions of power that fascinated people, not personal magnetism' " (p. 434). Perry, seeing Charles as an " 'exploded myth' " also gets free: " 'Now you're old and done for, you'll wither away like Prospero did when he went back to Milan, you'll get pathetic and senile' " (p. 399). Actually, Perry is not far from the truth; James, also, has urged Charles to end his life as a celibate uncle priest, an idea Charles derides, but one that nonetheless sticks in his mind. Certainly such a role in these last years would be an improvement over his past role and would provide him, in Buddhist terms, with better *karma* in the next existence.

For it has been the main occupation of James to free Charles. This goal has involved, most importantly, his rescue of Charles from a literal as well as metaphorical experience of death, and is perhaps the turning point in the lives of both men. Nevertheless, the mysterious rescue has its tragic aftermath, illustrating again the pervasiveness of causality, for in saving Charles from Minn's Cauldron, into which he has been pushed by Perry, James undergoes such an expenditure of energy that he needs days of physical and mental replenishment, and is still in a weakened state when Titus, caught in a wild sea and drowning, needs him. But James sees to it that Hartley is returned to Ben, and he is also able to convince his cousin of the need to leave the sea behind and return to London. Then, having finished his work, James too returns to London to prepare for his "journey."

Buddhist teachings explain that to experience the Clear Light of the Void, the *yogi* must be aware of "the supreme moment of quitting the body." He must be conscious, able to recognize the Light and thus to become one with it.[21] At this moment all sangsaric bonds of illusion can be broken. In James's words, " 'At the moment of death you are given a total vision of all reality which comes to you in a flash. . . . if you can comprehend and grasp it then you are free . . . out of the Wheel' " (p. 385). This belief helps us to understand exactly what has transpired at James's death, as described to Charles by way of a letter from the Indian doctor who has discovered the body. There is no doubt about the nature of James's achievement, for the doctor writes:

> He was sitting in his chair smiling. . . . Mr. Arrowby died in happiness achieving all. I have written for cause of death on the certificate "heart failure," but it was not so. There are some who can freely choose their moment of death and without violence to the body can by simple will power die. It was so with him. . . . He has gone quietly and by the force of his own thought was consciousness extinguished. . . . he was an enlightened one.
>
> (pp. 472–73)

So James finds release from bonds. But what of Charles? First, he must leave his seacoast world. After the departure of James, however, he suffers a rather severe illness that is like an experience of death. This experience seems to signal a new beginning for him, because when he recovers from it, his view of life is altered. Furthermore, this alteration seems to follow the patterns of awakening described in *The Tibetan Book of the Dead* as the *bardo* experience.

Like the *bardo* stages, Charles's consciousness seems closest to genuine understanding immediately following his illness. At this time he begins to assume some responsibility for his actions toward others. Especially remorseful over the death of Titus, he reflects, "Causality kills. The wheel is just" (p. 453), which is hardly his characteristic way of speaking, much less thinking. In another, rather unusual comment about Titus that also reflects James's influence, he says, "My vanity destroyed him" (p. 459). He sees a different kind of relationship with the boy, a more fatherly one that might have been possible had he not allowed his attention to be diverted by selfishness and ego. For if the sea has been the literal killer of Titus, the "ocean of *sangsara*" has been the real culprit.[22] Now Charles is also able to surrender his hold on Hartley. But his greatest discovery at this time concerns his own role as a drowned man, for he is finally able to confront his experience of descent into Minn's Cauldron, his thrashing about with the serpent, and, more important, the deeper mysteries involved with the actions of James, who, he now recalls, has scaled an impossibly high cliff, walked across the water to him, seized him under his arms, and deposited him on dry land. Pondering James's strange power, he is suddenly "filled with the most piercing pure and tender joy, as if the sky had opened and a stream of white light had descended" (p. 470). Furthermore, he now feels himself at the threshold of a new and better relationship with James. Yet while all of James's knowledge and strange abilities come back to him, James's power no longer threatens him. Charles is also able to glimpse at this moment the problematic nature of magic. He speculates that "white magic is black magic." Perhaps, he thinks, James has also recognized the tragic results of a "less than perfect meddling in the spiritual world," and has decided to abjure magic (p. 471).

At this point in his awakening love for James, Charles receives word of James's death. Now alone, he realizes how strong his attachment to his cousin has been. Thinking of James's death, his "journey," his last trick, Charles, with unusual acumen, wonders if James didn't want to "lay down the burden of a mysticism that had gone wrong, a spirituality which had somehow degenerated into magic" (p. 474). In his last encounter with the sea Charles at last sees the seals mentioned by James early in the story. The seals, sea creatures like the serpent, but benign instead of destructive, are symbols of Charles new consciousness, and he is able to recognize them as "beneficent beings come to visit me and bless me" (p. 476).

So ends Charles's seacoast life and the "real" novel. The final section of the book—the "Postscript"—describes Charles's return to London where, as James's heir, he comes to reside in James's apartment among James's "fetishes" (for Buddhists such objects, images, or reliquaries are used in mediation and symbolize the Buddha's body, speech, and mind).[23] As he now takes up his life again, his special understanding fades away and he enters, at least metaphorically, the second and third stages of *bardo*. He begins to believe James mad. He decides that James is not dead at all but has returned to Tibet on a secret mission. He sees strange "orientals" on the street below and believes them to be agents—although he later discovers they are waiters from an Indian restaurant. Nonetheless, Charles persists in his debunking of James and now observes him to be a " 'sphinx without a secret' " (p. 488), and his own great illumination becomes "a kind of nonsense" (p. 492).

Which of these views are we to accept? Perhaps an answer can be found in James's "demon casket," as Charles calls it. On the final page of the book, the casket falls to the floor and Charles observes, "whatever was inside it has certainly got out. Upon the demon-ridden pilgrimage of human life, what next I wonder?" (p. 502). Here Charles seems to have left his metaphorical *bardo* stage behind and, in terms of James's language, has entered life on the Wheel—that demon-ridden pilgrimage of the *sangsara*.

One final comment on the nature of art and morality. *The Sea, The Sea* is notable in structure for its reflexive features. When Charles goes into retirement, he intends to write some kind of philosophic journal, although his goals are, at this juncture, rather fuzzy. James, upon hearing of Charles's writing efforts, asks if they will be about theater, " 'Anecdotes about actresses,' " giving us an indication of how James views both Charles's life and his attitudes. Charles, however, is offended, and insists that he wants to do "the deep thing, real analysis, real autobiography" (p. 175). James sees the difficulty of such a task for Charles, since Charles is obviously so little aware of himself. But the writing, beginning as diary and memoir, changes into a novel and back into a memoir, as the divisions "Prehistory," "History," and "Postscript" suggest.

In the opening section, called "Prehistory," Charles chronicles events that have occurred literally "before the writing," i.e., before his retirement to the sea. This writing, being rather different from the writing of the second part of the book, is a jumble of diarylike entries. The true novel begins, not surprisingly, after a series of portentous occurrences—the sea serpent, the letter from Lizzie, the "haunting" by Rosina, and the appearance of Hartley, all of which serve to energize both the obsessional tendencies of Charles and his creative abilities as well, in other words, his art. But here we must remember that Murdoch recognizes two kinds of art. The first is "a form of fantasy-consolation," a reflection of the writer's personal obsession.[24] Surely Charles's "novel" is of that kind.

Murdoch is also interested in another kind of art, however, the kind where personal obsession is transcended by the artist's "just and compassionate vision":

> The great artist sees his objects (and this is true whether they be sad, absurd, repulsive or even evil) in a light of justice and mercy. The direction of attention is, contrary to nature, outward, away from the self.[25]

This is the kind of art, according to Murdoch, practiced by Titian, Velasquez, Tolstoy, and, of course, Shakespeare. Murdoch also uses Buddhism, particularly Zen, as another means to get at the higher art. In *The Fire and the Sun* she argues that, while Western art, "separated and grand," has become an authority in itself, Eastern art is more loosely connected with religion and therefore is less likely to impose authority. Eastern art maintains mystery, a "deeper relation to the spiritual." "Zen," she says, "is prepared to use art so long as art does not take itself too seriously." She also notes that Zen is "well aware of the way in which art imagery may provide false resting places."[26]

We may feel uncomfortable with Murdoch's juxtaposition of art and morality, but the two do seem to blend, both in Prospero's epilogue and in the ultimate thematic concerns of *The Sea, The Sea*. In *The Tempest*, for example, it could be argued that Prospero delineates the obsessional side of his creator, Shakespeare. Still, Prospero possesses not only magical powers, but an understanding of the need to surrender them, to practice forgiveness, compassion, and justice, and thereby to redeem the other characters. But we also remember that *The Tempest* is a reflexive play. Prospero himself calls attention to this fact when he addresses the audience and asks to be "relieved by prayer," to be set free from the "show" the audience has just been witnessing. By breaking down the barriers between art and so-called real life—both of which are, in the Buddhist view, illusory—he forces the audience to participate in the show and demands that they respond on moral grounds. Murdoch, Charles, and his "novel" form a slightly different triad because Murdoch has created James, and both characters represent two different types of art. Charles, it should be recalled at this point, has observed the theater to be a place of obsession, and his audiences as victims of trickery, while at the same time he has recognized Shakespeare's ability to turn theater into "something spiritual" (pp. 33–34). It is not surprising, then, to find Charles creating his most provocative art while most under the bondage of his own obsessions. Nevertheless, the reflexive features of the entire work call attention to these obsessional aspects of art as well as to the kind of art where the personal and obsessive are transcended. Murdoch's text, like the epilogue of *The Tempest*, breaks down the barriers between itself and the reader and demands moral involvement. Does that imply that Charles's art is a failure? Perhaps the answer can be found in James's comment on art. " 'If there is art enough,' " he tells Charles, " 'a lie can enlighten us as well as the truth' " (p. 175). Like Shakespeare, Murdoch is able to present her audience with a fantasy while she calls attention to the fact, always keeping before the reader the obsession and the fantasized consolation it produces. What she gives the reader is a lie that enlightens, and when the "show" is over, both the characters and the "audience" have achieved some kind of liberation.

Notes

1. See especially studies by Linda Kuehl, "Iris Murdoch: The Novelist as Magician/The Magician as Artist," *Modern Fiction Studies*, 15, No. 3 (Autumn 1969), 347–60; Zohreh Tawakuli Sullivan, "Enchantment and the Demonic in Iris Murdoch: *The Flight from the Enchanter*," *Midwest Quarterly*, 16, No. 3 (Spring 1975), 276–97, also "The Contracting Universe of Iris Murdoch's Gothic Novels," *Modern Fiction Studies*, 23, No. 4 (Winter 1977–78), 557–69.

2. Kuehl, p. 349.

3. William F. Hall, *"Bruno's Dream*: Technique and Meaning in the Novels of Iris Murdoch," *Modern Fiction Studies*, 15, No. 3 (Autumn 1969), 429.

4. See Robert Hoskins's study, "Iris Murdoch's Midsummer Nightmare," *Twentieth Century Literature*, 18 (July 1972), 191–98, and June Sturrock's "Good and the Gods of *The Black Prince*," *Mosaic*, 10, No. 4 (Summer 1977), 133–41. There is also a book-length study of Murdoch's use of Shakespeare: Richard Todd's *Iris Murdoch: The Shakespearian Interest* (New York: Barnes and Noble, 1979).

5. Hall discusses Murdoch's use of Indian myth in *Bruno's Dream*, focusing especially on the mystical vision of Nigel, which he likens, I think correctly, to the Buddha's "Great Struggle," pp. 436–38.

6. Elizabeth Dipple's study, *Iris Murdoch: Work for the Spirit* (Chicago: Univ. of Chicago Press, 1982), pp. 277–305, the fullest study of Murdoch to date and one of the best, discusses Buddhism in *The Sea, the Sea*, but only as one of the many ways Murdoch employs to treat the problem of power, the presence of demons, and the "dangerous road" to goodness. Dipple tends to view Buddhism as another failed approach to the problem of goodness and sometimes seems uncomfortable with its mystical aspects and their implications. She likens James to other Murdochian converts to Buddhism, and describes such characters as people who are "genuinely spiritual beings" who "finally do not quite make it" (p. 293).

7. *The Sea, the Sea* (New York: Viking, 1978), p. 35. Hereafter cited parenthetically in the text.

8. *The Tempest*, ed. Northrop Frye, Pelican Shakespeare series (Baltimore: Penguin Books, 1970). Subsequent references are to this edition.

9. Murdoch in *The Sovereignty of Good* (New York: Schocken, 1971), p. 67, defines fantasy as "the proliferation of blinding self-centered aims and images . . . a powerful system of energy and most of what is often called 'will' or 'willing' belongs to this system."

10 Dipple, p. 292. She also observes that "This spiritually highly developed man has indeed taken a wrong turning as Charles has so long intuited" (291). In all her commentary, she maintains a kind of ambivalence about James which is, perhaps, what Murdoch intends us to do.

11. Sir John Woodroffe, Forward, *The Tibetan Book of the Dead*, ed. W. Y. Evans-Wentz (London: Oxford Univ. Press, 1960), p. lxxii.

12. *Tibetan Book of the Dead*, p. 1.

13. Alan W. Watts, *The Way of Zen* (New York: Random House, 1957), p. 49, says of *karma* that "man is involved in *karma* when he interferes with the world in such a way that he is compelled to go on interfering, when the solution of a problem creates still more problems. . . . *Karma* is thus the fate of everyone who 'tries to be God.' He lays a trap for the world in which he himself gets caught."

14. Woodroffe, p. lxxiii.

15. Woodroffe, p. lxvii.

16. Alexandra David-Neel, *Buddhism* (New York: Avon, 1979), p. 232.

17. Woodroffe, pp. lxxiv–lxxx.

18. Dipple sees Charles's *bardo* experience as beginning when he retires to the seacoast (p. 301), but I rather think Murdoch is applying the concept of *bardo* more precisely.

19. Evans-Wentz, p. 84, emphasis added.

20. David-Neel, p. 233.

21. Evans-Wentz, p. 89.

22. Evans-Wentz, p. 67.

23. Geshe Lhundup Sopa and Jeffrey Hopkins, *Practice and Theory of Tibetan Buddhism* (New York: Grove, 1976), p. xvi.

24. Murdoch, *The Sovereignty of Good*, p. 64.

25. Murdoch, *The Sovereignty of Good*, pp. 65–66.

26. Murdoch, *The Fire and the Sun* (New York: Oxford Univ. Press, 1978), p. 71.

The Problem of the Past in Iris Murdoch's
Nuns and Soldiers

Margaret Scanlan

In any of the conventional senses, *Nuns and Soldiers* is not a historical novel. The time of the novel is roughly contemporary with the time of its writing; it begins in November, 1977, and ends a year later. While written in the revisionist version of realism that Murdoch always favors, the novel lacks the kind of careful social and political documentation that allowed Michael Holquist to say of nineteenth century novels that "there is a sense in which they are all historical novels" (145). The one public event of 1977–1978 that the novel records is the election of a nameless "Polish pope," the occasion for an outburst of "For he's a jolly good fellow" at a cocktail party. The social context is blurred: characters go on National Assistance, have trouble finding teaching jobs, do volunteer work among native speakers of Urdu, or regard Northern Ireland as a place where being killed by a terrorist bomb is a distinct possibility, but these isolated details are never linked to a historical process that might include, for example, the policies of the Conservative party or Idi Amin.

All the same, the word "history" recurs frequently in *Nuns and Soldiers* as a signal of the book's concern with how people remember, tell, and respond to their own past. One is reminded of Carlyle, whose *Frederic the Great* fascinates the novel's insomniac Pole. For Carlyle the difficulties we experience in telling the truth about our past are deeply connected to the problems of writing public history: "All men are historians . . . our very speech is curiously historical," for we usually "speak only to narrate . . . what we have undergone or seen." In our memory, he continues, we find our own history, "the whole fortunes of one little inward kingdom, and all its policies, foreign and domestic" (56). Murdoch's characters are such historians, each seeking a relationship to a past denied easy continuity with the future. The novel criticizes each character as an interpreter. *Nuns and Soldiers* is deeply pessimistic about the possibility that a true past is ever recorded, told and understood: it is a novel in which what Murdoch has called the "essential elements of trickery and magic" in aesthetic form seem more apparent than its ability, at least where the past is concerned, "to communicate and reveal" (FS, 78).

From *Renascence* 38, no. 3 (Spring 1986): 170–82; © Marquette University Press. Reprinted by permission.

The implications of the past tense in fictional discourse have been discussed. Whether one stresses the notion that the past tense is used ordinarily to convey a sense of presence, or agrees with Hamburger that "it creates no time at all, no past, it obliterates time" (64), we can certainly agree with Roy Pascal's conclusion that "the meanings of the tenses cannot be equated with the temporal functions they have in normal discourse" (11). This insight, when coupled with the Jamesian tradition of telling, not showing, may explain the discomfort we feel when an author seems as determined as Murdoch, in the first hundred or so pages of *Nuns and Soldiers*, to use the past tense to create a past that we experience as just that, a world of previous experience that has already ended. Guy's death and Anne's departure from the convent are deeply connected, "endings," "eternal partings" that must be accepted as such from the beginning (356). Murdoch indulges in long selective expositions of the characters' pasts: Anne's theological crises, the Count's childhood, education, and career; Tim's childhood, and Daisy's, the history of Gertrude and Guy's marriage. The past is thematized in other ways: Anne has a degree in history, a subject that preoccupies the Count, whose reading is limited to historians like Gibbon, Thucydides, and Carlyle and to novelists with a strong sense of the past—Trollope, Tolstoy, Proust. We become aware from the beginning that even minor characters will be defined in terms of their relationship to history. Thus "les cousines et les tantes," Guy's extended family who function as a chorus throughout the book, are introduced in terms of their complicated relationship to Openshaw family history. Ethnically Jewish or half-Jewish, where religion is concerned they are a confusing mixture of pious converts to Roman or Anglo-Catholicism, converts in name only, highly assimilated agnostics, devoutly Orthodox Jews. Their return to Orthodoxy suggests that some Openshaws feel the intractability of Jewish identity, but on the surface they all appear comfortably adapted to British upper middle class life. The historical dangers of being Jewish are articulated only in the Count's vivid nightmare in which he becomes a Polish Jew on his way from the Warsaw Ghetto to Treblinka.

Defined in large measure by their characteristic ways of responding to the past, the Count, Tim, and Gertrude become vehicles for an exploration of the ways in which human beings generally respond to their history. Each of these responses needs careful analysis, but let us begin with the most obviously "historical" figure, Wojciech Szczepanski, the Count. The child of emigrants, he had once wished to evade the implications of history. To some extent his identity is still suppressed, his "dog's breakfast of a name" having long since fallen victim to the Anglo-Saxon disdain for foreign sounds (11). Instead, he is known by more allegorical titles, Tolstoyan and Biblical: "Count" or "Pierre" or "Peter": "I love not Christ but Peter," Anne thinks (304). In both English and Polish, he speaks with a foreign accent; he lives alone in "featureless" rooms (20). The Count's life seems to be conducted almost exclusively in the past tense, its direction ruthlessly determined by historical accidents: his father's failure to die for Poland, his brother's death in the bombing of a London church at Christmas, the crushing of the uprisings first of the Warsaw ghetto and then of the Polish Underground Army. As a child he had been "determined not to be damaged by" such "horrors," but of course he is (9). As a child, too, he had personified history as a force that destroys Poland: "obviously history intended . . . Poland to be subservient to Russia" (9). As an adult the Count has "*interiorized Poland, he was his own* Poland, suffering alone" (13). "Polishness" becomes a "private disaster" (42).

Poland in fact comes to stand for public history in the novel, its generals and politicians and dates enumerated as their counterparts in English history are not—Kosciuszko, 1226, Mickiewicz, the Poznan riots. The English characters are so oblivious to this history that the Count wonders if Poland is invisible (13). Even Guy has no books about Poland, though the Count believes that "every intelligent person must be interested in Poland" (390). For him and for the novel, Poland becomes a "symbol" of "the sufferings of oppressed people everywhere" (39). Closer to home, the Joycean overtones of "nightmare" suggest that Poland is a good deal like Ireland, as the Count finally realizes (451).

In *Nuns and Soldiers*, then, to be ignorant of Poland is to refuse one's affinities with either the victims or the oppressors in the history of small nations. Yet the haunting of the Count by Polish history cannot be seen as ideal. For the Count Polish history is a version of Quentin Compson's South; like Quentin's his body is "an empty hall echoing with sonorous defeated names" (Faulkner, 12). The Count is paralyzed by his tragic sense of Polish history; as unable to die for Poland as his father was, he becomes passive in every human relationship, compulsively reading this myth of Poland back into his personal story: "The image of Gertrude shone in sad Warsaw like the image of Christ in Limbo" (228). Quite appropriately the woman he loves is inaccessible throughout most of the novel; losing her for good only confirms his personal myth: "Maybe it's all to do with being Polish. My country has had nothing but persecution and misery and the destruction of every hope . . ." (445). On the evening that the Cardinal from Crakow becomes Pope—this other Peter the embodiment of a more positive reading of the Polish myth—the Count, reduced in the reader's eyes, settles for mediocre happiness as an adjunct to Gertrude's marriage to Tim.

Obsession with history, as the Count suspected as a child and demonstrated as an adult, is dangerous. The extreme alternative is to be like Tim, who is always "prepared to settle for the contentment of 'the man who has no history' " (77). In a novel in which each of the major characters first appears to be neatly opposed to another, Tim seems to be the counterpart of the defeated Polish exile. His "history . . . is unsatisfactory" (74), the story of a deserted consumptive mother, an anorectic sister and a feckless father, all dead by the time he is fourteen. His Irish father, who might have nurtured an identification with oppression like the Count's, has bequeathed instead an instinct for avoiding a settled adult life. Like the Count he is imaged as one of the novel's soldiers, but instead of seeing himself committed to a "soldier's dullness and circumscribed lot and extremely small chance of glory" (14), he sees "himself sometimes as a soldier of fortune, a raffish foot-loose fellow, a drinker, a wandering cadger, a happy-go-lucky figure in a shabby uniform (not of course an officer) who lived from day to day avoiding unpleasantness . . ." (77). And, of course, Tim, after a brief courtship, wins the woman whom the Count has loved futilely for years.

Most significantly Tim opposes to the Count's steady diet of historical novels, memoirs, and history books an aesthetic sensibility divorced from history. He haunts the British Museum, enraptured by "Greek vases and Etruscan tombs and Roman paintings and Assyrian reliefs," but knows "nothing of their history" (81). This inability to make historical distinctions, this "magpie taste" parallels and perhaps causes Tim's inability to develop a style of his own (81). He has "no identity, no 'personal style' "; he paints "pseudo-Klees, pseudo-Picassos, pseudo-Magrittes, pseudo-Soutines" (80). He goes from purely formal works that resemble elaborate diagrams or networks to sentimentalized pictures of cats that by the novel's end have already appeared on ceramic mugs and may soon appear on matchbooks.

This artist without a history illustrates the sorts of reservations about art that Murdoch analyzes in *The Fire and the Sun*. Tim is a copyist whose copies always remain inferior to the originals; a "destiny as a great faker" evades him only because he lacks patience, talent, knowledge of chemistry (80). Murdoch has analyzed this practical incompetence, which Tim repeatedly illustrates, as one of Plato's fundamental objections to artists—the painter of beds who cannot make a bed (FS, 6). Even more importantly, he is what Plato thought artists were always likely to be, a liar. For Tim wishes to escape notice ("his motto was *Lanthano*") and to think of himself as a child: London's pubs are "innocent places" where he and Daisy are "innocent children" (83). These impulses connect to his lack of respect for history and motivate lies about his past: "He had . . . to rewrite history so as to obliterate Daisy from it. But without Daisy it was a false history . . ." (341).

"That pure clean blessed beginning-again feeling" (154–155) is perhaps Tim's happiest emotion, setting him outside of time, free of consequences and responsibility. A certain kind of art collaborates in this fantasy: "Gertrude would save him, as good women have always saved sinful men in stories. He thought again about . . . the 'new innocence and the fresh start' " (214). Traditionally Christianity also has fostered this notion of being purified of the past, born again as a little child. Tim in fact is "baptized" twice in the novel in near-drownings described in language both religious ("he prayed," 423; "he blessed," 424) and Wordsworthian ("there was a presence in the glade," 417). Yet the encounter with the "Great Face" does not permanently change Tim, who cannot integrate these moments into the history of his life. At the end of the novel he is still hedging to himself about whether he will ever lie to Gertrude, still painting cats.

Whether such secular baptisms are ever efficacious is an idea more seriously explored in the case of Anne Cavidge, nun to Tim's soldier. Having lost faith "in a personal God" (65) and "the anti-religious idea of life after death" (66) she comes back into the world and nearly drowns there. As is the case in Tim's near-drowning, Gertrude is the first person Anne sees after she comes ashore. Anne's life does seem to change after her drowning. A convert, like so many of the Openshaws, she had sought in Catholicism what Tim has always sought in the world, a "quiet conscience": "she would regain her innocence and keep it under lock and key" (56). Always a Protestant's idea of a nun (impossibly unaffected by Vatican II, apparently knowing only the King James version of the Bible), Anne has lived as much outside time as possible for fifteen years. Life in the convent meant wearing medieval garb, marking the hours in patterns prescribed by the order and by the "holy repetition" of the liturgical year (236). Life with Gertrude, on the other hand, means acquiring a few fashionable clothes and falling in love with the Count. When the convent ethic of self-sacrifice meets the world of sexual love, both are distorted. Anne, ceasing to be "God's spy" (303), starts spying on Daisy and on the Count. She lies to Gertrude about Mrs. Mount's letter, withholds from her the information that Tim has gone back to Daisy, then that he has returned to Les Grandes Saules. At the time, she thinks she is behaving selflessly but has no regard for the harm to others that might come from her behavior, as she finally realized; absorbed in defeating her own hopes, she had no "thought to spare for catastrophes which her selfless masochistic morality might be bringing about in Daisy's life" (495).

A new secular beginning proves as impossible for Anne as for Tim; yet, unlike him, she is also involved throughout the novel in an effort to make historical sense of her life. This slower less dramatic change is at the heart of her vision of Christ and allows her at the end to preserve an intention of going into the world to help the poor, to understand her mistakes and to make a serious effort to prevent their recurrence. The Christ Anne sees does not wholly correspond to the myth that had drawn her into the convent; he particularly does not correspond to paintings of him. He criticizes her desire for innocence as "sentimental"; repeatedly he says that salvation, goodness, and miracles depend on her. The scene is full of echoes of Julian of Norwich's *Revelations of Divine Love*, which Murdoch admires for the "evident combination of purity and realism" that it shares with "the Gospels, St. Augustine, and parts of Plato," and that also characterizes "good art" (FS, 83).

Elizabeth Dipple discusses this scene at some length, perceptively analyzing the "ironic connection" between Anne's vision and Julian's. Julian's

Christ "encourages a human resting on his divine power to perform what looks impossible to the human mind"; Anne's Christ teaches that "she alone is responsible . . . for whatever shall be well in the world" (Dipple, 329). The two Christs agree on only one issue, "the size of the universe," but the dissimilarity of the inferences they draw is seen in the differences between the objects they use to illustrate the point. Anne guesses that her Christ is holding a hazelnut because she has read Julian; actually he hands her a small gray stone. Anne's Christ is also, Dipple points out, "wrenched . . . from his traditional indentification with life to an equivalence with death" (326). Like Guy and like Murdoch's *The Sovereignty of Good*, Anne's Christ emphasizes the value of contemplating death: " 'Indeed it is one of my names' " (291).

For our purposes it is most important to note that Anne's ambiguous vision—we are probably meant to take it as real but the psychoanalytical escape hatch is left open—not only "domesticates" (Dipple, 309) Christ but also historicizes him. The vision does not restore Anne's faith in the church's Christ but continues a change that had begun in the convent. When she thinks of the Passion it is "now like something she had read about in the newspapers": "Now there were no angels, no Father, only a man hanging up in an unspeakable bleeding anguish, of which for the first time she was able to grasp the details" (354, 355). The goal of her personal religion is to follow a "nomadic cosmic Christ" who is, nonetheless, conceived historically, "a pathetic deluded disappointed man who had come to an an exceptionally sticky end" (500). The question becomes whether she can "relive his journey and his passion while knowing that he was after all not God" (500). This movement from a conception of time figured in transcendent moments to a conception of the ordinary time of slow historical process is also reflected in a changed evaluation of her relationship with the Count. Anne realizes that she had been wrong to live on "perfect moments," "the pure honey of love": "I was afraid to move on with him into the horrors of history" (496). In this movement of mind, Anne reverses the procedure by which the Count had made Polish history into a tragic personal myth and makes herself an actor rather than a victim.

Anne then chooses a relationship to the past while the Count sees himself historically determined to have no choice. Tim, desiring to live without history, is commited to making himself safe from the past: "He must be able to speak of Daisy as something belonging to the past, and so he had better wait until she *was* past, or rather more past than she was now. But when was this pastness going to begin?" (223). The old question of when it is decent for a widow to remarry becomes such a question in the novel. Gertrude wonders whether she has only "fallen in love with the first man with whom, after Guy's death, she has been really alone? How quickly can the past lose its authority; what *is* its authority?" (195). For Gertrude herself the answer is *"very* quickly." When Guy dies she loses any connection with philosophy, with the systematic examination of moral issues that he always engaged in. "Model," "king," "judge" (1), this patriarch seems to embody what he says he despises, the idea of God the Father (65). His death issues in a time of moral uncertainty in which his widow's major task appears to be making herself happy, as he wanted her to be.

According to conventional wisdom, Gertrude's marriage to a shiftless young man who used to steal from her refrigerator should make her unhappy, but it doesn't. Art, religion, history and philosophy variously mediate the responses of the other major characters, but Gertrude lives entirely for personal relationships. Among the damaged and dying she is a natural survivor, an emblem of the healthy self-seeking ego. She learns the double-think of survival: "There are terrible things which cannot be different, and which the mind stores and deals with in the process of surviving" (466). She does not ask too many questions about why Guy would have disapproved of her love pact with the Count; she does not notice that Ann is in love with him, or see any harm in her desire to have everything, "like a sheepfold with the sheep gathered in" (467).

Through each of its four major characters, then, the novel presents a way of looking, or failing to look, at the past. Forgetting and rewriting are presented as fundamental, perhaps even necessary impulses. Still there is the question of the content of the past, the difficulty of knowing the truth not only about Hannibal or the Soviet Army, but about one's own history. Looking back, characters in the novel are always "reinterpreting" (296), afraid that a present act may violate or "spoil" the past (35). But Murdoch does not allow the reader to remain an innocent spectator; the novel becomes an interpretative trap in which we are continually caught in our own too hasty judgments. At its simplest the technique consists of deferring vital information, forcing us to re-interpret what we have read. We must reach the end of the novel to discover that Anne had taken charge of Sylvia Wicks during a period when we had thought she was given over exclusively to mystical visions, migraines, and the activities of unrequited love. Manfred has really been as much in love with Anne as she had been with the Count; Guy, on his deathbed, had spoken Yiddish.

Of course from one perspective such revelations are simply unfair, though they may be justified as a reminder of the limits of our knowledge of any fictional character, whom we will not permit to have a life between the pages. But Murdoch's traps are more sophisticated; if we look back we can see that what Murdoch has called "the instinctive completing activity of the client's mind" has been at work in us (FS, 85). Like Stanley Fish's students, who can turn a list of famous linguists into a seventeenth century poem, we have required only the smallest scraps of information to build an interpretive whole to defend against further information. Many readers, for example, will rush to judge Guy's significance in the novel. The family's instinctive reverence for him, his patriarchal role, the words "king" and "royal," even his name, encourage the equation, Guy = God. And, as we have already said, this interpretation has some validity and usefulness. Nonetheless, toward the end of the novel Murdoch shakes that interpretation by introducing a secondary meaning: the Count thinks of Tim as "a sort of guy or faked-up devil" (449). Of course Guy is much too charitable and scrupulous to turn into Satan, but we are forced to consider evidence that his views were not always as infallible as his wife and friends had wanted them to be. We perhaps recall that he had told Tim that "it did not matter, having no identity" (80), or that he had "often" said to Gertrude "that time was unreal," a line she finds consoling when she contemplates re-marriage (279). Tim and Gertrude's behavior suggests the limits, event the dangers, of such views; when they are acted on, they encourage a denial of consequences. The final revelation that Guy had spoken Yiddish on his deathbed is deeply moving, not only because it suggests previously unknown dimension of this outwardly assimilated Jew, but because it suggests a return to a historically grounded identity that his family is still denying or at least deferring. "I shall be there myself tomorrow," says Veronica Mount. "Chattering Yiddish in Abraham's bosom" (492).

One of the novel's traps is imbedded in the binary opposition its title suggests. *Nuns and Soldiers* is a nineteenth century title, a presumably deliberate echo of *The Red and the Black* or *War and Peace*. Obviously, Anne is a nun and the Count always thinks of himself as a soldier; almost immediately, however, we mush acknowledge that Tim and Daisy "soldier on" (73). Gertrude says a "widow is a kind of nun" (103); she has worn "her mourning like a nun's veil" (305); the Shakespearean allusions remind us of how Hamlet used that word. Then, too, the Count's life, with its poverty and isolation, is more monkish than military; Daisy and Tim's favorite pub has an "ecclesiastical atmosphere" and "little cubicles, like confessionals" (71). Daisy fears being "reduced to drinking the left-overs in the pubs, like bloody Frog Catholics living on the Eucharist" (88).

The opposition of nun and soldier—peace vs. war, contemplation vs. actions—begin to seem less important than the similarities that both take vows/oaths, wear uniforms/habits, submit to discipline/order, set themselves apart from civilian/worldly life. As the reader proceeds the apparent interpretive convenience of the terms dissolves; the classification scheme they suggest breaks down. The difference between the words seems to be of the sort that Barbara Johnson has called "critical difference." According to her,

> Difference . . . is not what distinguishes one identity from another. It is not a difference between (or at least not between independent units), but a difference within. Far from constituting the text's unique identity, it is that which subverts the very idea of indentity, infinitely deferring the possibility of adding

up the sum of a text's parts or meanings and reaching a totalized, integrated whole.

(4)

What is at issue is not a nihilistic denial of any distinctive meaning whatsoever but a sense of the deep connection between the concepts of nun and soldier. Meaning seems to reside in the impossibility of effecting a perfect separation between the words, for the most contemplative life can have consequences in the actions of other people. Anne seems to speak for the author when she tells the Count that his isolation does not make suicide acceptable: no one "can tell where his life ends"; there is an "infinite responsibility" that arises from our deep and largely unconscious connection to other people (446).

The novel continually proposes such facile oppositions: the Day Nurse vs. the Night Nurse, Guy ("the man who has everything") vs. Tim ("the man who has nothing" 307), God vs. Mammon, Mary vs. Martha, Christ vs. Peter, liars vs. truthtellers, the selfish vs. the selfless. The opposed terms remain meaningful, but are not the shorthand for avoiding thought that we may at first think they are. Anne, for example, is deeply connected to Daisy and Tim by her search for innocence, to the Count by the dream vision of a garden with a great copper beech, to Tim by baptism, to Manfred by the capacity for unrequited love. She is no one's opposite number, requires constant attention and remains morally a little enigmatic even at the end.

Expectations that the reader brings to the novel as a form can be another kind of trap. Dipple correctly points out that "Nuns and Soldiers is in relatively small measure about the subject of its greatest area of expansion," the Gertrude-Tim plot. "This bourgeois surface" does indeed "skirt the domain" of what Dipple unhappily calls "women's fiction" (307). "The reader's impatience with the pair," says Dipple, ". . . is part of the strategy of the novel, which offers their marriage," ironically, to "satisfy the conventional hunger of readers for traditional material" (312). Murdoch's ironic intentions seem clear enough; the reader's desire for a happy ending, satisfied in the case of the mediocre characters but denied the more admirable ones, points to the insufficiency of his or her own reflexes about happiness, domesticity, what Dipple refers to several times as "at-homeness in the world." Much as this view fits into my own sense of Murdoch's strategies, I would add that Murdoch has not avoided all of the dangers of provoking the reader's impatience, that the longueurs of the love story must inevitably strike many readers as crying aloud for editing.

More successful are the illusions. Murdoch's belief in the ethical value of great literature is complicated, as we have already said, by her sensitivity to the seductions of form and the capacity of art to gratify the desire for a simplified view of the world. Allusions can supply such a convenient pattern for the reader, who is thereby trapped into substituting a literary past for the present. We observe how the Jamesian formula, "we shall never be as we were" (367) seems to suggest that the characters are willing to believe the story that Tim and Daisy had plotted to live on the proceeds of a rich marriage because they unconsciously tie that "plot" to *The Wings of the Dove*. Similarly, if Murdoch names a character Manfred and tells us that he is handsome and writes an "affected Italianate script" we are likely to use these scraps to build a character for him that excludes the charity and restraint that are finally revealed in his behavior.

The most obvious of the novel's allusions are to *Hamlet*, as we could see even from the plot synopsis: an attractive widow named Gertrude marries hastily an indecisive younger man who spends his spare time at a pub called The Prince of Denmark. He calls her his "queen" (230), behaves with her like "a hereditary price in a peaceful happy feudal state" (256), and worries as little as possible about the feeling that her dead husband was "like a father to me" (478). The tragedy we may expect the allusion to supply never occurs. Murdoch takes the latent Freudian content of the tragedy, which a twentieth century reader cannot help seeing, and plays it out. Let Hamlet marry his mother; they will not do so badly, after all. In a world of uninhibited gratification, there is no tragedy, only a mediocre settling for a nursery atmosphere of games and orality, "incompetent chess" and "another bottle of Beaujolais" (473, 474).

The end of the novel refuses its implied reader's desire for order, pattern, certainty. We are back with Anne, the character who seems, after Guy, the only one to choose her actions in ethical terms, and find that even she is flirting with the idea of giving up on goodness as "too hard to seek and too hard to understand" (504). Even as Anne looks forward to her future in America, the text's literary allusions draw the reader back into the past. In the last scene, the silence, the falling snow, the "hissing" of the street lamps, the color brown, the subdued puns (Anne thinks of the heavens as "countless"), all take the reader back into that model of literary ambiguity, the final epiphany of *Dubliners*. Joyce's journey westward associates itself with death, but for Gabriel Conroy "the west" is also rich with the history of his own people, which he had long ignored. Anne's westward journey ("tomorrow she would be in America") is a shade darker, heavy with the irony of another new beginning at the end of the novel that begins with death and connects new beginnings to moments of illusion. In the "hypnotic silence" the scene reminds her of a "picture or a dream," looks *like* the heavens spread out in glory, proclaiming the presence and goodness of its Creator" (504; emphasis added). Anne is left "*feeling* lightened of her burdens" (505; emphasis added). The verbs reinforce the sense that she looks to a world of appearances and wishful thinking, or automatic consoling responses conditioned by art.

Readers of *Nuns and Soldiers*, then, must to some extent share with the characters the problem of understanding the past, if only as it is figured in their reading of earlier sections of the novel; they must particularly acknowledge the inadequacy of a response based on the finding of forms and the completing of patterns. All too successfully, Murdoch frustrates the reader's desire for a character who will serve as a model, for the illusion of having once and for all understood (gained mastery over) a character, but especially for the consolation of form. In a negative way, the novel seems to offer conclusions—that the human task is to examine one's past and to live faithfully within it without becoming its victim. Change is painfully slow and transcendent moments are illusory unless slowly contemplated and understood. A philosophy, aesthetics, or theology that presents the possibility of transcending this sort of historical process is not conducive to good behaviour, a point Murdoch makes in *The Sovereignty of Good*, where she connects the concept of "individual history" to moral perfectability (26). The question that remains is whether the novel allows for the possibility of communicating more than the problem, as Murdoch characteristically argues that art ought to: "The great artist, while showing us what is not saved, implicitly shows us what salvation means" (FS, 80). This novel, exemplifying a relationship between the telling of stories about the past and lying, seems to insist on the intractability of the barriers between human beings. Anne's quiet charities commend a persistent obscure goodness in her to our attention, but the last two images of her—drinking alone in a bar while overhearing a lying story about her past, walking along in the snow—seem more than accidentally linked to this goodness. It is easy to see why Dipple argues that the "main point" of the novel "is that although the characters of the good . . . may yearn for a place in the comfortable middle space of the world, their essential state is one of alienation and separation" (322). "The Son of Man hath not where to lay his head" (NS, 105).

The novel's fragmentary and negative association of public and private histories hedges this vision of alienated goodness. Murdoch goes to some length to show the intersection of Polish history with the Count's life and to suggest how unsatisfactory the lot of the assimilated British Jew is. A reasonably attentive view of one's link to the history of a people that yet preserves a sense of a separate personal identity is suggested as psychologically and morally desirable. Yet a similar sense that her characters might benefit from closer attention to the public history of the time and place in which they are living is altogether missing. And this absence at the heart of a novel filled with so many references to "history" is perhaps the novel's most chilling statement about the possibilities of constructing, telling, and responding to a truthful version of the past. Enmeshed in the permanent crisis of a largely uncommunicable personal past, they "do not even know they do not know" a shared world of public history. Perhaps in a world where an unspecified "cosmic disaster" (309) seems scientifically credible—the novel's famous astrophysicist has seriously considered suicide—public history is simply either too remote or too difficult for most people to face. Abetting the characters' ignorance, the narrator suggests that we must fear not only our tendencies to apply to public history the whole deceptive apparatus we erect for our own lives, but our desire to avoid looking altogether.

Works Cited

Carlyle, Thomas. "On History," in *A Carlyle Reader*. Ed. G. B. Tennyson. New York; Random, 1969.

Dipple, Elizabeth. *Iris Murdoch: Work for the Spirit*. London: Methuen, 1982.

Faulkner, William. *Absalom, Absalom!* New York: Random, 1936.

Hamburger, Kate. *The Logic of Literature*. Trans. Marilynn J. Rose. 2nd ed. Bloomington: Indiana, 1973.

Holquist, Michael. "Whodunit and Other Questions: Metaphysical Detective Stories in Post-War Fiction." *New Literary History* 3 (Autumn 1971): p. 145.

Johnson, Barbara. *The Critical Difference: Essays in the Contemporary Rhetoric of Reading*. Baltimore: Johns Hopkins, 1980.

Murdoch, Iris. *The Fire and the Sun: Why Plato Banished the Poets*. London: Oxford, 1977. Referred to as FS.

Murdoch, Iris. *Nuns and Soldiers*. New York: Viking, 1980. All references to this text.

Murdoch, Iris. *The Sovereignty of Good*. London: Routledge and Kegan Paul, 1970.

Pascal, Roy. "Tense and Novel." *Modern Language Review* 57 (1962).

New Directions: Iris Murdoch's
Latest Women

CHERYL BOVE

Iris Murdoch's greatest contribution to the novel lies in the area of characterization. Her aesthetic and philosophical writings propose the creation of
characters who are free from the prejudices of their authors, and she strives
to create unique individuals who "seem realistic and valid," and who are not
"mere extensions of her own emotional and philosophical bias."[1] While some
critics praise Murdoch's characterization, she has also been criticized for
developing a male point of view in her novels, particularly through first-
person male narrators, and she consistently refuses to "write as a woman,"
saying, instead, that she wants to present "the human case."[2] This paper
would argue, however, that several interrelated factors account for the pre-
dominance of male voices in her novels and for her problematic portrayal of
women: first, Murdoch's aesthetics, mainly her ideas about the novel and
characterization, preclude her consciously writing "as a woman"; second, she
writes in the realist tradition, portraying human beings as they are, and does
not believe that the novel is the proper place for social commentary; third,
she does not recognize gender distinctions and insists that people are "at a
higher level" androgynous.[3] Nevertheless, her characterizations of women
and her reliance on the male voice are in themselves a comment on the social
position of women, a condition about which she has frequently expressed
concern. Feminist writers such as Deborah Johnson have thus noted that
Murdoch touches on vital feminist issues in her writing, both through what
she says and what she does not say. However, Murdoch's most recent novels,
The Book and the Brotherhood (1987) and *The Message to the Planet* (1989),
reveal subtle changes in her perspective and offer representations of women
which are more extensive and varied, in part because these later works are
narrated to a greater extent through the consciousness of women characters.

Murdoch's desire to "create characters who are like real people" (Chevalier, 74), entails a conscious effort on her part to do what she argues that all
good artists must do, namely, remove themselves from the characters and
avoid becoming entangled in political or emotional biases that might produce

A shorter version of this paper was given at the Modern Language Association Annual Convention,
Chicago, December 1990. This longer version was commissioned especially for this collection.

188

characters who appear to speak for their authors. For example, while admitting an admiration for George Eliot, Murdoch also views Eliot as "driven to develop an intellectual vision through reaction to her situation as a woman."[4] Such an emphasis, Murdoch feels, limits the artist and narrows the artist's vision. She particularly wants to avoid having her own emotional concerns govern her works and expresses the hope that they do not present her own personal fantasy about the world. Murdoch has commented extensively, both in her philosophy and in interviews, on the artist's difficult duty to adhere to truth. "Great art," she has said, "is connected with courage and truthfulness. There is a conception of truth, a lack of illusion, an ability to overcome selfish obsessions, which goes with good art, and the artist has got to have that particular sort of moral stamina."[5]

Consequently, she tries to avoid politics in her novels: "I think it's a novelist's job to be a good artist, and this will involve telling the truth, and not worrying about social commitment. I think social commitment, in so far as it interferes with art, is very often a mistake. It can make the novelist nervous and anxious and not able to open himself to the whole of reality as he understands it."[6]

Nevertheless, although she does not believe that the primary concerns of the novelist should involve social commentary, Murdoch also admits that her novels contain "a lot of social criticism."[7] She recently made a similar point to Jeffrey Meyers: "A novelist is bound to express values, and I think he should be conscious of the fact that he is, in a sense, a compulsory moralist" (219). Thus Murdoch intentionally makes a social statement in her portrayal of Axel and Simon, a homosexual couple in *A Fairly Honorable Defeat*, a portrayal of which she is particularly fond. Because she has known many happy homosexual couples, her rendering of Simon and Axel is sympathetic (Chevalier, 76).

More problematic is Murdoch's attitude about the "masculine" or "feminine" mind. When Veronica Groocock reminded her that she had been praised for having a "masculine mind" when *The Bell* was published in 1958, Murdoch indicated a distaste for this kind of discrimination. The idea of a feminine consciousness is equally unacceptable. To Sheila Makay she offered the following comment:

> Women will be liberated not when they perceive themselves as "us great women who are superior to men, who have intuitions which men don't possess, who will read only books written by women." That's going back to the ghetto. Human beings are very much the same for the purposes of how intelligent they are, whether they're male or female, and to see them as otherwise is very bad for human beings and very bad for literature.[8]

For Murdoch the primary social hindrance for women involves education: "The problem for women is the way they think about themselves. Education is fundamental to their socially conditioned behavior of inferiority. The wretched girls are demoralized at each age by fobbing off with soft subjects: unless there is a positive move for women's education, there is no hope" (Hale, 180). Nevertheless, she disdains a separatist outlook for women, primarily because "women who think of themselves as something separate are forming a kind of inferiority movement, like women's clubs" (Hale, 180). Such separatism "fosters a dangerous double standard. . . . One wants to be part of the general stream of education, culture, thought and art" (Groocock, 817). And she concludes, "the point is to join the human race, the general scene that men have kept to themselves."[9]

One method by which Murdoch presents her beliefs about gender in her novels is through her representations of androgyny. The numerous androgynous characters that inhabit her works can be explained as a result of her belief that on a spiritual level gender differences cease to exist. For example, at Caen she remarked, "I so much want to say that there isn't any difference between us! But at a higher level—a more spiritual level—I think the difference vanishes" (Chevalier, 83). Whatever difference there may be, it has little place in serious fiction, and she has told Hale that she "dissents from the thesis that gender, whether of author or of imagined audience, is of the slightest importance" in this area (180). Thus her androgynous characters reflect her belief that "most people are androgynous: there is certainly no difference in terms of mental make up. There are fewer women in public life, men are better educated; but there are not different kinds of mind" (Hale, 180).

Indeed, the names and behavior of several Murdoch characters can be taken as either masculine or feminine. Lindsay Rimer, for example, has a dual role in *An Unofficial Rose*: as the Peter Pan figure who acts both as secretary-companion-love interest for Emma Sands, and as lover for Randall Peronett. In *The Black Prince* Bradley Pearson, who is probably homosexual, consummates an affair with sprite-like Julian Baffin-Belling only after she dresses up as Hamlet. Elizabeth Fisher in *The Time of the Angels* has the "appearance of a favorite page."[10] She also smokes cigars and wears shirts, trousers, and the "male version" of a surgical corset (*TA*, 47). In *The Message to the Planet* Irena Vallar's sex and age confound Alfred Ludens. When he stumbles upon her during the night, he takes her for a child of ten or twelve, "more probably a boy."[11] Later he describes her as "the mysterious boy" (*MP*, 84). But when he sees her in daylight, he mistakes her for an old charwoman (*MP*, 83). Finally, Emmanual (Emma) Scarlett-Taylor, the Irish counter-tenor in *The Philosopher's Pupil*, displays transvestite tendencies and has bisexual emotional attachments and attractions.

During a 1982 interview, Iris Murdoch related another example of androgyny: [I]t just occurs to me . . . there is a character who appears at intervals [in a novel I have just completed] and it is never clear what sex was the character. I can reasonably reply I don't know, in fact I have an idea what sex this character is, but it doesn't matter. As far as the novel is concerned the character is of indeterminate sex."[12] As this unnamed character is a minor figure, Murdoch felt she could creditably present "the human case," rather than the "male case" or the "female case." But perhaps more revealing about the human tendency to classify and define is the possibility that few of Murdoch's readers noticed that the character was of "indeterminate sex" because they had already made their own decisions about its gender.

Since Murdoch does not recognize distinctions between the genders and wants to "write about things on the whole where it doesn't matter whether you're male or female" (Chevalier, 82), many critics have questioned her frequent use of a male narrator. Murdoch herself responds that she "describe[s] the world, and we live in a male world."[13] Since she wants to write about the human condition, she must do so as a male. "You'd better be male," she says, "because a male represents ordinary human beings, unfortunately, as things stand at the moment, whereas a woman is always a woman!" (Chevalier, 82). Her response is, she says, a comment on the social position of women. "Unfortunately it's still a man's world. A man doesn't have to explain what it's like to be a man but a woman has to explain what it is like to be a woman. . . . If you portray an intellectual woman, part of her role in the book is to be an intellectual woman, but an intellectual man can just be a man."[14]

Perhaps even more unsettling is Murdoch's frequent statement that she identifies more with men than with women,[15] that she has "no problem in imagining the man's outlook on the world,"[16] and that writing as a man is "instinctive" (Chevalier, 82). It would seem that Murdoch's intelligence, literary stature, and Oxford associations have given her acceptance in a male-dominated world, but while she insists that "at a higher level" there are no gender distinctions, many critics find her acceptance of a male role for herself disturbing.

The truth is that while Murdoch may feel fortunate in her own acceptance in the male world, the women that people her novels usually enjoy a far different status.[17] As Johnson has shown, they are most usually victims.[18] Barbara Stevens Heusel, noting that none of Murdoch's women characters appeared to have her own strength, but were, in the main, more like Harriet Gavender in *The Sacred and Profane Love Machine*, often "just a piece of ectoplasm," was told by Murdoch, "Yes, often that is an aspect of—not being good, because nobody is totally good—but being . . . like teachers who lack identity. They're not self-assertive: I think that a lot of such people who are goodish may seem like that. Incidentally, it isn't a remark made by me, but by one of the characters. It's a very unjust description of someone who is not self-assertive" (Heusel, 12).

Because for Murdoch selflessness is an important criterion for goodness, Murdoch has acknowledged the difficulty in creating a good character who also exhibits strength. Instead, male characters who do approach goodness, such as Bledyard (*The Sandcastle*), Brendan Craddock (*Henry and Cato*), and Tallis Browne (*A Fairly Honorable Defeat*), usually have minor roles in the novels or appear vacuous and are unable to act assertively. Indeed, such men can be seen as having the so-called "female virtues of humility and interest in others."[19] Women who display qualities associated with the good, such as Ann Peronett (*An Unofficial Rose*), Anne Cavidge (*Nuns and Soldiers*), Harriet Gavender (*The Sacred and Profane Love Machine*), and Franca Sheerwater (*The Message to the Planet*), also lack forceful wills and their behavior is therefore frustrating to the reader who has been conditioned to identify with strong characters.

In sum, good and gentle people who exhibit humility, selflessness, awareness of others, and correct vision and action are not very interesting characters when placed against the confirmed egoists who prominently hold forth in Murdoch's novels. Also, because "selfishness is absolutely ingrained in human beings . . . very often the people who do climb out [of egoism] are people who appear very simple or dull to the outsider" (Chevalier, 90). They are also difficult to represent in fiction. As Murdoch has said, "writing about good people is difficult for novelists, because they may often be nearly invisible, not needing to make great waves of self-assertion."[20]

The situation is complicated by the fact that those characters who lack egoism and self-assertiveness, who often appear as victims, are not necessarily good either. Murdoch's novels also contain a number of characters who want to be manipulated by others. Indeed, Murdoch claims that this subject is of great interest to her, and goes on to say, "people are not only manipulated by others but want to be so. . . . People very often elect a god in their lives, they elect somebody whose puppet they want to be, and . . . almost subconsciously, are ready to receive suggestions from this person" (Chevalier, 76). Such behavior becomes a way of avoiding truth, of living safely and without responsibility. Forcing others to take up positions of power removes responsibility for actions and continues the illusions that one finds comfortable.

Thus, Murdoch's interest in the balance of power between individuals comes to involve issues relating to gender, and she often depicts women in social situations that deny them equality. For example, the courtly lovers who frequent her novels behave toward women in ways that belie their own power. In *The Unicorn* Hannah Crean Smith becomes the love object of several courtly figures including Effingham Cooper, Jamesie Evercreech, Denis Nolan and Pip Lejour. And in Murdoch's latest novel, *The Message to the Planet*, both Alfred Ludens and Jack Sheerwater fall at Franca Sheerwater's feet, inviting Franca to do what she will with them. Equality in marriage is also a rarity, and there are a number of husbands like Martin Lynch-Gibbon in *A Severed Head*, who claims "in almost every marriage there is a selfish and an unselfish partner. . . . In my own marriage I early established myself as the one who took rather than gave."[21] Often male characters are attracted to or linked with women whom they can control because of age or social difference. Johnson has noted such relationships as that of Hilary Burde and the Indian servant Biscuit, and Martin Lynch-Gibbon with his older wife, Antonia, and his younger mistress, Georgie (8–9).

However, in recent novels Murdoch appears to have altered her narrative strategies, correcting what Johnson has pointed out as the problem with first-person male narrators and their tendency to decenter the female point of view (8). Recognizing that the problem with first-person male narrators is also related to strong plot lines, Murdoch has said:

> The danger with a very strong plot and a few very strong characters is that other characters, perhaps haven't got any space in which to develop themselves. I think there's more detail in general in the later novels. They are longer novels, and there's more opportunity for descriptions of all kinds, and I think they're more realistic. The characters are better, and I think this is the main thing, to be able to invent characters who have a life of their own, who seem to exist.[22]

Thus while the earlier novels primarily represent the woman's voice by undercutting the reliability of the narrator, the later novels, although they continue to have obsessive male characters, also move closer to what Murdoch describes as her ideal novel:

> My ideal novel—I mean, the novel which I would like to write and haven't yet written—would not be written in first person, because I'd rather write a novel which is scattered, with many different centres. I've often thought that the best way to write a novel would be to invent the story, and then to remove the hero and heroine and write about the peripheral people—because one wants to extend one's sympathy and divide one's interests (Chevalier, 81).

One important result of this decentering strategy is that it allows for more narration through the consciousness of her women characters. An examination of the women in Murdoch's two latest novels, *The Book and the Brotherhood* and *The Message to the Planet*, will demonstrate the effectiveness of this new strategy in more fully representing the female voice.

In *The Book and the Brotherhood*, Rose Courtland, a central character, is another representation of the female as victim. Although she is intelligent and educated, having "studied English literature and French at Edinburgh,"[23] she wastes any creative talents she might have waiting for a relationship with Gerard Hernshaw to develop, a wait that has lasted for thirty years: "her life always seemed so provisional, a waiting life, not settled like other people's" (*BB*, 227). When Gerard eventually tells her that he needs a research assistant and wants them to live together, Rose, subordinating her own talents, once again agrees. Even though she also requests "some sort of security" for herself

(*BB*, 573), it comes to rest, Gerard tells her, first on her place in his life as Sinclair's sister, and last on her role as his love.

Yet in many ways Rose seems to understand problems of power and gender. Her observations about the relationship of her friend Jean Kowitz Cambus and David Crimmond accurately reflect such an understanding of the misuse of male power: "You are living inside an illusion. It's all so one-sided, so unfair. . . . As far as I can see, you have no relationship now except with him, a sexual relation which is part of his life and all of yours!" (*BB*, 309). And she is aware of her own position, telling Gerard, "You've always taken me for granted, and I'll always be there to be kind and useful" (*BB*, 556). But Rose does not act on her own vision; instead, she resigns herself to Gerard's direction. While her decision could be interpreted as an act of love, a sublimation of self, it reinforces the view readers have of women as submissive.

Another woman character in the novel, Tamar Hernshaw, is a good example of the woman who responds to unfair treatment with her own problematic exercise of power. As an illegitimate child whose mother has never hidden her regret at not having an abortion, Tamar has never felt wanted. Forced to leave Oxford to go to work to support herself and her mother who is incapable of holding a job, she, ironically, does have an abortion after becoming pregnant during a brief encounter with Duncan Cambus. The abortion leaves Tamar a maimed creature, crippled by guilt and self-hate, who proclaims "nobody *can* love me. It's impossible. I'm a person *outside* love and I have always been" (*BB*, 370).

Thus in the early stages of the novel, Murdoch's character appears as yet another victim of women's social situation. Nevertheless, following a strange religious conversion, Tamar is transformed and even becomes powerful. Sleek-looking and recovered (*BB*, 489), she is also described as cold and ruthless when she dismisses her mother, "endowed with an extraordinary authority" and "ready to trample on anyone," (*BB*, 515, 516). Father McAlister fears she has used him, and worries, "Have I liberated her not into Christ, but into selfish uncaring power?" (*BB*, 516). In fact, Tamar's acquisition of power does remove her from the good, even as it denies her clarity of vision, and she is left to wonder, "could she see more clearly now or less clearly?" (*BB*, 548). Murdoch, in her creation of Tamar, has offered her readers another victim who, struggling to be free, acquires power that then interferes with the ability to love.

In *The Message to the Planet* Murdoch creates another character similar to that of Tamar. Irina Vallar is an uneducated but strong-willed young girl who nonetheless appears to be a helpless and sequestered virgin, and is pursued by a number of courtly lovers. Irina, much like Tamar, becomes something of a power figure, but because she is a more complex character, her acquisition of power does not automatically render her separated from good, nor does it mean her vision is thereby clouded. Unlike Tamar, Irina remains perceptive. For example, she realizes that Alfred Ludens (one of the courtly lovers of the novel) is more attached to her father than he is to her, and manipulates him into helping her take her father to a sanitarium. She also skillfully avoids a sexual liaison with Ludens and manages a disappearance and reunion with a former lover. And despite her responsibilities for her father, Irina moves consistently from positions that disadvantage her to those that give her what she wants. Murdoch's strategy of withholding from the reader information about Irina's past relationships and the mental state of her father makes for the creation of a character that is more rounded than, for example, Hannah Cream Smith (*The Unicorn*), another sequestered figure who is also driven to the exercise of power.

Perhaps Murdoch's most interesting minor character in *The Message to the Planet* is (as Murdoch has admitted) the Jamesian character Maisie Tether.[24] Her uniqueness may be explained in part by her resemblance to her creator, at least in terms of her background. Like her author, Maisie too is an only child ("I did well having the individual attention of those two superior beings," she says [*MP*, 267]); she also has been educated in girls' schools and trained in the classics.[25] Maisie also shares Murdoch's affinity for Japanese culture. She is also remarkably vocal—"brisk, tart, downright Bostonian" (Russell, C20). Her forthright disgust over Franca Sheerwater's acceptance of a ménage à trois is evident in her words to Franca: "You are degrading yourself and you are degrading womankind" (*MP*, 250). Maisie also despises "female masochism" (*MP*, 268). Seeing herself as a "natural therapist" (*MP* 322), she also tells Franca that "the best way to rid yourself of a bad useless craving is to open your heart to other people, find new people to love" (*MP*, 322). Unusually developed for a minor character, Maisie is also Murdoch's most assertive spokeswoman for the good. Yet Maisie avoids egoism and remains interesting despite her goodness, thus escaping the fate of so many of Murdoch's good characters who become uninteresting to the reader.

More important is the fact that *The Message to the Planet* is narrated extensively through Franca Sheerwater, a character who is also the most fully developed of the novel's women. Involved in a triangle with her husband, Jack, and his mistress, Franca's situation initially parallels that of Harriet Gavender in *The Sacred and Profane Love Machine* or Rachel Baffin in *The Black Prince*, both of whom are married to men who attempt to maintain ménages with the support of the victimized wives. Franca seems particularly doomed to the role of object. When Jack tells her that as an object her role is "to restore silence," she seems to comply without resistance, willing to be "for him, beneficiently, life giving, a thing" (*MP*, 27).

Franca is also a kind of mother figure, not only to Jack but to the gravely ill Patrick and is considered selfless and good by her fellow characters. She might even be said to have saintly traits. Yet Franca's helplessness masks a struggle for survival that eventually leads her to experience feelings of rage and hatred, "even . . . fierce cruel fantasies" (*MP*, 141). Finally, these always hidden feelings become her "great deception," and a source of power to her, a "cruel triumphant power by which she [holds] her husband trapped and blinded" (*MP*, 180), even as she contemplates his murder. However, as she cherishe[s], nourishe[s] and develop[s] her suffering (*MP*, 141) she also succumbs to what in Murdoch's view are the consolations of egoism. Instead of freedom, her "wicked vicious ill-intentioned lying to Jack" (*MP*, 153) causes her own entrapment: "As she entrapped him she was entrapping herself" (*MP*, 153).

Unlike Rachel Baffin, who murders her husband, or Harriet Gavender, who flees under the burdens of the ménage à trois, Franca finds her freedom, paradoxically, not in leaving Jack but in returning to him. This she does with full knowledge of her position. She tells Alfred Ludens, who has encouraged her to get away from Jack and to thereby find "freedom and happiness," that he does not know "what love is like. The things you mention are *shadows, fantasies*, they are *nothing*. Jack is reality, to consider leaving him, to plan to leave him, was to tear myself out of myself" (*MP*, 528). In so doing, however, Franca gains her freedom. Her intense suffering has been accompanied by a purification, a defeat of the self that, in Murdoch's view, brings freedom and moves the individual closer to the good.

In many ways the conclusion of *The Message to the Planet* is unsettling. Many readers may feel that justice would be better served if Franca were to leave Jack and begin a new life. Yet Murdoch deliberately undercuts the fantasies of those readers who expect some degree of happiness for Franca. Such an ending would be a consolation and thus an illusion. Instead Murdoch's careful focus on Franca's struggles with the good suggests her more highly developed state of spirituality.

As an artist, Murdoch feels a serious obligation to present the truth, to avoid offering consolation. Neither Murdoch's novels nor her moral philosophy present an optimistic view of human life or its relationships; however, the good artist can help us contemplate the whole of the real world, Murdoch has said, "including what is terrible and absurd."[26] As with all human endeavors, the relationship between the sexes has its basis in power, not love. Murdoch creates characters who find it nearly impossible to interact without the protective masks of lies or of unequal social distinctions; those who do conform to Murdoch's moral philosophy and return abuse with love shift the balance of power even further against themselves. Yet Murdoch would have her readers and her characters resist the formulation of optimistic fantasies: "The message is, everything is contingent. There are no deep foundations. Our life rests on chaos and rubble, all we can try to do is to be good."[27]

Notes

1. Ruth Heyd, "An Interview with Iris Murdoch," *University of Windsor Review* (Spring 1965): 140.

2. Rein Zondergeld and Jorg Krichbaum, "De Filosofie van Iris Murdoch," *Hollands Diep* (December 1976): 32. Translated for the author by Catherina DeJonge of Indiana University.

3. Jean-Luis Chevalier, ed. *Rencontres avec Iris Murdoch* (University of Caen, France: Centre de Recherches de Litterature et Linguistique des Pays de Langue Anglaise, 1978), 83; hereafter cited in the text.

4. Sheila Hale and A. S. Byatt, "Women Writers Now: Their Approach and Apprenticeship," *Harpers and Queen* (October 1976): 180: hereafter cited in the text.

5. Jeffrey Mayers, "The Art of Fiction CXVII: Iris Murdoch," *The Paris Review* 115 (Summer 1990): 218; hereafter cited in the text.

6. W. K. Rose, "Iris Murdoch Informally," *London Magazine* 8 (June 1969): 60.

7. Michael Bellamy, "An Interview with Iris Murdoch," *Contemporary Literature* 18, no. 2 (Spring 1977): 133.

8. Veronica Groocock, "Names and Faces," *The Listener* (31 December, 1981): 40; hereafter cited in the text.

9. Adam Mars-Jones, "Conversation with a Mastermind," *Sunday Times* (London) 29 September, 1985, [n.p.].

10. Iris Murdoch, *The Time of the Angels* (London: Chatto & Windus, 1966), 39; hereafter cited in the text as *TA*.

11. Iris Murdoch, *The Message to the Planet* (New York: Viking, 1990), 78; hereafter cited in the text as *MP*.

12. Heide Ziegler and Christopher Bigsby, eds. *The Radical Imagination and the Liberal Tradition: Interviews with English and American Novelists* (London: Junction Books, 1982), 217.

13. Didier Eribon, "Les Paves d'Oxford," *Le Nouvel Observateur* 39 (January 1986): 5. Translated with the author by P. J. Anderson and Karola Anderson.

14. Barbara Stevens Heusel, "An Interview with Iris Murdoch," *University of Windsor Review* (Spring 1965): 12; hereafter cited in the text.

15. See Bellamy, "An Interview with Iris Murdoch," 133.

16. Kevin Hull, producer, *Bookmark: A Certain Lady*, BBC Television, Channel 2, 29 December, 1989.

17. In more recent years Murdoch claims not to have experienced sex typing, but she recalls seeing other women in the position of having to adjust their behavior, physically, due to social pressure: "I realize I am lucky. I have never felt picked out in an intellectual sense because I am a woman; these distinctions are not made in Oxford. But I do notice when I come up to London that people under social pressure develop sexual masks, adjust their behavior at a physical level—giggling and so on. This is something I dislike and which doesn't happen in my world" (Hale, "Women Writers Now," 180).

18. Deborah Johnson, *Iris Murdoch* (Bloomington: Indiana University Press, 1987), 61; hereafter cited in the text.

19. Christine Sizemore, *A Female Vision of the City: London in the Novels of Five British Women* (Knoxville: University of Tennessee Press, 1989), 117.

20. Rosemary Harthill, "Iris Murdoch: Flight to the Enchantress," *Writers Revealed* (London: BBC, 1989), 84.

21. Iris Murdoch, *A Severed Head* (London: Chatto & Windus, 1961), 18.

22. Richard Todd, ed., *Encounters with Iris Murdoch* Amsterdam: Free University Press, 1988), 101.

23. Iris Murdoch, *The Book and the Brotherhood* (New York: Viking, 1988), 13; hereafter cited in the text as *BB*.

24.   John Russell, "Under Iris Murdoch's Exact, Steady Gaze," *New York Times*, 22 February 1990, C20.

25.   Murdoch has observed about her childhood, "I had marvelous parents. I was an only child, you see, and had their complete attention" (James Atlas, "The Abbess of Oxford," *Vanity Fair* 51, no. 3 [March 1988]: 76). Murdoch attended Badminton School, Bristol, and Somerville College, Oxford, where she studied classical Greek. For a poem about a course she had in Agamemnon see "Agamemnon Class 1939," *Boston University Journal* 25, no. 2 (1977): 57–58; she claims that she can "scarcely overestimate the influence of her classical education" on her work ("An Arion Questionnaire: 'The Classics and the Man of Letters' " *Arion* [Winter 1964]: 66–67).

26.   Iris Murdoch, *The Fire and the Sun: Why Plato Banished the Artists* (Oxford: Clarendon Press, 1977), 80.

27.   Linda Wortheimer, "All Things Considered," interview broadcast, 26 February 1990, on Monitor Radio.

Index

♦